Gainsborough Pictures

Gainsborough Pictures

Edited by Pam Cook

CASSELL
London and Washington

Rethinking British Cinema
Series Editor: Pam Cook

This series is dedicated to innovative approaches to British cinema. It expands the parameter of debate, shedding new light on areas such as gender and sexuality, audiences, ethnicity, stars, visual style, genre, music and sound. Moving beyond narrow definitions of national cinema, the series celebrates the richness and diversity of British film culture.

Cassell
Wellington House
125 Strand
London WC2R 0BB

PO Box 605
Herndon
Virginia 20172

First published 1997

British Library Cataloguing-in-Publication Data
A catalogue record for this book is available from the British Library.

Library of Congress Cataloging-in-Publication Data
Gainsborough Pictures / edited by Pam Cook.

     p. cm. — (Rethinking British Cinema)
     Includes bibliographical references and index.
     ISBN 0–304–33708–0.—ISBN 0–304–33707–2 (pbk.)
     1. Gainsborough Studios—History. I. Cook, Pam. II. Series.
PN1999.G35G35 1997
384'.8'0941 — dc21   97–17081
                                                        CIP

ISBN 0–304–33708–0 (hardback)
     0–304–33707–2 (paperback)

Designed and typeset by Ben Cracknell Studios
Printed and bound in Great Britain by Creative Print and Design Wales, Ebbw Vale

Contents

Notes on Contributors

CHARLES BARR is a Senior Lecturer in film studies at the University of East Anglia. His numerous publications on British cinema include the influential *Ealing Studios* (revised edition, Studio Vista, 1993) and (as editor) *All Our Yesterdays: 90 Years of British Cinema* (BFI, 1986). He is currently working on two Hitchcock projects: a book about his British films, and a study of *Vertigo* for the BFI Film Classics series.

TIM BERGFELDER is a Lecturer in film studies and German at the University of Southampton. He has taught and published on film in Germany, and is currently researching co-productions and cross-cultural influence in popular European cinema.

PAM COOK is a Senior Lecturer in film studies at the University of East Anglia. She is editor of *The Cinema Book* (BFI, 1985) and co-editor of *Women and Film: A Sight and Sound Reader* (Scarlet Press, 1993). Her last book, *Fashioning the Nation: Costume and Identity in British Cinema*, was published in 1996 by the British Film Institute. She is currently working on *I Know Where I'm Going!* for BFI Film Classics.

K.J. DONNELLY is a Lecturer in film, media and cultural studies at Staffordshire University. He is a specialist in film music, although he has also published material on ecology. He has just completed a doctoral thesis on popular music and British cinema at the University of East Anglia.

DENIS GIFFORD began as a cartoonist, with collating film information as a hobby. Gradually the latter took over, and he has written many definitive cinema books, including *British Animated Films*, *Illustrated Who's Who in British Films*, *Pictorial History of Horror Movies*, *American Animated Films* (silent era) and *The British Film Catalogue*, now in two editions, *Entertainment Films* and *Non-Fiction Films*.

SUE HARPER is Reader in film history at the University of Portsmouth. She first published material on Gainsborough costume melodramas in

1983. She has written widely on British cinema of the 1930s and 1940s, and in 1994 the British Film Institute published her *Picturing the Past: The Rise and Fall of the British Costume Film*.

ANDREW HIGSON is chairperson of the Film Studies sector at the University of East Anglia. His publications include *Waving the Flag: Constructing a National Cinema in Britain* (Clarendon Press, 1995), *Dissolving Views: Key Writings on British Cinema* (Cassell, 1996), which he edited, and *'Film Europe' and 'Film America'* (University of Exeter Press, 1998), which he co-edited with Richard Maltby.

PHILIP KEMP is a freelance critic and film historian, a regular contributor to *Sight and Sound, Film Comment, Variety* and *Metro* (Melbourne). His last book was *Lethal Innocence: The Cinema of Alexander Mackendrick* (Methuen, 1991). He is currently working on a biography of Michael Balcon.

JUSTINE KING teaches film studies at the University of East Anglia, and English and cultural studies at City College, Norwich. She is researching a PhD on women film-makers in British cinema at the University of East Anglia.

GEOFFREY MACNAB is a freelance writer based in London. He contributes regularly to *Sight and Sound, Moving Pictures International* and *Time Out*, and is the author of *J. Arthur Rank and the British Film Industry* (Routledge, 1993). He is currently working on a book about the British star system for Cassell.

ROBERT MURPHY was educated at the London Film School and the London School of Economics. He teaches film studies and scriptwriting at Sheffield Hallam University. He has written two books on British cinema: *Realism and Tinsel* (Routledge, 1989) and *Sixties British Cinema* (BFI, 1992), and edited (with Sue Aspinall) *Gainsborough Melodrama* (BFI, 1983) and *The British Cinema Book* (BFI, 1997).

DUNCAN PETRIE is Director of the Bill Douglas Centre for the History of Cinema and Popular Culture at the University of Exeter. He has published several books on aspects of British cinema, including *Creativity and Constraint in the British Film Industry* (Macmillan, 1991), *New Questions of British Cinema* (BFI, 1992), *The British Cinematographer* (BFI, 1996) and *Inside Stories: British Cinema Diaries* (BFI, 1996).

Acknowledgements

A book such as this, exploring relatively uncharted areas, depends heavily on its contributors. It has been my good fortune to work with a dedicated group of historians whose enthusiasm for British cinema has produced some fascinating, and in more than one case original, material. Simon Davies deserves special mention for his tireless efforts with the filmography, which have resulted in an invaluable resource for future researchers.

Justine King provided sterling editorial assistance and moral support under difficult circumstances, coping admirably with knotty technical problems. Tim Bergfelder, Philip Kemp, Andrew Higson and Robert Murphy offered valuable advice and comments. I am particularly grateful to Jane Greenwood at Cassell for her commitment to the project, and for her patience, and to desk editor Helena Power for her professionalism and calm efficiency.

Grateful thanks are due to the British Film Institute's Stills, Posters and Designs Department, who supplied all the photographic material for this book. I am indebted to the Research Committee of the School of English and American Studies at the University of East Anglia, who provided funds for editorial assistance. The song 'Let's Get Hold Of Hitler' (p. 93) by Noel Gay and Frank Exton, © 1941 Cinephonic Music Co. Ltd/ Richard Armitage Ltd, 8/9 Frith Street, London, W1V 5TZ, is used by permission. All rights reserved.

Last, but not least, special thanks to Charles Barr and Andrew Higson, my colleagues in the UEA Film Studies sector, where British cinema is something of a passion. And, of course, to Sam Cook for many kinds of support.

For Sam

Introduction

Pam Cook

Gainsborough and British film culture

There is an element of flag-waving associated with British cinema. The myth of a plucky, impoverished British film industry struggling against the might of Hollywood is one that informs promotional discourses, political arguments about government subsidy, and many British cinema histories. Like all myths, it contains elements of truth, and of heroic fantasies that have deep roots in our national culture. At the same time, it has had some detrimental effects. The perception of our national cinema as disadvantaged has resulted in two kinds of compensatory critical approaches: one that celebrates its high spots, whether they are perceived in terms of key historical periods, auteurs, charismatic producers or successful film cycles, and one that defines 'British cinema' in parochial terms, confined by national boundaries, criteria of domestic production and local subject matter.

Both these positions have certain strengths, but they do depend on a defensive view of British cinema, and of British film culture. The broader histories that conceive of British cinema as an intrinsic element of British popular culture generally, and therefore organically rooted in that culture, are few and far between. Even rarer are those that define national culture as a mixed bag of national and trans-national cross-currents. Such a view would demand that British film culture be seen, both in terms of production and reception, as an amalgam of the indigenous and the 'foreign'. In this sense, the term 'British' stands for a specific manifestation, or manifestations, of cultural in-mixing that change at different historical moments. In defining themselves against Hollywood, many British film-makers have tended to adhere to purist notions of a core British identity rather than embrace cultural hybridity.

This is not, of course, universally the case. There is a rich seam of internationalism running through British cinema that consciously penetrates national boundaries, and crosses frontiers between 'high' and 'low' culture – in the films of Powell and Pressburger, Hitchcock, Alexander Korda and Gainsborough, to mention but a few. However, the hostile reception of some of these films at the time of their release suggests that they were not perceived to be authentically British, a position echoed, ironically, by more recent revisionist accounts that place such films outside the cultural mainstream, identifying them as a transgressive undercurrent in British cinema. As I maintain elsewhere, such arguments have contributed to the critical marginalization of whole areas of popular British cinema (Cook, 1996a). In the case of Gainsborough Pictures, which from its inception in 1924 until its demise in 1950 produced films that were both successful at the box office and, side by side with movies imported from Europe and the USA, made a significant contribution to British film culture, this marginalization appears almost perverse. For more than 25 years, Gainsborough film-makers actively participated in debates about the future direction of the British film industry, debates which are constantly being revived, and are still relevant today.

This anthology starts from the premise that, far from representing an undercurrent, Gainsborough has played, and continues to play, a central role in British cinema and in British film culture. This role extends far beyond the production of the cycle of melodramas and costume dramas in the 1940s, although, as several contributors point out, connections can be made between these flamboyant efforts and Gainsborough films of the 1920s and '30s. In the articles collected here, the emphasis is less on constructing a coherent, core identity for the studio than on tracing shifts of identity across different historical moments and cultural contexts. The focus is primarily on the 1920s and 1930s – partly because the 1940s has received an unprecedented amount of critical attention, and partly because those earlier decades are characterized by important developments in British cinema (the 'Film Europe' initiative, for example) that have scarcely been touched upon, and which have considerable implications for the way our national cinema is perceived.

We have not provided a complete studio history here: that can be found elsewhere (see, for example, Murphy, 1983). The aim is rather to provide a wider picture of British film culture, and Gainsborough's place within it, through selected moments or snapshots of the past. Nor do we claim to have solved the riddle of how to accommodate the hybrid nature of the studio's output within 'British cinema' generally. Instead, we foreground the question of the multiple identities that make up any studio, any national cinema, and any national culture. This is quite a different agenda from those that have informed earlier critical reassessments of Gainsborough. Issues of gender, sexuality and class, though they are dealt with by several contributors, have been subsumed here within those of national identity and cultural exchange. This shift of historical conjunctures has taken more than a decade, and deserves further discussion.

Time flies: then and now

The seeds for this book were sown fourteen years ago. In 1983, a season of 1940s Gainsborough melodramas played to packed houses at London's National Film Theatre. As the accompanying dossier published by the British Film Institute explained, this cycle of costume dramas and melodramas had been just as enthusiastically received by audiences when they were released in wartime and post-war Britain, though critics had generally dismissed them as tasteless trash (Aspinall and Murphy, 1983, p. 1). The age of the NFT audiences suggested that many of their number had taken the opportunity to enjoy another look at films that had captured their imaginations 40 years previously – though some, no doubt, had had their appetites whetted by more recent daytime television screenings.

The organizers of the NFT season had their own agenda. In their introduction to the dossier, Sue Aspinall and Robert Murphy established the context for re-viewing the films, indicting a general critical distaste for popular culture as the reason for the melodramas' continuing neglect in histories of British cinema. They also cited a prevailing attachment to realism, the preferred aesthetic for British cinema, as a deterrent against taking the determinedly non-realistic Gainsborough melodramas seriously (Aspinall and Murphy, 1983, p. 1). They argued that the films demanded a new critical approach:

> A critical approach needs to be developed which can appraise such films without elevating them falsely into works of 'art' and without reducing them to mere socio-economic objects. Such a new approach would have to account for their appeal through attention to the whole range of factors involved in film production, distribution and consumption. It would have to take into account the historical, political and ideological as well as the economic, industrial and technical determinants of a film text and its effects (Aspinall and Murphy, 1983, p. 2).

The dossier provided interview material with Gainsborough personnel and examples of contemporary critical reception which contextualized the films at the moment of their production and release. At the same time, it included essays that discussed the melodramas from the perspective of recent feminist debates. This modest publication, which sadly has long been out of print, offered an interesting example of conjunctural analysis. It represented the convergence of two historical periods with different but interlinked agendas. The feminist debates around melodrama as a devalued genre, and its implications for theories of female spectatorship and pleasure, intersected productively with arguments made 40 years earlier about the status of popular texts in British cinema. The dossier's determined assault on the prevailing critical preference for a national cinema defined in terms of quality and restraint challenged the consensus that Britain lacked both an indigenous popular cinema and a popular audience of cinephiles. The sophistication of the Gainsborough films, on the levels of scripts, and set and costume design, suggested that audiences were and are attracted to more than the opportunity to indulge in star-gazing.

There had been other Gainsborough histories and part-histories (see, for example, Seaton and Martin, 1982; Brown, 1977a). But it was the melodrama dossier's insertion of the studio into a debate about the nature of British cinema and its audiences that broke new ground. However, although it was influential in bringing about a revaluation of 1940s Gainsborough melodrama, it did not result in a historical reassessment of the place of the studio itself in British film culture – despite the fact that Robert Murphy's studio history (Aspinall and Murphy, 1983, pp. 3–13) suggested that Gainsborough, and the associated company Gaumont-British which absorbed it in the late 1920s, had been key players in industry policy since the 1920s.

Fourteen years on, a different matrix of events has produced the conjuncture that makes that reassessment possible. The world-wide resurgence of ethnocentric nationalist movements, the rise of trans-national communication systems and the political debates about Britain's relationship with Europe all connect in interesting, though not necessarily direct, ways with the cultural developments affecting Gainsborough in the 1920s, '30s and '40s. The history of those developments has only been touched on here; what we have tried to do is to sketch in the discursive context for the fluctuating pattern of the studio's output during this period.

This unevenness is often put down to changes in administration: the internationalism of Michael Balcon in the 1920s and '30s giving way to Edward Black's domestic, regionalist policies, which were then superseded by the Ostrers' renewed internationalism in the 1940s. The management changes consequent upon the absorption of Gainsborough by the

Gaumont-British corporation, and later by the Rank Organization, should also be taken into account. Yet the idea of studio heads controlling output – which is often the way in which studio histories are written – is somewhat misleading. Not only does it invest certain individuals or groups with power they may not actually have, but it ignores the extent to which the film-making process is part of wider cultural dynamics which may have a profound impact on the decision-making process, on the kinds of films that are made, and on the ways in which they are received. Studio histories tend to offer a version of auteur theory in which control is simply shifted from directors to producers. This anthology attempts to construct a different kind of studio identity for Gainsborough, one that recognizes its sensitivity to social change and the complexity of the discursive contexts within which it operated, and also takes account of the current conjuncture and its role in generating such an enterprise.

Such a project implies a particular view of history. Rather than provide a complete picture, we recognize that histories are always partial and incomplete, subject to vagaries of fashion, lapses of memory and personal agendas. The reconstruction of a historical moment always produces a hybrid fabrication of past and present. The activity of historical research inevitably throws up methodological inconsistencies and contradictory interpretations of evidence as well as conflicting data. This is particularly the case with this anthology, where a certain amount of overlap occurs because contributors write about similar events and evidence from different perspectives, sometimes using different sources. We have not attempted to iron out such inconsistencies; instead, we have seen them as part of the historical process. Where it is a matter of conflicting sources, the source is given. Where contributors differ in their interpretations, such differences are allowed to stand. Thus the collection makes its own statement about history, participating in current debates about historical research.

New history, new problems

Perhaps the most dramatic development in film studies over the last ten or fifteen years has been the recourse to history. The return to the archive has been seen as a necessary corrective to the abstractions and unsubstantiated assertions generated by 1970s film theory, particularly in the area of spectatorship. The 'historical turn' has brought with it a renewed self-consciousness about the theory and practice of film history itself. Historians have become more than storytellers, or chroniclers of events; they are more like scientists and philosophers. They must be aware of the ideological and methodological pitfalls that beset any historiography: the accuracy, originality and completeness of their findings, the strengths and weaknesses of different approaches, the status and value of empirical evidence in relation to general argument. Above all, they are required to situate themselves in relation to other histories, to comment on and engage with them. History has always been vigorously contested when it comes to the 'truth' of what happened when and where; under pressure from modern political agendas, the question of who and why – the ideological issue of who writes history, for whom and with what motives – has become an essential feature of contemporary historiography. With the huge expansion of history as an academic discipline has come the proliferation of meta-discourses on history and historians which attempt to define their function and methods.

Metaphors for the historian's activity abound. Following Michel Foucault, a favourite is the one of the archaeologist working synchronically to situate historical objects and events in their wider discursive contexts, to uncover the underlying (often unconscious) social rules and cultural forces that made them possible. Foucault's work has been extremely influential in the shift from text-based theory to historicism in film studies, and has inspired a number of revisionist histories which aim to contextualize the traditional object of study – the film text itself – in relation to the discourses surrounding it. What is studied in this process is not so much a single text as the complex interrelationship between different texts and artefacts, and what is produced is an explanation of the multiple forces affecting selected events and objects. By implication, the forces at work in the selection process, the discourses governing the historian's choices and methods, are also significant factors in the writing of histories, overdetermining who writes them and why.

Despite the persuasiveness of Foucault's ideas, many different models of historical enquiry still co-exist, and many different kinds of history are written. The traditional chronology and the diachronic narrative exist side by side with conjunctural approaches and symptomatic analyses. The postmodernist dismantling of master narratives and grand designs, and the explosion of new technologies and global communications networks, have contributed to the dispersal of traditional hierarchies and the challenging of accepted categories. Notions of origin, truth and authenticity have been substantially decentred in favour of multiple, often dissenting versions competing with one another for validation. Readers and writers of histories increasingly find themselves adrift in a sea of relativism where one version carries as much weight as any other. How does the historian cope with this problem? The 'facts' of history, and the 'objectivity' of the historian, are and always have been contested. Nevertheless, history is still wedded to the idea that it is possible, through careful attention to original source material, to arrive at more complete, more convincing, more authentic explanations.

In the face of this renewed challenge to the authority of history, ironically occurring just as the New History movement gathers momentum, the status of evidence has become crucial. Suspicion of secondary sources, and of assertions based on unsupported evidence, has sent historians scurrying to the archives in search of primary materials, which are then endowed with authority in their own right. The importance of primary sources in historical enquiry cannot be overestimated – however, it is not always recognized that 'primary' evidence is often as mediated, as con-taminated, as secondary sources, and that when historians come to interpret it, they insert it into another highly mediated context. Historians who present their work supported by a mass of references to primary sources may seek to endow that work with greater authenticity – but equally, they are offering to other historians the opportunity to read the evidence differently and arrive at different conclusions.

This brings us back to relativism, one of many conundrums facing historians today. In their overview of theory and practice in film history, Robert C. Allen and Douglas Gomery deal with this problem by citing Realist theories of science inspired by the work of Roy Bhaskar and Rom Harre, an approach which attempts to reconcile the validity of empirical data with the subjectivity of the scientist. They quote Russell Keat and John Urry:

> 'Scientific theories must be objectively assessed by reference to empirical evidence. This evidence is such that all scientists who are competent, honest, and lacking in perceptual deficiencies can agree upon it, though not necessarily with total certainty.' ... One such way of testing a theory is by the principle of *non-contradiction*. Frequently the same phenomenon will be investigated by scientists with differing philosophical orientations, theories, and methods. On most points we would expect the resulting explanations to differ as well. Where they do not, where there is non-contradiction among them, there is evidence of a finding that is valid (Allen and Gomery, 1985, p. 16).

Despite the apparent attractiveness of the Realist approach in rescuing history from the anarchy of relativism, this formulation does not completely solve the problem. It is entirely possible for historians to agree on certain points, yet disagree in their interpretation of them; who is to arbitrate? Moreover, the principle of history (or science) governed by a consensus among historians seems fraught with difficulty, particularly if it is put in the service of a search for authoritative versions. Surely it must be history itself that decides what is valid and what is not. The notion of hegemony developed by Antonio Gramsci suggests that, at any given historical moment, a number of competing versions of history are in conflict, and that through a process of debate and negotiation some are accepted while others are relegated. The dominant versions do not achieve ascendancy by virtue of their authenticity, or 'truth', but through consent. In this situation it is entirely possible for people to subscribe to more than one version simultaneously – or to consent to the dominant versions, yet to believe in others that have been devalued. By the same token, it is possible to doubt a particular version of history, and yet behave as though one consents to it because the situation demands it. What is at stake here is not the authority of historical accounts, but the agency of history itself, to which we are all subject.

The idea that it is history itself that confers validity on the historian's work does not imply either that historians are powerless instruments, or that they are free to construct whatever unsubstantiated histories they please. (It is true, of course, that histories that break the bounds of credibility are produced – see, for example, versions of the Holocaust dreamed up by the extreme Right, or Baudrillard's notorious contention that the Gulf War was entirely a media phenomenon. It is a frightening thought that such histories may achieve consent in certain circumstances, and in some cases inspire horrendous atrocities.) However, it does suggest that history is less a matter of policing other versions of the past and more a question of recognizing the limits of historical enquiry and its status as provider of evidence and explanation. In the case of Holocaust denial, for example, evidence and explanation seem to carry little weight. It is an extreme and chilling instance of the notion that 'truth' depends upon the perspective of the individual or group perceiving it. It is also a salutary reminder that the struggle for historical veracity must take place in the terrain of the imagination as well as that of rational analysis.

This has momentous implications for the study of history. The texts and objects that the historian chooses to scrutinize are the result not only of external social forces but of internalized emotions and aspirations. Yet the dynamic between personal desires and public events, though it provides the motivating impulse behind historical fiction, is rarely considered to be the subject of proper history – which is not, of course, regarded as fiction. As well as being sensitive to conjuncture – not only the context of the 'primary' materials under consideration, but also of the secondary texts and commentaries consulted (which are, after all, also historical documents) – historians need to be aware of their own situation and imaginative investment in the project. The historians' interpretations and analyses are as much part of personal and public histories as the past events they study, and historians are as vulnerable to lapses of memory and perception as the diarist or the popular historical novelist. By the same token, these personal and popular fictions are part of the imaginative landscape not just of their own time, but that of the historians' too, and they contribute to our understanding of history. I have discussed elsewhere the relegation of popular period romances by officially sanctioned discourses on history, and by progressive revisionist historians (Cook, 1996a). The recognition that historical fictions play a significant role in our perceptions of history often brings with it a distrust of the free play with history that motivates them. But rather than vehicles of false consciousness, or even agents of subversion, these popular fantasies might better be seen as texts that comment on historical analysis, foregrounding elements of masquerade, invention and pastiche that are generally elided in more serious histories. The investment in history as authority, involving as it does the expulsion of contradictory elements, produces secondary discourses which travesty those legitimized discourses that see historical enquiry as a process of correction.

Conjunctural analysis, though it may not answer all the problems of (re)writing history, at least has the virtue of displacing correction models of historical investigation which place today's historians in authority over those of the past. The analysis of the interrelationship between different discourses at different historical periods, and of their conjunction in the present, could be said to offer a more convincing interpretation of how history works than one that relies on a notion of succeeding generations of historians laying down the law to those who went before, and producing more complete and adequate explanations. Such an approach has the advantage of locating the historian inside and outside history at once, as both observer and participant. And it also suggests that 'lost' histories – those versions devalued or relegated at certain moments – may not be lost for ever. They remain as traces which can find their way to the surface when the moment allows.

Studio style and identity

Just as there are many different ways of writing history, there are different kinds of studio history. There are those that give a chronology of events, featuring key personnel such as producers, directors and stars, significant films, occasionally a genre particularly associated with the studio. Some locate the studio in the context of the film industry itself, explaining its existence and output in terms of industrial and economic forces (for example, Balio, 1976). Others assess the impact of social change, working methods and power hierarchies on the films themselves (for example, Barr, 1993), and the part they play in creating and maintaining studio identity. These are generally the ones that tackle the question of studio style, often citing producers, creative personnel such as scriptwriters and directors, genre and stars as key elements. Writing in 1974 about Warner Bros during the 1930s, Edward Buscombe assessed the current state of studio histories:

> Studio style is a term which occasionally crops up in film criticism, but in a loose kind of way. Thus MGM went in for large-budget costume dramas and, later, musicals. Paramount had a taste for raciness and decadence (Lubitsch and von Sternberg), Columbia equals Capra. But such study as has been made of the studios during their heyday of the 30s has not gone beyond a few random observations on a small proportion of the output and has generally been concerned only with the films themselves. What seems to be lacking is any conception of the relations between the economic structure of the studio, its particular organisation and the kind of films it produced (Buscombe, 1974, p. 52).

Buscombe goes on to analyse, in thematic terms, how the films directed by Raoul Walsh after he joined Warner Bros in 1939 were typical of studio policy and output. Despite his call for a broader perspective, and for an approach that would link economics, institutional history and aesthetics, Buscombe himself deals primarily with a specific cycle – the crime melodramas – and his discussion is couched in terms of content. Buscombe's article must be seen in the context of the authorship debates that motivated the Walsh anthology in which it appeared (Hardy, 1974), which no doubt accounts for his focus on a specific period and cycle. But his argument that studio identity is often narrowly conceived, depending on an association with a particular genre and a repertory company of stars, directors and scriptwriters remains convincing. MGM is still known primarily for its musicals, Ealing for its comedies, Hammer for its horror and Gainsborough for its melodramas, despite the fact that all these studios produced many different types of film. The survey histories that provide a more general picture of studio output tend to skirt the question of house style altogether.

Despite this narrow focus, studio histories can provide a useful antidote to accounts of cinema history that confer agency and power on charismatic individuals or groups. They remind us that film-making is a collaborative process subject to cultural and economic forces. They encourage us to view style as the end result of a series of negotiations between managerial, creative and technical personnel, rather than the realization of a single personal vision. They suggest that both films and film-makers are embedded in structures over which they may have little control. This is the view taken by many in this anthology, though not by all. Several contributors follow the established pattern of constructing a studio history through the policies of those producers who managed Gainsborough at different times; in some cases a conscious effort has been made to locate those figures within the cultural and industrial forces that they were bound to negotiate, rather than present them as solely responsible for decisions that were made. In other cases, an argument is made that these producers had overall responsibility for policy-making, and were therefore primarily responsible for studio output.

No single chapter provides a comprehensive history of Gainsborough; taken together, the contributions view Gainsborough's history from the perspectives of different aspects of the production process. Several chapters are devoted to areas that are rarely discussed by studio histories – for example, music, cinematography and design, all of which help to create a distinctive studio style. Under-researched genres such as musical comedies and comedy, and influential but neglected directors such as Victor Saville are also featured. Although, as I have discussed above, the emphasis is on diversity rather than coherence in Gainsborough's output, some interesting patterns have emerged. More than one contributor has noted a consistent preoccupation with history and with revisiting the past; themes of masquerade and mistaken identity also surface across a range of genres and periods; and there is considerable evidence for what has been described as Gainsborough's obsession with 'life across the Channel' (Seaton and Martin, 1982).

As with any history, as one agenda displaces another, new gaps appear, and historians become aware that, in attempting to solve a particular historical problem, they have created a number of others. Just as the '40s melodramas were the tip of the iceberg in relation to Gainsborough's overall output, so this anthology reveals a relatively small amount of the studio's distinguished contribution to British film culture. That contribution itself represents a fraction of popular British cinema production between 1924 and 1950. However, this is a cause for celebration rather than regret, as avenues for further research open up.

It is hoped that this collection will help to carve out new directions in the study of British cinema as well as provide a valuable resource for researchers. But that is up to history to decide. With this in mind, the last word goes to Walter Benjamin: 'To articulate the past historically does not mean to recognize it "the way it really was" (Ranke). It means to seize hold of a memory as it flashes up at a moment of danger' (Benjamin, 1992, p. 247).

Note

In the interests of consistency in film titles and dates, Gainsborough and Gainsborough-related films cited in the text have been checked against the filmography in this volume. Non-Gainsborough films have been checked against Salmi, 1982.

Not for Peckham:
Michael Balcon and Gainsborough's
International Trajectory in the 1920s

Philip Kemp

Early in 1925, less than a year after the newly formed Gainsborough company had moved into Islington Studios, Michael Balcon sounded a challenge to his fellow film-makers. Writing in the trade journal *The Film Renter and Moving Picture News* under the heading 'A Plea for Wider Vision', he denounced the British film industry for its insularity, and for good measure lambasted the national press for abetting such narrow-mindedness. 'Bernard Shaw,' Balcon reminded his readers, 'says that starvation is the stimulus of genius, and certainly our present position should provoke us to think more clearly than during these last heedless years when, with a pittance in our pockets, we made pictures for Peckham and were pained with the world for not wanting our suburban crudities.'[1]

It was an audacious, not to say impudent, performance to come from a fledgling producer with just three feature films under his belt, one of them (*The White Shadow*, 1924) a financial and critical disaster. But Balcon was clearly in no mood to defer to anyone else's experience. 'To my mind,' he announced, by now firmly astride his soapbox,

> it is of the utmost importance that the Trade should be educated to the necessity of producing not only for this country, but for the world, otherwise it will lead to the further discouragement of British capital and a lamentable levelling down of the standards of production. ...British pictures, to be commercial successes, must comply with the accepted standards of picture production.[2]

For an example of these standards, he suggested modestly, his colleagues in the industry need look no further than his own debut feature, *Woman to Woman* (Graham Cutts, 1923).

The company concerned [Balcon, Freedman & Saville] chose an Anglo-French story and it is generally admitted that they had the courage to adopt an unconventional and artistic ending. The exteriors were taken in France and this country. The film director and his staff were English through and through, not one had set foot in an American studio. The only characteristic in which the picture was similar to American productions was the high standard of photography and all film technique generally. ...Making pictures 'international' is an art in itself which I and my colleagues have studied very closely. The process is expensive, but it is profitable – and much safer than pandering to Peckham. There is no doubt that British pictures with an international appeal will save British film production.[3]

It may seem surprising that a man generally regarded as the most staunchly English (or even, in Michael Powell's view, 'suburban'[4]) of producers, should have pursued so firmly internationalist a policy at the outset of his career. But Balcon, a much more complex and ambiguous figure than is generally conceded, was never parochial: even at Ealing he surrounded himself with a roster of non-English-born collaborators to rival Korda's – and drawn from a far wider catchment area. The output of that supposedly ultra-English studio was created *inter alia* by people hailing from Russia, France, America, Brazil, Czechoslovakia and Germany – not to mention Scotland, Wales and Ireland.[5] And in this, Balcon was following a policy he had begun to establish twenty years earlier at Gainsborough.

Balcon himself, as a member of the great nineteenth-century Jewish diaspora, belonged to a worldwide clan. Though born and brought up entirely in England, he had close relatives in Eastern Europe, South Africa, Canada and the USA. Thinking internationally came naturally to him, and from the first his films reached across national borders. In choosing to shoot part of the pre-Gainsborough *Woman to Woman* on location in France, Balcon and Cutts set the tone for much of Gainsborough's output in the 1920s, which displayed (as Ray Seaton and Roy Martin put it) a 'long-standing and at times obsessional involvement with life across the Channel'.[6] Of the entire Gainsborough output of the 1920s, all but three or four included scenes set (and in most cases shot) outside Britain. Even the company name, Gainsborough, at first sight so redolent of English decorum and good taste, may carry more exotic overtones. Thomas Gainsborough, as Pam Cook has pointed out, 'was influenced by eighteenth-century French painting and is considered to be the only British painter whose style is distinctively rococo', offering a blend of 'British subject matter with a European style associated with sexuality and passion'.[7]

Balcon's emphasis, in his 1925 article on the Englishness of Graham Cutts and his crew, was not mere flag-waving. Rather, it was a pre-emptive strike aimed at rebutting suggestions 'that the firm responsible have thoroughly Americanised their production'. At the same time he insisted that, 'Unpalatable as it may be, we must recognise that America still produces by far the best pictures from the point of view of technique.'[8] What he omitted to add was that, though he and his colleagues had learnt a lot from studying current American productions, the overseas technical expertise on which his company was chiefly drawing was German. Shortly before Balcon's article appeared, Graham Cutts had wound up principal shooting on Gainsborough's first co-production with Ufa, *The Blackguard (Die Prinzessin und der Geiger*, 1925).

This may have been deliberate caution. Seven years after the war anti-German feeling was still widespread. Not long since, one of the leading British distributors had been running full-page ads in the trade press announcing 'Will Exhibitors kindly note – That the Phillips Film Co. has NO GERMAN FILMS to offer them.'[9] Such chauvinist sentiments were weakening: films such as *The Cabinet of Dr Caligari* (1919 – distributed, in the event, by Phillips) and *Dr Mabuse* (1922) had been well received in Britain, and other British film-makers such as Herbert Wilcox (*Chu-Chin-Chow*, 1923) and George Dewhurst (*The Uninvited Guest*, 1923) had already shot films in Germany. But the national press still ran periodic scare stories about sinister Teutonic plots to swamp the world with German films; and with *The Blackguard*, Gainsborough's first super-production, due for release Balcon perhaps felt he should take no chances.

Balcon paid his first visit to the Ufa studios in 1924. He was not much taken with Berlin – 'The town and the people seem to be very second rate,' he wrote to his wife Aileen – but Ufa was another matter: 'The Ufa–Decla Studios are really wonderful and there is no doubt that the Hun intends to beat the Americans at film production.'[10] The contrast with the tiny Islington studios could hardly have been more striking. Formed from the merger of half a dozen German and Austrian film-making concerns, Ufa (Universum Film Aktiengesellschaft) was by far the largest production company outside Hollywood, turning out some 50 films a year.

Ufa's main studios at the aptly named Neubabelsberg (New Babylon) to the east of Berlin were the biggest and best equipped in Europe, quite possibly in the world, with multiple shooting stages covering 200,000 square feet plus huge exterior lots stretching out across the sandy Brandenburg plain. (Islington, by way of comparison, had just two stages totalling some 6250 square feet, and its sole exterior lot was the flat roof.) At Ufa, under the guidance of Erich Pommer, directors such as Fritz Lang, F.W. Murnau, G.W. Pabst and Robert Wiene were encouraged to operate as the heads of individual creative teams, free to experiment without interference from the front office.

Balcon was greatly impressed, both professionally and personally, by Pommer, so much so that his own style as a producer, with its strong emphasis on mutual personal loyalty, may well have been modelled on the older man's practices. Years later, the journalist Hans Feld sketched Pommer's working methods:

> He would say, 'I seek out my set designers, my cameramen, my directors. I make sure I get young people of promise. And then when I've got them together, I stand on guard in front of them, and let nobody get at them.' ... It wasn't just that Erich Pommer was loyal to his colleagues, he inspired loyalty in them. In his group, in his collective, you had this feeling of a 'Pommer spirit'.[11]

Change the name, and this could well stand as a description of Balcon at Ealing.

The Blackguard initiated an association that lasted nearly ten years. No other British producer developed so close or so fruitful a relationship with the German film industry as Balcon. Of the 22 features released by Gainsborough (or its related company, Piccadilly) up to the coming of sound, seven were Anglo-German co-productions. The association, which would continue after the company was absorbed into the Gaumont-British empire in the late 1920s and end only with the Nazis' accession to power, enriched the Gainsborough-Gaumont output with the contributions of German personnel in all fields. The producers Hermann Fellner and Josef Somlo; cinematographers Otto Kanturek, Günther Krampf and Mutz Greenbaum; art directors Oscar Werndorff and Alfred Junge; actors Conrad Veidt, Fritz Kortner and Renate Müller; these and numerous others lent Balcon's productions a professionalism, and a cosmopolitan sophistication and sheen, otherwise rare in British films before the advent of Alexander Korda.

The traffic was two-way. Balcon, always a great nurturer of talent, used the German industry as a kind of finishing school, sending there both seasoned professionals ready for their ultimate step up such as Alfred Hitchcock, and promising youngsters ripe for experience such as Robert

Stevenson. Not everyone, perhaps, found the experience liberating; Graham Cutts, for one, gives the impression of being inhibited by the Ufa environment. *The Blackguard* looks terrific, with massive sets (designed by Hitchcock and constructed on sets left over from Lang's *Siegfried's Death*, 1923) and moody chiaroscuro lighting (Theodor Sparkuhl), but Cutts seems terrified of moving his camera, preferring to cut clumsily within set-ups. Yet *The Rat* (1925), made by Cutts a few months later at Islington, is notable for its sweeping, fluid camerawork – though this may be simply because in the interval Cutts had discovered the use of the dolly.

Hitchcock, though, clearly revelled in the technical facilities available in Germany. While working at Neubabelsberg he had taken every opportunity to watch Murnau shooting *Der letzte Mann* (*The Last Laugh*, 1924) on a neighbouring stage, and Karl Freund's famous *'entfesselte Kamera'* (unchained camera), gliding and swooping and soaring around Robert Herlth and Walter Röhrig's intricate sets, left its mark on Hitchcock's own directorial début later that year. For all the well-rehearsed stories he would subsequently tell of mishaps and disasters during production, *The Pleasure Garden* (1926) fizzes with high spirits, playing exuberantly with witty angles and camera movements. (*The Lodger*, 1926, the first film he shot back at Islington, seems relatively static by comparison.) It is worth noting, though, that both *The Pleasure Garden* and *The Mountain Eagle* (1926) were shot, not at Neubabelsberg, but in the slightly less imposing studios of Emelka (Münchener Lichtkunst), a Munich-based rival to Ufa. But in general the German connection gave Gainsborough access to a lavish style of production the company could never have mounted on its home turf, productions that Balcon hoped would appeal to the international – and in particular the transatlantic – market.

Besides the specifically German production tie-up, Gainsborough absorbed a broader cosmopolitan influence through its links with the Film Society. Founded in 1925 by the left-wing intellectual, writer and table-tennis champion Ivor Montagu and the actor Hugh Miller, the society aimed to show experimental, avant-garde and controversial foreign films unlikely to find a general distributor in Britain. Among the European classics that received their British premières at the Society's meetings were *The Battleship Potemkin* (1925), *Man with a Movie Camera* (1928), Vsevolod Pudovkin's *Mother* (1926) and *End of St Petersburg* (1927), Paul Leni's *Waxworks* (1924), Pabst's *The Joyless Street* (1925), Jean Renoir's *Nana* (1926), Alberto Cavalcanti's *Rien que les heures* (1926) and Teinosuke Kinugasa's *Crossways* (1928). Not all the films shown were on this level of high seriousness: the society's members had a taste for comedy, and shorts by Chaplin and Keaton, Disney cartoons and burlesques by Adrian Brunel (made for Gainsborough) often featured on the programmes. But the prevailing view of the society by the film industry, which remained for the most part hostile and suspicious, was of 'Eton-cropped women and long-haired men'[12] gathered together to watch highbrow, sexually depraved Communist propaganda. It was accused, with oddly contradictory logic, of stealing audiences from regular exhibitors and of bringing the industry into disrepute by showing films no decent person would wish to see.

Several of the society's earliest members were closely connected with Gainsborough. Montagu, whose criticisms (both public and private) of Gainsborough productions Balcon had read with interest, was called in by him to help rejig Hitchcock's *The Lodger* after it had been rejected by C.M. Woolf. Subsequently, Montagu worked regularly for the company as supervising editor, screenwriter and scenario chief. Adrian Brunel, a member of the society's council, was taken on as a director by Gainsborough about the time the society was set up. (Montagu and Brunel also found work outside Gainsborough, editing foreign films for British consumption.) A fellow council member was Sidney Bernstein, Balcon's backer from his Birmingham days. Victor Saville, Balcon's first partner, Hitchcock, Ivor Novello and Angus MacPhail were society members and regularly attended screenings. Another founder member, the graphic artist E. McKnight Kauffer, designed title cards for several Gainsborough productions, including *The Lodger*.

There is some ambivalence about Balcon's own attitude to the Film Society. He too was a member, attending screenings whenever possible and maintaining (as he would throughout his career) an open-minded interest in the latest developments in world cinema. Yet he seems to have felt sceptical, initially at any rate, about the society's viability. Three days after the screening of the initial programme (which featured *Waxworks*, experimental work by Walter Ruttmann, comedy shorts by Brunel and Chaplin and a Broncho Billy Anderson Western from 1912), Hugh Miller wrote to Montagu:

> Michael Balcon told me quite simply and firmly lately that he did not think the society would go any distance. I had imagined Balcon to be more than a business man but I am afraid he is not. Really … our policy is simple and our ambition sincere but we can always rely upon the business man to misunderstand.[13]

Balcon's estimation of the society no doubt soon changed; years later he was to write nostalgically of it as 'the Mecca of all cineastes'.[14] But Adrian Brunel stated in his autobiography that he was obliged to resign from the council 'as my employers [Gainsborough] insisted that my association with the society would damage the prestige of the films I made for them!'[15]

Such an order may not have come from Balcon – it could have originated with Graham Cutts or C.M. Woolf – but he must certainly have known about it. However, no one at Gainsborough seems to have objected to Ivor Montagu's even closer association with the society – or if they did, he took no notice. At all events, the society's international-minded influence on Gainsborough's films, especially those of Hitchcock and Brunel (less so, perhaps, in the case of those directed by Cutts), can be seen in their scripting, editing, lighting and overall treatment of narrative. Hitchcock certainly learnt from Pudovkin. He famously liked to pre-edit his films, editing in the script and on the storyboard, editing in the camera. As he explained, 'The screen ought to speak its own language, freshly coined, and it can't do that unless it treats an acted scene as a piece of raw material which must be broken up, taken to bits, before it can be woven into an expressive visual pattern.'[16] This echoes Pudovkin's view: 'Film-art does not begin when the artists act and the various scenes are shot. ... Film-art begins from the moment when the director begins to combine and join the various pieces of film.'[17]

The Film Society contingent also made their influence felt on Gainsborough films in terms of casting. Montagu and Brunel had been much taken with Nadia Sibirskaïa's performance in Dimitri Kirsanov's *Ménilmontant* (1924), and persuaded Balcon to let them cast her in *Blighty* (1927). Unfortunately she proved sulky and temperamental, and nearly got herself thrown off the film.[18] In any case, it seems Balcon did not share Montagu and Brunel's high opinion of Kirsanov, since a subsequent letter found Sibirskaïa urging Montagu: 'I wish Mr M. Balcon would see *Sables* [1928], as I think it would change his views on Kirsanov.'[19] In general, however, Balcon relied a good deal on Montagu, the first of the well-connected young Oxbridge intellectuals he would surround himself with throughout his career. '[Mick] always listens to you,' Angus MacPhail observed to Montagu with a touch of malice, 'though perhaps not always understanding what you say.'[20]

While European cinema was coming to Gainsborough via the Film Society, Gainsborough films were being seen in continental Europe via Ufa. The exact terms of the Gainsborough–Ufa co-production deal varied from film to film, but the broad outline remained constant. Generally the agreement was that Ufa would provide the bulk of the finance and the studio facilities, while Gainsborough furnished the script, the director and much of the cast and crew. In return, Ufa retained all European rights, while English-language rights went to Gainsborough's regular distributors, C.M. Woolf's W&F Film Service. The association also allowed certain home-produced Gainsborough films access to Ufa's European distribution network, while others (such as *The Rat*) were shown through Emelka. But though Balcon welcomed the prospect of having his films shown throughout Europe and valued the cross-cultural fertilization that ensued, when he wrote of making 'British pictures with an international appeal'[21] what he primarily meant was an American appeal. His overriding ambition (shared with almost every major British producer down the years) was to 'crack the American market'.

From the first, Balcon had been determined to give his productions the best possible chance of securing American distribution. One obvious tactic, as Herbert Wilcox had already realized when he signed up such actresses as Dorothy Gish, was to import American stars; Victor Saville accordingly travelled to Hollywood (in those days a twelve-day trek by ship and train) to persuade Betty Compson to star in *Woman to Woman* (1923) at £1,000 a week – said to have been the highest salary ever paid to an actor in a British film. The generosity of the carrot was needed to induce Compson to risk working under supposedly primitive British conditions. 'I not only had to sell the screenplay,' Saville recalled, 'but all the technical aids as well – did the studio use a Bell & Howell camera, had the cameraman a good track record, how experienced was the make-up man, and so on and so forth – right down to the efficiency of the wardrobe mistress.'[22] That most British studios enjoyed so dismal a reputation bears out all Balcon's complaints of 'lamentable' standards of production.

Under Gainsborough, the practice of importing American stars continued. Nearly always they were female, to play opposite British male leads, presumably on the same theory as the teaming of Fred Astaire with Ginger Rogers: she gave him sex appeal, he gave her class. (There were exceptions, though, such as the Americans George Hackathorne, cast opposite Betty Balfour in *The Sea Urchin* (1926), and Carlyle Blackwell, who joined up with Balcon to form Piccadilly Pictures and appeared in several Gainsborough/Piccadilly productions.) The relatively low-budget *Pleasure Garden* boasted no less than three Hollywood imports, Virginia Valli, Carmelita Geraghty and Nita Naldi. But the presence of an American star, though it might help, was never enough to ensure Stateside distribution, as Balcon well knew. In 1923, with *Woman to Woman* completed, he made his first trip to America in the hope of interesting

American distributors in the film. None of the major circuits took the bait, but Lewis J. Selznick (father of David O. and Myron), who had his own independent distribution company, loved the film and sold it into the Paramount chain of cinemas. Such was Selznick's enthusiasm that he had the New York showing set up before the London date could be fixed, making *Woman to Woman* the first British picture ever to have its première in New York.

For Balcon and his partners, their satisfaction at this coup – and at some rave reviews for *Woman to Woman* in the American press – was tempered by Selznick's adroit bargaining; talked into signing away most of their rights, they saw precious little revenue from their transatlantic hit. Even worse, the Selznick Company soon afterwards went into receivership, dashing Balcon's hopes of striking a lasting distribution deal. Only in one respect did the Selznick connection have long-term consequences. Myron Selznick came over to London to inspect the Islington studios while the first Gainsborough production, *The Passionate Adventure*, was being filmed. Among the cast were Alice Joyce and Marjorie Daw. Finding London congenial, he married Daw, set up a talent agency in partnership with Alice Joyce's brother Frank, and became Hitchcock's agent. Fourteen years later the Joyce–Selznick agency negotiated a Hollywood contract for Hitchcock with Myron's brother, David O. Selznick.

At one point Balcon was offered a deal that might have solved his American distribution problems for good. Sam Eckman Jr, sent over by Louis B. Mayer to head MGM's London operation, was much impressed with *The Rat* and offered Balcon a contract for a series of Novello films to be wholly financed by Metro. Each one would be guaranteed to return at least £30,000 net to Gainsborough from its North and South American revenues alone. If it failed to do so, Eckman undertook to pay that sum as an indemnity. Balcon himself was then earning about £2000 a year. Under this deal, he realized, he needed to make only one film a year to pay his overheads and boost his and Cutts's salaries to unprecedented levels.

It was a Faustian deal, even if Eckman, whom Balcon personally liked and trusted, made an unlikely Mephistopheles. But behind him stood the might of Hollywood, and for Hollywood Balcon always felt an instinctive mistrust. He was hardly naïve enough to imagine that Metro would happily stump up the cash while leaving him free to make what films he liked; signing the deal would mean selling his soul as an independent producer. 'For days,' he recalled in his autobiography, 'I sweated over this MGM proposal ... and I came to the conclusion then, as I did again in later years, that the financial control of British films should remain in British hands. I turned down security, and never regretted it.'[23]

But if 'the financial control of British films', or of Balcon's films at any rate, did 'remain in British hands', the hands were not Balcon's. Unlike in America, where the Hollywood majors were turning themselves into vertical combines to dominate the industry, the controlling force in Britain lay not with the producers but with the distributors. British producers were caught in a vicious circle: with production (then as ever) seriously undercapitalized and financial institutions mostly fighting shy of an industry they distrusted, the best hope of financing production was securing an advance against distribution from one of the major film renters. But the distributors, most of whom had prospered on renting out American movies, looked askance at British films, regarding them as inferior and unprofitable merchandise – as, indeed, the bulk of them were, being made on the run with inadequate budgets. And so it went on.

Balcon was luckier than most. C.M. Woolf, head of W&F Film Service, had been persuaded to back *Woman to Woman*, albeit rather against his better judgement. But Woolf, an exceptionally shrewd film-buyer without much interest in production, had built up his company by securing distribution rights to the films of Harold Lloyd, Snub Pollard and other popular Hollywood comedians, and had no particular incentive to ensure continuity of production by Balcon or any other British producer. After the flop of *The White Shadow* he withdrew his backing, obliging Balcon to turn to Gaumont to fund Gainsborough's first production. The success of *The Passionate Adventure* made him reconsider, and thereafter he backed all Gainsborough's films. But there was no running contract between the two companies: Balcon had to renegotiate terms for each new project, giving Woolf effective control over what was made and by whom – a control he never scrupled to exercise. His antipathy to Hitchcock's films is well documented.[24]

Intent as he was on exploiting the home market, Woolf rarely troubled himself about the export potential of the films he financed. The same trade paper that carried Balcon's diatribe against the parochialism of British film producers also ran a long and rather sycophantic interview with Woolf on W&F's plans for 1925.[25] In it he expressed satisfaction that his company was now handling a few British-made films, but at no point showed the least awareness of America as anything but a source of product. From his experiences over *Woman to Woman* Balcon knew that he needed help in dealing with the Americans; it seemed unlikely to be forthcoming from his chief backer and distributor.

Six months after his previous article Balcon made a further attempt to rally his fellow producers. 'May I be allowed to register a protest against the chorus of despair?' he wrote in *Kine Weekly*. 'British film production is slightly damned, perhaps, but it is certainly not dead; and a few of us ... are resolved that, as far as we are concerned, the Americans are not going to get away with it entirely.' Rejecting the idea of 'grandiose schemes' costing 'millions and millions', he argued that 'a hundred thousand pounds are all that are necessary for a six-picture a year program ... which will be equal to any six-picture program made in America', and appealed to 'our American friends' to 'co-operate with us in choice of stories and casts' and to guarantee 'an outlet in their own home market sufficient to make profitable the modest program of British pictures which we are capable of'.[26]

This was Balcon's version of 'reciprocity', an idea being widely mooted at the time as an alternative to a government-imposed protectionist quota. The essence of it was that voluntary agreements should be sought with US producers and distributors on the lines of 'We'll take so many of yours if you'll take so many of ours' – always subject, of course, to acceptable subject-matter and quality. One of the chief advocates of this system was the journalist Charles Lapworth, a cosmopolitan Englishman who had lived in Paris, Rome, Berlin and the USA. He had edited the *Los Angeles Graphic*, and had acted as Sam Goldwyn's agent in London and as Chaplin's personal representative in California. Now back in London, he was writing a series of articles for *Kine Weekly* drawing on his recent transatlantic experience. One of them appeared in the same issue as Balcon's piece.

Lapworth's ideas chimed closely with Balcon's. 'If they are wise,' he wrote in the first of his articles, 'the British producers will not relinquish their efforts to supply a steady output of pictures that will get into the American theatres. ... There is no prejudice against British films as such. There is a prejudice against poor films, and if our British producers are honest with themselves they will admit that a lot of poor material has been offered for sale over the water.' And to create this 'steady output', continuity of production was essential: 'The one-picture proposition, either for production or for selling, is hardly worth the attention of serious persons. The single picture costs more to make than one of a series ... and then it is only rarely that it will interest anybody but the odd jobbers.'[27]

Such a coincidence of views could hardly have passed unnoticed by either man, and in August 1925, a month after his article and Balcon's had appeared within a few pages of each other, Charles Lapworth was invited to join Balcon and Cutts on the board of Gainsborough Pictures with the title of editorial director. It was generally recognized that Lapworth's Stateside knowledge and connections were the main reason for his appointment. 'Lapworth, with his valuable fund of experience in the U.S.,' commented *Kine Weekly*, ' … is a real gain to the studio *and* the commercial side of British production.'[28] His duties included screenwriting, and he supplied the story for *The Mountain Eagle*, Gainsborough's first film with an American setting (albeit shot in the Tyrol). A few weeks later another Englishman with American experience joined the company: George Hopton, who had started out in films with Thomas Edison, was appointed Gainsborough's general manager.

The months following Lapworth's appointment marked Gainsborough's most concerted westward push. In October it was announced that the company would be producing a series of films in association with Carlyle Blackwell, an American actor-producer based in Britain. The first of these would be *The Four Warriors*, to a screenplay by Lapworth, 'which is believed', wrote the *Kine Weekly* reporter, 'to be one of the most powerful stories designed for the screen based upon the great war. … Scenes are laid in England, in France, in Germany and in America, and already Gainsborough have received offers from New York for the American exploitation of this film.' Graham Cutts, the same article added, had also received a transatlantic offer of his own, in the form of a long-term contract from Hollywood, but had 'chosen to remain in England' with 'the personal satisfaction of knowing that all his productions have found a market in America'.[29]

The Four Warriors never materialized, but would by the sound of it have represented Gainsborough's most blatant attempt so far at pitching a story to the American market. A few weeks later there came a further announcement: the company had signed a contract to produce six films for distribution in America by the Lee–Bradford organization. Lee–Bradford was not one of the major distribution outfits, although the head of the concern, Arthur Lee, had something of a penchant for British films; during the 30s he would act as Gaumont-British's New York representative. Even so, the deal constituted something of a triumph for Gainsborough, as *Bioscope* jubilantly noted:

> By Mr Balcon's contract the Gainsborough output is not only guaranteed American release, but guaranteed it by what a cynic might say is the only consideration that has any meaning in American film circles – by the dollar itself. … The Lawson–Haris Productions group has contracted to put down in London, before a foot of film is turned, a cash amount representing their share of

the production cost. ... It would be difficult to express in words the tremendous significance of this contract at the present stage. It is, first and foremost, a reciprocity contract of unimpeachable genuineness – the first tangible evidence of reciprocity between this country and the States. But consider it further as to what it means in the revival of British production. ... It is more than a pretty compliment from our opponents in the struggle for markets; it is a revival in prestige for the British producer, a signal to him to hold up his head and go to work with renewed energy and artistic determination. Above all, it is a tribute to the thing which in this business is greater than any considerations of class, creed and nationality, namely the good picture.[30]

It was also, *Bioscope* could have added, a tribute to Gainsborough's ability to produce films suited to the American market. Indeed, Balcon may even have felt he had tipped the balance too far and laid himself open to a charge of pandering to American tastes. Some such misgiving could explain the announcement a few weeks later that Gainsborough were preparing a film to be called *Edward the Peacemaker*, 'based upon the brilliant and romantic career of Edward the Seventh, well-beloved of his people, respected and admired by the whole world'.[31] It was an oddly parochial choice of subject for so globally minded a company and, despite the alleged worldwide respect and admiration, it seems unlikely that such a film would have found a market outside Britain and the Common-wealth. But whether the material proved intractable, or whether it was felt the public was not yet ready for the 'romantic career' of the late monarch (Betty Balfour as Lily Langtry?), nothing further was heard of this patriotic endeavour.

With the signing of the Lee–Bradford deal Balcon saw his international production policy fully vindicated: he had exactly achieved his stated aim of a 'modest six-picture programme' that, with the co-operation of his 'American friends', would be guaranteed an outlet in the US market. 'Gainsborough are putting British Productions on the Screens of the Whole World'[32] exulted a full-page ad in the trade press. But within days of the announcement of the deal Balcon's thunder was stolen by Herbert Wilcox. The US rights to *Nell Gwyn* (1926), which Wilcox had directed for British National with Dorothy Gish in the title role, were snapped up by Famous Players–Lasky. The news was widely hailed as a further triumph for British production and beside FPL, whose Paramount circuit was one of the largest in the States, Lee–Bradford was a very small fish. It was no doubt in the hope of regaining the initiative that in March 1926

Balcon, along with Charles Lapworth and Gainsborough's financial director Arthur Rawlins, sailed for New York.

Balcon and Lapworth's aim, they told the press, was to accomplish 'certain business deals' as well as doing 'everything in their power to assist the general cause of British films in America'.[33] Their timing was singularly unlucky. Even while their ship, the SS *Cedric*, was still in mid-Atlantic, the Washington *Sunday Star* carried a statement by Will H. Hays, head of the MPPDA (Motion Picture Producers and Distributors of America) and widely dubbed the 'Tsar' of the US film industry. Alarmed at what he saw as the encroaching threat of European films, Hays warned that plans by governments such as the British to aid their native film industries by means of subsidies or quotas constituted 'a serious menace to the continued maintenance of our foreign film trade', which might accordingly have to be 'cut down with the consequent dislocation of the trade here at home'. Hays's article, felt *Bioscope*, amounted to 'an avowal of America's private intention to stifle her competitors at all costs'.[34]

Not surprisingly, Balcon and his colleagues arrived in New York to find the climate less than receptive, though the hospitality was as lavish as ever. They were lunched and dined by various industry bodies, invited to speak, politely heard and warmly applauded. 'These people are all expressions of goodwill,' Balcon wrote to his wife, 'and they don't mean a thing they say.'[35] One of the 'certain business deals' he had hoped to pull off was selling *The Rat* to one of the major circuits, but his efforts were hampered by the need to satisfy C.M. Woolf as well as any potential American partner. 'Metro and 1st National I have one or two quite good propositions on here,' he told Aileen, 'but unfortunately they do not include Master Chas Woolf so there is likely to be a great deal of trouble on when I return.'[36]

Lapworth and Rawlins left for England at the beginning of April. Balcon stayed on, lonely and homesick, still hoping to strike a deal for *The Rat* with one of the major circuits. Back in London Lapworth reported on his trip in ambiguous terms: he was 'very appreciative of the courtesy he and Mr Balcon received on all hands from members of the industry'. The British film situation, he added, 'is being watched with great interest over there'; Hays had told him 'it was at the present time the major concern of his own organisation'.[37] Finally, settling for what he could get, Balcon sold the North American rights of *The Rat*, along with *The Pleasure Garden*, *The Mountain Eagle* and *The Sea Urchin*, to Lee–Bradford and returned resignedly to London.

This was Balcon's last visit to America as the boss of his own independent production company. He never abandoned his intention to make films that would sell to America, and Gainsborough held to its international course. Within the next twelve months the company embarked on its first two films assigned to non-British directors: *One of the Best* (1927), directed by the young American T. Hayes Hunter, and the first of several screen versions of Arnold Ridley's stage thriller *The Ghost Train* (1927), directed by the Hungarian Geza von Bolvary, with studio scenes shot in Berlin and railway exteriors in England. But Balcon's New York experiences had made him sceptical about pursuing the chimera of the ideal American distribution deal; and in any case, as the decade wore on, his freedom of operation steadily diminished.

Three factors in particular led to the narrowing of his options. In the wake of the 1927 Cinematograph Films Act a proliferation of new production companies sprang up, eager to provide the 'quota quickies' demanded by exhibitors to fulfil their obligations under the Act. Balcon, whose commitment to quality product remained firm, had no intention of competing at this bargain-basement level, and the quickies were of course never meant for overseas consumption. None the less, they would be jostling for British screen time along with all the other films on the market, Gainsborough productions included; any company that hoped to survive had to be assured of distribution muscle in the home market. The passing of the Act locked Gainsborough still more tightly into its relationship with W&F.

So too did the imminent arrival of sound. In later years Balcon liked to portray himself as having been naïvely slow to recognize the revolution of the talkies, but a near-contemporaneous article describes him as one of those who 'tackled the talkie situation wholeheartedly'.[38] For a small, close-budgeted outfit such as Gainsborough, the financial implications of sound were serious, and not only because of the huge cost of re-equipping the studio. Sound would make the international co-productions so favoured by Gainsborough far more complicated, and far more costly. With dubbing techniques as yet undeveloped, any film that aspired to cross frontiers had to be shot in multiple-language versions, usually requiring several different casts. (Some films were shot in as many as seven different versions simultaneously.[39]) Shooting schedules and budgets expanded, and films that would have needed no more than a modest extra outlay on intertitles now involved major added investment.

Both these factors contributed to the third: the gradual erosion of Gainsborough's independent status. In June 1926, soon after Balcon's return from the States, a corporate reorganization was announced.[40] Piccadilly Pictures, which Balcon had formed in partnership with the American actor Carlyle Blackwell, acquired all Gainsborough's shares, making it the controlling company both of Gainsborough and of Piccadilly Studios Ltd, which held the lease on Islington. Balcon and Blackwell were appointed joint managing directors of Piccadilly, respectively 'in commercial control' and 'in control of production'. The other directors were Arthur Rawlins and Reginald Baker. Graham Cutts stepped down from his directorship of Gainsborough in order 'to devote himself to the company's increased production programme', but a few months later quit Gainsborough altogether. C.M. Woolf became chairman of Piccadilly, and Charles Lapworth resigned his directorship and left the company. Until now Balcon had been free to have his films distributed by any renter he cared to approach, and in theory he still was. But with Woolf as his chairman, he was in effect tied indissolubly to W&F.

A further upheaval followed in March 1927. Gaumont-British, now controlled by the Ostrer brothers and rapidly expanding its field of activities, made a bid for W&F. Woolf told Balcon of the offer; according to Balcon's account, they agreed that, 'despite the financial temptations nothing could compensate for the loss of independence, and I left him reassured that our association would continue unaltered'.[41] The next morning 'a smiling, cheerful C.M.' informed him that he had accepted Isidore Ostrer's offer.

With this deal, which also involved the Ostrers gaining control of another major distributor, Ideal Films, and of the Biocolor circuit of cinemas, Gaumont became the largest producer–renter–exhibitor in Britain and the dominant force in the industry. Balcon issued a statement denying that Gainsborough, or Piccadilly, would be involved in this or any other merger,[42] but it was clear that he was being ineluctably sucked into Gaumont's hungry maw. No one was surprised when, in April 1928, Gainsborough was relaunched as a public company, Gainsborough Pictures (1928) Ltd, with C.M. Woolf and Maurice Ostrer joining Balcon on the board.[43] Gaumont also retained the right to nominate two further directors. Whatever soothing noises were made about continued independent operation, Gainsborough was now a wholly-owned outpost of the Gaumont-British empire.

This absorption by no means put an end to Gainsborough's international trajectory. Quite the reverse: Gaumont-British, which already enjoyed its own strong overseas connections (having after all been founded as the British offshoot of a French company), eagerly embraced the tradition which continued in spirit – as Pam Cook has pointed out[44] – even throughout the war years in such post-Balcon Gainsborough movies as *Madonna of the Seven Moons* (1944). Balcon himself, as joint production chief of both Gaumont and Gainsborough,

was to be closely involved in the 'Film Europe' initiative of the early
'30s,[45] as well as in Gaumont's own bid to penetrate the American market.
But he was no longer his own man. Overall export policy now lay in the
erratic hands of the Ostrer brothers, and developed in ways that Balcon,
left to himself, would have hesitated to follow. As an independent
company, Gainsborough had been known (according to *Kine Weekly*) as
'one of the few British film undertakings which has consistently made a
profit out of its business'.[46] Under the Ostrers no such boast could be
made about Gaumont, and within a few years their ill-starred export
drive would bring the company down in ruins.

Notes

1. Balcon, M., 'British Film Production: Is the general conception too narrow? A plea for wider vision', *The Film Renter and Moving Picture News*, 3 January 1925, n.p.
2. Ibid.
3. Ibid.
4. Powell (1986), p. 236.
5. Monja Danischewsky and Sergei Nolbandov were Russian-born; Georges Auric and Françoise Rosay were French; Alexander Mackendrick and William Rose were American by birth; Alberto Cavalcanti came from Brazil via France; Otto Heller was Czech; Günther Krampf was German, and Henry Cornelius hailed from Germany via France and South Africa; Harry Watt was Scottish; Diana Morgan was Welsh and Jim Morahan was Irish.
6. Seaton and Martin (May 1982), p. 10.
7. Cook (1996a), pp. 81–2.
8. Balcon (1925), loc. cit.
9. Advertisement in *Kine Weekly*, 13 July 1922, p. 17.
10. Balcon, M. (1924), letter to Aileen Balcon, n.d. Held in the private collection of Jonathan Balcon.
11. Feld, H., interviewed in *Das Cabinet des Erich Pommer*, scripted and directed Hans-Michael Bock and Ute T. Schneider, Bayerischer Rundfunk, tx. 19 August 1989.
12. 'C.O.B.', *World's Picture News* (Manchester), 24 April 1927.
13. Miller, H., Letter to Ivor Montagu, 28 October 1925. Held in the Ivor Montagu Collection at the British Film Institute, file no. 47.
14. Balcon (1969), p. 51.
15. Brunel (1949), p. 114.
16. Hitchcock (1937), 'Direction', in Davy, *Footnotes to the Film*, p. 7.
17. Pudovkin (1958), pp. 166–7.
18. Brunel (1949), p. 128.
19. Sibirskaïa, N., Letter to Ivor Montagu, 17 January 1928. Held in the Ivor Montagu Collection at the British Film Institute, file no. 49.
20. MacPhail, A., Letter to Ivor Montagu, 20 November 1928. Held in the Ivor Montagu Collection at the British Film Institute, file no. 47.
21. Balcon (1925), loc. cit.
22. Saville, V. (n.d.), *Shadows on the Screen*, p. 25. Unpublished memoirs of Victor Saville – typescript held at the British Film Institute.
23. Balcon (1969), p. 23.
24. See, *inter alia*, Truffaut (1968), p. 42, and Taylor (1978), pp. 53, 106.
25. Unsigned article, 'Making Phenomenal Headway: W&F's amazing progress in 1924 to be

followed by even greater effort in 1925', *The Film Renter and Moving Picture News*, 3 January 1925, n.p.

26. Balcon, M., 'Will You, Sir William?', *Kine Weekly*, 23 July 1925, p. 49.

27. Lapworth, C., 'Organising the British Output: One Road to a Stabilised Market', *Kine Weekly*, 28 May 1925, p. 41.

28. Unsigned article, *Kine Weekly*, 27 August 1925, p. 41.

29. Unsigned article, 'Gainsborough's Progress', *Kine Weekly*, 22 October 1925, p. 44.

30. Unsigned article, 'Reciprocity in Black and White: Gainsborough's Outstanding Achievement', *Bioscope*, 28 January 1926, p. 48.

31. Advertisement in *Kine Weekly*, 11 March 1926, pp. 18–19.

32. Advertisement in *Bioscope*, 1 January 1926, p. 23.

33. Unsigned article, 'Off To America', *Bioscope*, 18 March 1926, p. 33.

34. Unsigned article, ' "Menace" of British Films: Extraordinary Washington Manifesto', *Bioscope*, 1 April 1926, p. 18, quoting Hays's article in the Washington *Sunday Star*, 14 March 1926.

35. Balcon, M., Letter to Aileen Balcon, 1 April 1926. Held in the private collection of Jonathan Balcon.

36. Balcon, M., Letter to Aileen Balcon, 13 April 1926. Held in the private collection of Jonathan Balcon.

37. Unsigned article, 'Charles Lapworth Home Again', *Bioscope*, 29 April 1926, p. 29.

38. The Editor of *Film Weekly* [Herbert Thompson], 'Famous Producer at 34 Years of Age: Michael Balcon's Romantic Career', *Film Weekly*, 9 December 1929, p. 6.

39. *The Doctor's Secret* (1929), directed in its original American version by William DeMille, was also released in French, Spanish, Italian, Swedish, Czech and Polish versions, each with a different director and cast.

40. See *Kine Weekly*, 1 July 1926, p. 25, and *Bioscope*, 1 July 1926, p. 11.

41. Balcon (1969), p. 31.

42. Unsigned article, 'Davis Halls Sold', *Kine Weekly*, 7 April 1927, p. 25.

43. Culmer, F.G., 'New Companies: Gainsborough Pictures', *Kine Weekly*, 3 May 1928, p. 55.

44. Cook (1996a), pp. 81–2.

45. For more about 'Film Europe', see Higson in this volume.

46. Culmer, F.G., 'Gainsborough Pictures', *Kine Weekly*, 10 May 1928, p. 44.

Surface and Distraction: Style and Genre at Gainsborough in the Late 1920s and 1930s

Tim Bergfelder

Alien methods

In the last ten years the Gainsborough melodramas of the 1940s, together with Hammer horror and the *Carry On* films, have become key elements in critical attempts to challenge traditional conceptions of British cinema. Vilified by the quality press, but cherished by their audiences, the Gainsborough costume melodramas have been invoked to address issues such as the high/low culture divide and its gendered bias, to reconstruct a history of female spectatorship in Britain, and to propose the possibility of a feminine discourse in British popular cinema (Aspinall and Murphy, 1983; Harper, 1994; Cook, 1996a). For Pam Cook, it is the notion of national cinema itself that is problematized by Gainsborough melodrama (Cook, 1996a). Drawing attention to their narratives of miscegenation set in foreign locales, and their disregard for authenticity in terms of visual style, art direction and costumes, Cook discusses these films as specific examples of a British cinema which, unconstrained by fixed notions of national community or identity, openly embraces cultural hybridity:

> The costume films deal in fantasies of loss of identity. They suggest that identity itself is fluid and unstable, like the costume genre itself, a hybrid state or form. And they suggest that national identity is not pure, but mixed (Cook, 1996b, p. 62).

Cook points out that the roots and antecedents of the Gainsborough costume dramas can be traced back to the 1920s and '30s, and to the 'Film Europe' movement, which, for a time, united the film industries in

Britain, Germany and France in a bid to fend off Hollywood hegemony (see also chapters by Higson and Kemp in this volume). In the following pages, I shall look in some detail at the interaction between the British and European industries during this period and its impact on films made by Gainsborough. In the process, a continuity in studio style and a persistence of 'gender' and 'cultural hybridity' as thematic and production concerns at Gainsborough, from the late 1920s to the 1940s, should become apparent.

In another article, I outlined the specific historical and economic conditions under which German and other European film technicians came to work in the British film industry from the late 1920s to the late 1930s (Bergfelder, 1996). One of my central arguments was that the rationale behind their employment had less to do with their stylistic preoccupations than with their technological expertise, which made them attractive to British producers. Yet it is evident that among British colleagues or apprentices there was a clear sense that the German artists contributed more to the British film industry than a few technical innovations. So, if there is indeed a 'German' style, how can it be characterized? I have objected to the use of the term 'expressionism' to define German film style of the 1920s and its legacy, mainly because it connotes a quite separate and clearly defined movement in art, stage and literary history. The relationship between German cinema and expressionism proper is more tentative than the characterization of Weimar film as expressionist allows. This generalization has obscured the diversity of German cinema during this period, locking it into the emblematic image of Dr Caligari and his somnambulist Cesare against misshapen landscapes. On the other hand, if such overdetermined associations could be put to one side, there is some credibility in describing Weimar cinema as expressionist. It is indeed a mode of film-making that placed great emphasis on *expressive* gestures, spectacle, décor and effects.

The legacy of continental artists who worked in the British industry in the 1930s is evident in the '40s Gainsborough films. For example, the costume designer Elizabeth Haffenden began her cinema career in the 1930s under the tutelage of René Hubert, a Paris-born designer who made his mark in the mid-1920s in France and Germany, where he worked in Erich Pommer's production unit at Ufa (Cook, 1996a, p. 129). When Haffenden collaborated with him in the mid-1930s he was working for Alexander Korda, whom he accompanied to Hollywood in 1940. It is interesting to note that Hubert's professional background was not that of a fashion designer; he had trained as an architect and initially worked as a production designer for stage shows (Schöning, 1993, p. 117). In the context of the production at Ufa in the 1920s, this expertise was certainly an advantage – scene composition and the close co-ordination of all visual elements (settings, photography and costumes) into a coherent overall design was a priority of Ufa directors and artists. Haffenden's costumes for the Gainsborough melodramas function in a similar way. They do not aim primarily for historical verisimilitude or accuracy; rather, they display an awareness of the film's overall 'look', emphasizing or mirroring the visual patterns set up by the art direction and the photography. The remnants of a Ufa approach to style in Haffenden's costumes were not lost on the more patriotic sectors of the British press during the war, who criticized some of her work for adhering to 'alien methods' and being 'pro-German' (Harper, 1987, p. 184).

The 'German' influence is far more apparent in art direction. Maurice Carter, who worked at Gainsborough in the 1940s, stated in an interview with Sue Harper:

> It developed from the German and not the American tradition. ... It came up from Ufa, and Craig and Appia. ... We were all very much influenced by films such as *Dr Mabuse*. They were design dominated (quoted in Aspinall and Murphy, 1983, p. 57).

Throughout the 1920s European stage design (for example, the productions of Max Reinhardt) and Ufa's visual style were widely admired and copied by British designers (Carrick, 1948, pp. 11–12). Alfred Junge and Oscar Werndorff, who arrived in Britain in the late 1920s and who became highly influential in introducing new design concepts and methods in British cinema, had worked in both the theatre and the German film industry. By the mid-1930s many art departments of major British film studios were headed by German or other European exiles: Junge led Gaumont-British's department at Lime Grove/Shepherd's Bush, Werndorff presided over the Gainsborough lot in Islington, and Hungarian-born Vincent Korda worked at Elstree and Denham (Bergfelder, 1996). In addition to these more established designers, there were those such as Ernö Metzner and Andrei Andreiev whose stay in Britain was temporary, but whose influence was felt none the less. John Bryan, art director in the 1940s for Gainsborough and David Lean, openly acknowledged the influence of Andreiev and the Viennese-born artist Ferdinand Bellan on his work (Aspinall and Murphy, 1983, p. 58). The main objective of these German or German-influenced art directors was, as with Haffenden's costumes, to convey both atmosphere and meaning through an overriding design concept, encompassing every visual aspect. Working conditions in British studios (at Gaumont-British and Gainsborough in particular) were geared towards achieving this goal. Art directors achieved a crucial position in the production process, and their influence on technical decisions was considerable. With an increasingly complex and expanding field of operation, art directors such as Junge became supervising design directors, or, as they were called from the late 1930s onwards, production designers (Carrick, 1948, p. 12).

Similar developments, though with less dramatic impact, can be seen in photography. Throughout the 1930s European cinematographers such as Günther Krampf, Curt Courant, Otto Kanturek, Franz Planer or Eugen Schüfftan had been praised by the press for their work on British films, and their expertise in lighting technique and trick devices (or special effects) was emulated by their British colleagues (Brandlmeier, 1993, pp. 72–6). This is not to say that the Ufa style of photography translated fully or uncompromised into the context of the British film industry. Günther Krampf, in particular, felt the constraints imposed on him by the requirements of British film-making when he complained in an article in *World Film News* (February 1937):

> The cameraman in Germany was the king of the studio. He worked closely with the director on the preparation for the film and his job was to convey the true meaning of the story through the camera and the camera only. … British producers do not give this power to their cameramen.

Krampf believed in the supreme power of the image – in fact, like many of his German colleagues, he resented the invention of sound as an aberration (the title of the above article was 'The Curse of Dialogue'). Krampf's aesthetic credo, 'The thing of fundamental importance is to tell the story by the picture, to stick closely to the visual effect', might not have become the *leitmotif* of the British cinema that followed, but it has certainly persisted as a noticeable undercurrent (most obviously in the works of Powell and Pressburger, and in the Gainsborough melodramas).

In the following pages I shall look at the German influence on two genres produced at Gainsborough in the 1920s and '30s, the film operetta and Ruritanian romance, and 'white-collar-worker' musicals. These were not, of course, the only genres that Gainsborough specialized in at the time. However, according to Annette Kuhn, during this period 'among British cinema-goers, the most consistently popular type of film was without doubt the musical comedy', both in its European and American varieties (Kuhn, 1996, p. 180). Many of Gainsborough's ventures in this field had some kind of continental connection. Some were multilingual co-productions, some were remakes of Ufa films, or based on German stage plays or novels. Many of them had a substantial contribution from continental cinematographers, art directors, composers and costume designers. In other words, one can see these films as cultural hybrids. However, it is not just the Gainsborough genres that can be characterized in this way. It is my contention that the 'original' German or European sources did not conform to a fixed or 'pure' national identity, but fed upon a variety of different stylistic and generic influences as well as international market considerations. Drawing on these trans-national interactions and on contemporary discourses, I shall investigate the relationship between narrative and visual style in these films.

Ruritanian pleasures

In the first five years after the foundation of Gainsborough in 1924, Michael Balcon established links with Erich Pommer at Ufa, with the Emelka studios in Munich, and with Felsom, the company of producers Josef Somlo and Hermann Fellner. Fellner was also running Fox's German distribution subsidiary, thus linking Balcon to the operations of an American major in Europe. It was at the Ufa studios of Neubabelsberg in 1925, during the shooting of the co-production *The Blackguard* (*Die Prinzessin und der Geiger*) that Balcon's protégé Alfred Hitchcock, then a screenwriter and art director, first came into contact with German studio methods. According to Wolfgang Jacobsen, Hitchcock witnessed and studied the production of Murnau's 1924 film *Der letzte Mann* (*The Last Laugh*) (Jacobsen, 1989, p. 62). A year later, Hitchcock began his directing career at the Emelka studios in Munich with *The Pleasure Garden* (*Irrgarten der Leidenschaft*, 1926) and *The Mountain Eagle* (*Der Bergadler*, 1926).

In terms of generic content and style, Gainsborough's output during this period was a far cry from Balcon's later attempts at building a national consensus in the Ealing films. (In his autobiography Balcon claims that most of this Euro-enthusiasm came from Isidore Ostrer; see Balcon, 1969, pp. 55–67.) Ivor Novello tangoed his way through the underworld of Paris as a roguish *ersatz* Valentino in *The Rat* (1925) and, after its success, in two sequels. *The Constant Nymph* (1928), based on Margaret Kennedy's bestseller about the love of a young girl for a selfish musician and, according to Rachael Low, 'Balcon's most important film during this period' (Low, 1981, p. 51), opts for a setting in the Tyrolean mountains. Even those films that seem to reflect a coherent British identity are not without ambiguities. In the First World War drama *Blighty* (1927), the sombre patriotic tone is somewhat derailed by the presence of the decidedly un-British Nadia Sibirskaïa, whose melodramatic register is in jarring contrast with the more restrained acting style of her British co-actors. Hitchcock's *The Lodger* (1926) clearly manifests the influence of German studio style. The London in this film, with its skilful employment of lighting techniques, mobile camera and optical effects, is no longer the city of Mrs Belloc Lowndes's novel. It could well be the backdrop for the activities of Dr Mabuse.

The cultural ambiguity described above is even more obvious in the Gainsborough film operettas of the late 1920s, and the studio's remakes of German 'white-collar comedies' in the early 1930s. The operetta, and its dramatic sibling the 'Ruritanian' romance (named after the imaginary Middle-European fairyland monarchy in Anthony Hope's literary prototype, *The Prisoner of Zenda*, 1894), was a staple film genre during the 1920s, not just in Europe but in the United States as well. One of the most prominent directors of this genre in Hollywood was Ernst Lubitsch. During his formative years in Germany, he made his mark first with his own brand of cosmopolitan, Berlin-Jewish comedy, and later with historical spectacles such as *Madame Dubarry* (1919), *Sumurun* (1920) and *Anna Boleyn* (1920). After he moved to America he became an expert in the Ruritanian romance, the most notable example being *The Student Prince in Old Heidelberg* (1927), based on the American stage operetta by Dorothy Donnelly and Sigmund Romberg. *The Student Prince*'s muddled cultural identity (a German play turned into an American operetta, to be filmed as a non-musical romance by a German exile in Hollywood) is instructive, because a similar indeterminacy can be seen in Gainsborough's ventures into this genre.

The international success of *The Student Prince* might also explain why Balcon and other British producers frequently returned to this genre – it provided a model for breaking into American as well as European markets. The Gainsborough–Ufa co-production *The Blackguard* (*Die Prinzessin und der Geiger*) had all the narrative hallmarks of the classic Ruritanian romance: a commoner in love with a princess against the backdrop of a fragile and decadent European monarchy (in this case, a ruritanized Russia) under threat from revolutionary assassins. Judging by production stills, the film (directed by Graham Cutts, designed and written by Hitchcock and photographed by the German Theodor Sparkuhl) made no attempt to recreate an accurate impression of Russia. In vintage Ufa style, it turned the masses into ornamental structures, dividing space into geometrical patterns.

The Queen Was in the Parlour (*Die letzte Nacht,* 1927) was originally a successful British stage play by Noël Coward, and might already have been conceived as a pastiche. When Graham Cutts shot it at Neubabelsberg, it starred the French actress Lili Damita as another princess in love (this time the country in question is called 'Zelgar'). Costumes and uniforms, as usual in this genre, were widely eclectic, creating a vaguely central European impression by combining Prussian, Austrian and Eastern influences. *Bioscope* noted in its review the 'lavish setting' and singled out for praise the spectacle of 'the ceremonial of the court and an elaborate carnival'.[1] The cinematographer was the Czech Otto Kanturek and the art director was Oscar Werndorff, both of whom would follow Balcon's call to Britain soon after. For Damita, on the other hand, roles such as this provided her entry ticket to Hollywood. A year later Samuel Goldwyn brought her to the United States.

The international dimension of this genre, and in particular its American market appeal, is equally apparent in *The Gallant Hussar* (*Der fesche Husar,* 1928). Shot in Germany and co-produced by the German subsidiary of the American major Fox, the film conformed for the most part to the narrative conventions of the Viennese operetta, but with an American twist. It starred Ivor Novello as a supposedly Austro-Hungarian army officer with the unlikely name of Alrik who is more interested in parties, drinking and gambling than his career, but who is reformed by the daughter of an American millionaire (played by Evelyn Holt). This temperance of European hedonism with American success ethic was clearly aimed at a moralistic US public. The film was directed by the Hungarian Geza von Bolvary, who had worked for Balcon a year earlier on the co-production *The Ghost Train* (*Der Geisterzug,* 1927). Designed by Werndorff, *The Gallant Hussar* is a perfect example of the incongruous combinations of cultural conventions characteristic of the film operetta or Ruritanian romance of the late 1920s. In its review, *Bioscope* noted 'the beautiful scenery, and many luxurious interiors' and concluded with regard to the narrative: 'This charming picture is convincing proof that fragility of plot is no bar to enjoyment.'[2]

It is clear that with these films both the German producers and Gainsborough were reacting to an international vogue which yearned for a pre-modern, feudal, Middle-European arcadia of pleasure. With their formulaic narratives, the operetta and the Ruritanian romance invoke a hedonist Utopia based on mobility of class and national identity. However, this vision is not necessarily democratic or progressive. In the Ruritanian romance narrative action often revolves around the threat posed by the amorphous, uncontrollable masses, represented by bomb-planting anarchists and assassins. For Thomas Elsaesser, the operetta, particularly in its Viennese variant, enacts an alliance between the aristocracy and the 'Lumpenproletariat', who drink and 'enjoy themselves in the same places, because their common enemy is the hard-working, production-oriented, upwardly mobile bourgeois' (Elsaesser, 1993, p. 33). Writing in the 1920s, Siegfried Kracauer voiced his suspicions about the operetta's regressive politics in a review of Ludwig Berger's film *Ein Walzertraum* (1925): 'There are well-mannered arch-dukes and tender flirts ... , the common people, continuously drinking and singing in winegardens, Johann Strauss, Franz Schubert, and the old and venerable Emperor' (quoted in Bock and Töteberg, 1992, p. 148).

However, such an analysis is not altogether appropriate in its approach to this genre. For example, it ignores the knowing artificiality and irony of the narratives. More importantly, as contemporary press reviews – such as those from *Bioscope* quoted above – indicate, it is not the narrative that provides the paradigmatic framework for this genre, but visual style. It is a style which has no other referent than itself; it is not a mode of representation, but one of display. Thomas Elsaesser has pointed to the significance of the genre's invocation of late Imperial Vienna. Like the film studio or the cinema, the Austrian capital in such films is presented as a space of make-believe, masquerade and *mise en scène*. In other words, Viennese society, with its enacted hierarchies and rituals, its simulated reality, and its illusions and self-delusions, becomes a metaphor for cinema itself and its social functions (Elsaesser, 1993, p. 33).

Throughout the 1920s, issues of style, self-referentiality and spectacle were widely discussed and theorized in Weimar culture, by Siegfried Kracauer among others. Like his contemporary Walter Benjamin, Kracauer perceived the mass cultural forms of his time as giving rise not only to new modes of cultural production, but also to new forms of cultural consumption. For him, this new paradigm expressed itself in 'surfaces' and 'appearances' and, although his critique deals with modern culture in general, one can make a connection with the style-dominated look of the films of this period. If modern culture was seen as ephemeral, then the corresponding mode of cultural consumption was 'distraction'. Rather than condemning this concept out of hand, Kracauer believed in its progressive or subversive possibilities, particularly as a means of breaking down the bourgeois high/low culture divide:

> This also meant rejecting the belief that art ... was, and always would be, irreconcilable with more superficial pleasures and less permanent involvements. Distraction not only represented a valid alternative to the paradigm of high culture, its practices also

demanded a redefinition of mass culture based on the ideological nature of such distinctions (Hake, 1993, p. 261).

Kracauer remained ambivalent about the subversive potential of cinema (as the above comments on *Ein Walzertraum* indicate, he disliked the operetta intensely). On the one hand, in its ephemeral surface attractions it accelerated the dissolution of fixed identities (class, gender, nationality) into pleasure and desire. On the other hand, it could reinforce these same identities and become a medium of oppression and social coercion. According to this critical framework, the film operetta and Ruritanian romance are open to both interpretations.

After the conversion to sound the Viennese operetta became a crucial factor in Ufa's strategy, which was launched with *Der Kongress tanzt* (1931), directed by the impresario Erik Charell, whose stage production of the operetta *Zum Weissen Rössl* (*White Horse Inn*) had been a phenomenal success with German and British audiences (Claus, 1996). *Der Kongress tanzt* (*The Congress Dances*) was shot simultaneously in three language versions (German, English and French), a common practice in the years to come. Balcon, under his agreement with Ufa, had the contractual option for the British distribution rights of these multilinguals, and he had influence over the casting and other aspects of the English versions. On the whole, however, he was less than happy with this form of production, and he recalls in his autobiography: 'The difficulties of working in this way are infinite, and impossible to exaggerate. And the boredom!' (Balcon, 1969, p. 60). During the following years, Balcon more often opted for a different form of international co-operation, producing remakes in British studios of German films that were adapted for British audiences. Furthermore, the vogue for the operetta in its Viennese variant had begun to recede slightly in the early 1930s as it made way for more contemporary forms of musical comedy. Still, operettas continued to be made in British studios throughout the decade, mainly to provide star vehicles for continental singers such as Richard Tauber, Jan Kiepura and Joseph Schmidt. Hitchcock's *Waltzes from Vienna* (1934), a romanticized account of the lives and music of the elder and younger Johann Strausses, shot at Lime Grove and with sets designed by Alfred Junge, is another example. Despite Hitchcock's own reservations about the film ('The lowest ebb of my career', Truffaut, 1978, p. 91), it might be worth taking another look at one of the least discussed entries in Hitchcock's *oeuvre* and reconsider it in a generic framework.

Shopgirls, secretaries and impostors

The prototype for a more contemporary type of musical entertainment, *Die Drei von der Tankstelle* (*The Three from the Petrol Station*), had come out before *Der Kongress tanzt* in 1930. Directed by Wilhelm Thiele, the film was a fast-moving musical comedy set in the present day and centred around three unemployed and penniless friends who, after being evicted from their home by a singing bailiff, decide to run a petrol station. Watching the film today, *Die Drei von der Tankstelle* has aged well – in its urbane charm, it invites comparison with Hollywood's New Deal comedies or René Clair's '30s films, rather than with the doom-laden austerity usually associated with German cinema. The thematic and stylistic affinity between these different national genres certainly owes a lot to the internationalist strategies of the European and American film industries in this period, and it also suggests cross-influences between countries which need to be investigated further. At the time of *Die Drei von der Tankstelle*'s initial release, contemporary reviewers noted the ironic uses of the new technology of sound and the facility with which the songs and tunes were integrated into the plot (Rother, 1992, pp. 272–6). Some were taken aback by the way in which real social issues such as financial ruin, poverty and unemployment were represented by snappy dance numbers and song lyrics. The film critic Ernst Jäger, however, openly welcomed this aspect:

> All you deadly serious people out there in your poor life of today: you are just wearing a costume, throw it off, be as carefree as these three happy station attendants. Whether you're wearing a tuxedo or the rags of a beggar, there is always a body underneath which ought to dance, which ought to move (quoted in Jacobsen, 1989, p. 110).

The implied reader of this review, and the addressed audience of the film itself, would have been the German white-collar worker, a class which had been seriously affected and derailed by the immediate post-war years and the economic crisis of the late 1920s.

Musical comedies of the early 1930s such as *Die Drei von der Tankstelle*, *Die Privatsekretärin* (1931), *Ich bei Tag und Du bei Nacht* (1932), and *Viktor und Viktoria* (1933) can be seen in the context of this social background. Like the operetta and the Ruritanian romance, they open up Utopian possibilities. However, as Richard Dyer points out in relation to the Hollywood musical:

Entertainment does not ... present models of Utopian worlds. ... Rather the Utopianism is contained in the feelings it embodies. It presents, head-on as it were, what Utopia would feel like rather than how it would be organised. It thus works at the level of sensibility, by which I mean an effective code that is characteristic of, and largely specific to, a given mode of cultural production (Dyer, 1981, p. 177).

In the early 1930s films, adherence to a rigid work ethic is abandoned in favour of idleness and hedonistic pleasures, and the figures of the social scrounger and the impostor become positive role models. The heroines, trapped in uniforms behind shop counters or in assembly lines of office typewriters, break free from their monotonous work routine by marrying their boss, becoming show stars, or running off with a charming and frighteningly happy scrounger into dance-floor heaven. Boundaries of class and gender are, if not dissolved, then at least open to revision: cross-dressing (for example, in *Viktor und Viktoria*) and the crossing of class barriers (in *Die Privatsekretärin*) are frequently employed narrative devices. Again, it is primarily through visual means that these cross-overs and desires are brought to the surface – in the deceptive appearances of dresses, uniforms or costumes, in the flashing billboard signs and city lights, reflecting the fragmented and virtual yet exciting geography of the modern metropolis, or in the simulated reality of the stage sets and nightclubs doubling and mirroring the films' construction of an illusion.

Die Privatsekretärin was the first of this genre that Balcon brought to Gainsborough, as *Sunshine Susie* (1931), which was a phenomenal box-office success in Britain (Kuhn, 1996, p. 180). Although Balcon considered the film as merely a universal 'Cinderella story' (Balcon, 1969, p. 55), the British version retained many of the generic characteristics of the German original. Renate Müller was cast in the female lead as the secretary out to catch the boss (the economic aspect of love was always clearly signposted in these narratives). Müller, who had starred in the German version, brought to *Sunshine Susie* a chirpy, tomboyish independence typical of female characters in German musical comedies of the time. The film also captures the visual emphasis of the Ufa productions, for example, by fetishizing the heroine's typewriter – an emblem of female working life in the 1920s – as a central image. It was photographed by the German cameraman Mutz Greenbaum, who became one of Gainsborough's most prolific cinematographers in the 1930s and who later anglicized his name to Max Greene (see Petrie in this volume). Rachael Low has commented that *Sunshine Susie* has a 'disembodied air' and 'placelessness' about it

(Low, 1985, pp. 93–4), a criticism that is often levelled against multilingual versions and remakes of the 1930s (and, for that matter, against international co-productions in general). However, one could argue that these characteristics are precisely what the German variant of this genre is about – the pleasure involved in loss of identity. Müller was husband-hunting for Gainsborough again in *Marry Me* (1932), a remake of the German *Mädchen zum Heiraten* (1932). *Marry Me* had a much stronger British presence in terms of personnel: the script of the German original was adapted by Angus MacPhail and Anthony Asquith, and the photography was by Bernard Knowles.

The continental origins of the genre became increasingly camouflaged in Gainsborough's subsequent films. The British stars who took over from continental performers such as Müller, and who became most closely associated with the remakes of German films, were Jessie Matthews and Jack Hulbert. The comedies starring Hulbert recaptured the fascination of Weimar society with modernity in their emphasis on cosmopolitan lifestyle, consumer culture and new technologies, but they transported this fascination into a distinctly British context (see Harper in this volume). For Marcia Landy, however, *Love on Wheels* (1932), based on a German screenplay and photographed by Greenbaum, adhered to 'a different mode from that of many of the British comedies of the era', evoking the style of the Weimar avant-garde director Walter Ruttmann (Landy, 1991, p. 345). The influence of a 'German' style of photography is indeed evident in Greenbaum's work for this film: for example, in its frequent use of low angles. Like *Sunshine Susie*, *Love on Wheels* manifests a fascination with inanimate objects (mainly commodity products and machines), a characteristic of Fritz Lang's '20s films as well. The overall narrative style, however, has an editing pace that conforms to a classical mode of film-making (namely, the Hollywood standard) and is far removed from the rhythm of Ruttmann's work.

Jessie Matthews's version of modern femininity, on the other hand, was close to the style of female stars in early '30s German cinema. Her gamine, slightly androgynous physique, her non-classical prettiness and her frantic vitality were all qualities she shared with actresses such as Renate Müller, Elisabeth Bergner or Dolly Haas (all of whom worked on British films at some stage in their careers). Incidentally, Matthews's first film at Gainsborough was *There Goes the Bride* (1932), a remake of the German *Ich bleib' bei dir* (1931), whose star Jenny Jugo bore a striking physical resemblance to Matthews. In writings on British cinema history, Matthews's screen persona of a shopgirl Cinderella has often been contrasted to the working-class authenticity of her contemporary

Gracie Fields (see Higson, 1995). Jeffrey Richards has referred to the Matthews films as 'Art Deco fantasies', another foreign art movement that, like expressionism, is easy to invoke and difficult to define (Richards, 1984, p. 208). Richards perceives these films as being concerned with the middle class in Britain in the 1930s. In other words, the genre's original social focus, the white-collar worker of Weimar society, had shifted in translation to the British middle class, necessarily resulting in new ideological configurations.

I would argue, however, that this translation process, far from providing these remakes with a more pronounced national identity, accentuated the genre's ambivalent social dimension further. As I have indicated above, in the German examples of the genre, social, national and gender identities are in a state of flux, which related to the experiences of a particular class in Germany at the time. For many left-wing Weimar critics (see, for example, Kracauer's *Die Angestellten*, 1924), it was this social 'placelessness' that rendered the white-collar worker a potentially progressive force. Transposed into the context of the British class system, this discourse can be seen as posing a challenge to the rigid class distinctions of the time. In British film criticism, however, there does not seem to be a comparable tradition that assigns progressive potential to the middle class or to social mobility. Instead, categories such as 'community' and 'national cultural tradition' are invoked more or less unquestioned, which not only perpetuates a contradiction-free view of British society and culture, but also precludes a more complex discussion of social difference and change. The static binary opposition between working and middle class is evident in Jeffrey Richards's evaluation of Matthews's and Gracie Fields's respective characteristics: 'While Gracie maintained her popularity by being the people's heroine with her roots in the community, Jessie gained hers by becoming the embodiment of an essentially individualist middle-class success ethic' (Richards, 1984, p. 224).

In his discussion of Matthews's Gaumont film *Evergreen* (1934), Andrew Higson remains uncertain about the film's social significance. He registers, with some ambivalence, the way in which it abandons fixed notions of social and cultural identity:

It does not do much in the way of imagining a national community, nor does it particularly seek to invoke a distinctively national cultural tradition. Indeed, its project might be seen as the effacement of such difference, rather than its celebration (Higson, 1995, p. 163).

What both Richards's and Higson's comments fail to take into account, however, is the way in which the Matthews films intertwine the issue of social mobility and class with questions of gender and sexuality. Such a consideration provides us with a markedly different perspective on the issue of 'imagined national communities' (bearing in mind that it is always important to enquire by whom such constructs are imagined), but I would argue that in this respect the films are at their most socially poignant and potentially radical.

Marcia Landy, in her reading of Gaumont's Jessie Matthews film *First a Girl* (1935, a remake of *Viktor und Viktoria*, 1933) claims that all Matthews's films for Gaumont-British and Gainsborough revolved around issues of sexual identity (Landy, 1991, p. 341). As in the German antecedents, this issue was dealt with primarily through appearances and illusion, through costume codes, masquerade, performance and a corresponding excess of style and décor in the film sets. Traditional social and gender roles were dispersed into a variety of options: in *First a Girl*, for example, Matthews plays a woman who plays a man performing on stage as a woman. The change of gender is accompanied by a change in social status: the poor shopgirl is transformed into a highly successful female impersonator. *First a Girl* places much greater emphasis on the social dimension of this transformation than the German original: the heroine of *Viktor und Viktoria* is introduced into the narrative as an unemployed opera singer and thus already part of a Bohemian environment. In the British remake, on the other hand, social mobility is presented as facilitating sexual transgression, and vice versa.

It is not so much that the film casts the heroine's own sexual identity in doubt, but that her character becomes a catalyst for homoerotic reactions in those surrounding her. Both men and women fall in love with the image of a man who is really a woman, leading in the first instance to homosexual desire being resolved in heterosexual practice, and in the second instance to heterosexual desire disguising an unfulfilled homosexual yearning. The artificial ambience of nightclub and theatre sets functions as a containment of these desires within the narrative (stressing the film's fantasy nature), but at the same time it emphasizes them on a visual level. The camp aesthetic, evident in the choreography of Matthews's dance numbers and her overall performance style, equally highlights a discourse the film is anxious to contain. It has been argued that *First a Girl* is less radical in these allusions than the German original. Ginette Vincendeau attributes this to the casting of Matthews, who 'takes the film in the direction of her "clean and cheerful" persona, the opposite of the highly ambiguous rendering of the same character by Renate Müller in the German version' (Vincendeau, 1988, pp. 38–9). Marcia Landy claims that the British film keeps a transgressive potential at bay with its overall homophobic tone and ultimate affirmation of traditional gender roles (Landy, 1991, p. 343).

It is also noteworthy that the original film's flirtation with specifically lesbian possibilities (rather than exclusively gay male ones) is far less pronounced in the British remake. Instead, we find a less ambiguous form of female friendship and bonding, particularly in the camaraderie between shopgirls in the all-female environment of the fashion house. Nevertheless, as Andrea Weiss observes, the spectacle of Matthews in male attire still projects an 'image with lesbian overtones', as it is clearly concurrent with lesbian fashions of the time (Weiss, 1991, p. 293). The British press in the 1930s were quick to reassure audiences that the film avoided unsavoury issues in a 'tasteful' manner.[3] One could argue, however, that the tension created by the narrative possibilities (underlined by the film's visual style), and the frantic attempts to keep them under control, heightens rather than diminishes awareness of the film's subversive message.

Traces of a legacy

As I have tried to show, international cross-cultural exchange and influence at Gainsborough in the 1920s and 1930s operated on a variety of levels. In terms of personnel, it was motivated by economic imperatives compelling European film industries in the 1920s to combine forces against the market hegemony of Hollywood. As Andrew Higson has argued, film technicians and artists of various nationalities became pawns in a distinctive production strategy which began as the Film Europe project but which ended in redefining the parameters of the respective national cinemas (Higson, 1993). It is important to keep this industrial background in mind when determining the stylistic and generic influence the continentals had on the films produced at Gainsborough. Designers such as Alfred Junge or Oscar Werndorff were employed by British producers primarily for their technological expertise, and it is in this respect, the innovations in production and studio design and, to a lesser extent, in cinematography, that the continental influence was strongest and had its most lasting effects.

Trying to determine the influence of a German style on Gainsborough in the 1920s and 1930s is a far more complex and difficult task. 'German' approaches to style in the design and photography of British films had to compete and compromise with the studio's standards of screenwriting, editing and directing, which were informed by the model of classical

(Hollywood) cinema (indeed, during the 1930s, many Americans worked in the British film industry precisely in these fields). The ideal of a purely visual film style, as espoused by Günther Krampf, mostly remained an unfulfilled ambition. What can be found in the British films of the 1930s (and later at Gainsborough in the 1940s) are traces, flashes and echoes of this ideal, in the disorientating camera movements and angles intruding into the narrative, in the ostentatiously baroque or ultramodern décor of stage sets calling attention to its own spectacle, and occasionally in attempts to recreate the psychologized lighting for which Weimar cinema was famous. In many cases, these stylistic techniques were nothing more than fleeting or marginal effects. However, in the case of the film operetta and the remakes and versions of early '30s German musical comedies, these stylistic devices not only replicated the iconography of these genres, they can be seen as pointing to an underlying discourse about the relationship between style, spectacle and modern society. With respect to Gainsborough's remakes of German comedies, this discourse, originating in the confusing and fluctuating context of Weimar society, translated into the British context as a potential challenge to the 1930s British class system and as a space to address and question sexual identities and gender roles. It was a challenge Gainsborough's costume melodramas would take up a decade later.

Notes

1. *Bioscope*, 5 May 1927.
2. *Bioscope*, 19 September 1928.

3. For example, *Film Weekly*, 9 November 1935.

4

Desperate Yearnings:
Victor Saville and Gainsborough

Charles Barr

Lovers are parted; years go by; the absent one returns. It is one of the most potent of romance plots, forming the basis of tales as diverse in time and culture as *The Odyssey*, *The Winter's Tale*, Ibsen's *Terje Vigen*, and Tennyson's *Enoch Arden*. As cinema developed, after the polymorphous early years, into a predominantly, and systematically, storytelling medium, it began to make fertile use of this structural archetype. Griffith worked many poignant variations on his initial two-reel version of *Enoch Arden* (1910), Victor Sjöström's 1916 adaptation of *Terje Vigen* was an important work in the development and international marketing of Swedish cinema, and three of the most successful of Gainsborough's early sound films use this basic framework.

Lovers are parted, years go by, the absent one returns. Always, there are children. In *Woman to Woman* (1929), an English officer, on leave from the trenches, falls in love with a French dancer, but is called back to the front before they can marry. Shellshocked in the next attack, he loses his memory, and goes home to acquire an English wife. Years later, the dancer turns up with their son. In *Michael and Mary* (1931), the young woman finds herself alone and destitute when her caddish husband decamps abroad with her jewels; Michael befriends her, and they go on to risk a bigamous marriage. A quarter of a century later, on the day their son becomes engaged, their prosperous family life is threatened by the first husband's return. In *The Faithful Heart* (1932), a young sailor promises his lover that he will come back to her, but twenty years go by in the space of another fade-out and fade-in, and he has become a distinguished soldier preparing, at the end of the Great War, to make a marriage appropriate to his status. A young woman then comes to see him and identifies herself as his daughter, whose mother died in childbirth.

These three films have the same director, Victor Saville. All of them are based on successful West End melodramas: modern ones, in that they were written, and are also set (at least in their 'present-day' scenes), in the period since the end of the war. *Michael and Mary* was filmed shortly after the play came off in June 1930, with the five leading actors repeating their stage roles; both *Woman to Woman* and *The Faithful Heart* were first staged in 1921, and they too had quickly been filmed (though with fresh casting), for release in 1923. Those silent versions, unlike the early sound remakes, do not seem to have survived, which is especially regrettable in the case of *Woman to Woman*, given its status as, surely, the main prototype of the Gainsborough film. The first feature to have Michael Balcon's name on it, it brought together five individuals who would be key players in the new company: Balcon and Victor Saville as producers, Graham Cutts as director, Alma Reville as editor, and, as writer and art director, the man she was soon to marry, Alfred Hitchcock.

Donald Spoto's biography records the moment in 1979 when Hitchcock, less than a year away from his own death, acknowledged that he would make no more films:

> On May 8th there was news of the death of Victor Saville – who had known Hitchcock since 1923 [in fact, 1922], when Balcon, Saville, and John Freedman formed a production company and engaged Alfred Hitchcock as a crew member. ... Peggy Robertson arrived at the office early the next morning, to tell Hitchcock gently before he heard it from the media or a telephone call. She told him that, regretfully, there was sad news – and then, without any expression, Hitchcock said he had sad news to report too. He was closing the office. Today (Spoto, 1983, pp. 550–1).

Linked so closely at the very beginning and at the very end, the two men's careers have some striking parallels. Both worked prolifically as directors in the British industry through the late 1920s and most of the 1930s, sometimes for other producers (including John Maxwell at British International Pictures), but mainly for Balcon at Gainsborough and Gaumont-British. Both of them left for America in 1939 (to Balcon's dismay), and both became American citizens in the 1950s, although Saville, unlike Hitchcock, would eventually return to settle in Britain.

A glance at the Gainsborough filmography reveals that the dominant directors of the company's early years were, successively, Cutts, Hitchcock and Saville. After working on four more Cutts films after *Woman to Woman*, Hitchcock branched out to direct five of his own, starting with *The Pleasure Garden* (1926), and his reputation soon overtook that of

Cutts. Saville had already left to produce a series of Maurice Elvey films for Gaumont (still a separate concern), and then to direct *Tesha* and *Kitty* for his own company, Burlington. By the time he returned to Balcon in 1929 to make the first Gainsborough all-talkie, the *Woman to Woman* remake (Brown and Low, 1984), Cutts had gone elsewhere, and into decline, and Hitchcock was with BIP. After *Woman to Woman*, Saville would, in the next eight years, make sixteen more films for Gainsborough or for Gaumont-British; midway through this period, in 1933, Hitchcock returned from BIP. These movements can be set out schematically (see Figure 1).

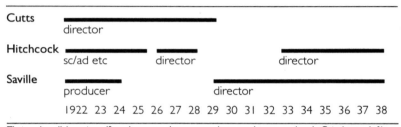

Their only collaborations (first three-way, then two-way) are on the pre- and early Gainsborough films directed by Cutts before 1925.

Figure 1: Three early Gainsborough (and G-B) directors: a basic chronology

The story of Cutts, to his chagrin, being quickly supplanted by Hitchcock as Gainsborough's star director is a familiar one (see, for instance, Taylor, 1978); the central role of Saville in the development of Gainsborough, and of British cinema on either side of the conversion to synchronized sound, has commonly been overlooked. He is seen as important, if at all, mainly for the set of mid-'30s musicals that began with *Evergreen* (1934): see, among many others, Roy Armes, who refers disparagingly to Gainsborough's earlier reliance on an 'endless succession of adaptations of popular West End theatrical successes' (Armes, 1978, p. 68). My own survey article on British cinema, the introduction to *All Our Yesterdays*, does not mention Saville, though it makes much of the early work of Cutts and Hitchcock, and of Anthony Asquith (Barr, 1986). Laurence Kardish, in contrast, in a perceptive essay written to accompany the big 1980s Michael Balcon retrospective in New York, argues that Saville's 'work for Balcon between 1929 and 1936 is as rich as that of any auteur in British cinema' (Kardish, 1984, p. 46). Kardish does not have much space to elaborate on this, and in a sense that is what I want to do in the rest of this article, with the aim not so much of promoting Saville within a hierarchy of British authors (the standard disclaimer – though I do not see this consideration as being an altogether disreputable one), as of getting a fuller sense of Gainsborough by taking a line through his work, and giving due weight to the kinds of melodrama and of theatrical adaptation that characterized his early films.

At the time of the industry's conversion to synchronized sound, both Saville and Hitchcock were associated with BIP. Each of them made a late all-silent film whose prospects were crippled by the sudden upheaval in the market (*Tesha*, 1928, and *The Manxman*, 1929), and followed this with a hybrid, released in two versions after a hurried adjustment to the new technology (*Kitty* and *Blackmail*, both 1929). *Kitty*, Saville's last production before he rejoined Balcon at Gainsborough, was, and has remained, an unlucky film. The rather wet impression created by the title (which is that of the source novel by Warwick Deeping) is reinforced by the tone of the only clip by which it is known: the scene in the synchronized version where dialogue breaks in for the first time, and the lovers carefully enunciate their feelings (this was used again in Kevin Brownlow and David Gill's television series for Channel 4, *Cinema Europe*).[1] The film's dialogue scenes are indeed rudimentary, compared with the intricate ingenuity of *Blackmail*:[2] after the silent version was complete, the last two reels were reshot for sound in a New York studio, resulting in some poor matching of backgrounds and a disastrous loss of overall momentum. Unlike *Blackmail*, this had no chance of being accepted as an authentic talkie either by critics or by audiences.

Yet *Kitty*, in its silent version (and in the first six reels of the synchronized one, which are visually identical), is a remarkably potent melodrama. In terms of Hitchcock, it counterpoints within the one story the lower-middle-class milieu of *Blackmail* with the upper-class intrigues of his 1927 Gainsborough film *Easy Virtue* (adapted from the Noël Coward play). The latter contains the first of Hitchcock's pathologically possessive mothers, fighting successfully to detach her son from his new wife. In *Kitty*, it is as if that son were marrying the Alice White of *Blackmail* (both she and Kitty live and work in modest parental shops whose layouts are virtually the same); this gives a bitter class dimension to an Oedipal struggle that is worked out, in a Great War context, in startlingly vivid terms. Almost literally, the mother castrates her son. An inexperienced pilot with the Royal Air Force in France, Alex is on the point of taking off on a mission when he reads a letter from her giving false information of his new wife's adultery. Traumatized, he loses control, crashes, and is invalided home. His mother pulls strings to get him delivered to her rather than to his wife, imprisons and infantilizes him, and sends to her rival an exultant message: 'Let us be frank. My son is coming back as a helpless cripple – as a husband, useless.' From this midway point the film charts the drive to reunion, regained potency, and final family reconciliation.

Though not a Gainsborough film, *Kitty* indicates the kind of strengths, and concerns, that Saville had developed by the time he rejoined the company as a director. Except in the tacked-on dialogue scenes, the realization does full justice to the thematic potential, with some sophisticated handling of interior sets and locations, and of point-of-view structures. As for Saville's preceding film *Tesha*, no viewing copy is currently available, though the National Film and Television Archive has plans to make one; the plot synopsis points to a similarly bold family melodrama, with a woman taking a lover in order to conceive the child that her husband cannot give her. In Saville's words, 'A desperate yearning for a child was the theme that interested me. ... The film delved into the psychology of parenthood, the causes of sterility and its problems.'[3]

And so to Gainsborough, to the 100 per cent talkie, and the trio of films with the *Enoch Arden* structure: the long-absent one returns (they are interspersed with other projects, but are made in the space of three years). One could call it, alternatively, the *Mary Rose* structure, after the J.M. Barrie play whose heroine disappears for 25 years and then returns, in uncanny circumstances, to visit the son whom she had left as a small boy; and let's not forget that Hitchcock, to the end of his life, cherished the desire, repeatedly frustrated, to make a film of this play which he had first seen in the famously formative theatre-going days of his youth (it ran in the West End for nearly a year, from April 1920). (See, among many references, Truffaut, 1968, pp. 257–8, and Spoto, 1983, pp. 474 ff.) Perhaps if he had gone back to Gainsborough when Saville did, rather than four years later, he might have done it then, since it was so much the sort of thing that the company was favouring at the time. In the event, compared with the full-bloodedness of the contemporaneous Saville projects and the 'desperate yearnings' that they dramatize, the stage adaptations which Hitchcock made for BIP after *Blackmail* look rather tame and shallow: *Juno and the Paycock* (1930, from O'Casey), *The Skin Game* (1931, Galsworthy) and even the much richer *Number Seventeen* (1932, Jefferson Farjeon).

'So many people lost their memory in the war, according to the silents. Now they have commenced to do it in the talkies.' *Variety*'s aside on *Woman to Woman*[4] is echoed by Kardish's comment on the play: 'Its plot device was amnesia, a condition the British aristocracy in purple fiction suffers with the frequency of a common cold' (Kardish, 1984, p. 44). The pattern would recur in the 1940s and attract similar scepticism ('I am not aware that amnesia and schizophrenia are stock parts of our social life' – Harold Wilson, in a parliamentary debate on the film industry in 1948). But, as I have suggested elsewhere, amnesia can operate as a powerful metaphor, able to crystallize common experiences of loss, and of the fading or repression of memory, on the part of an individual and/or a society (Barr, 1986, pp. 14 and 26).

The peculiarly complex rhetoric of flashback and of audiovisual echo that is available to cinema has been exploited in some profound Hollywood dramas of amnesia, among them *Only Yesterday* (John M. Stahl, 1933), *Random Harvest* (Mervyn LeRoy, 1942) and *Letter from an Unknown Woman* (Max Ophuls, 1948); in many respects the Saville trilogy anticipates them. It dramatizes three varieties of memory loss, followed in each case by the dramatic return of the forgotten or repressed: (1) *Woman to Woman*, the Army officer's amnesia through shellshock (as in *Random Harvest*); (2) *Michael and Mary*, conscious repression (of an early marriage); (3) *The Faithful Heart*, less conscious repression (of an early love affair, as in the Stahl and Ophuls films).

It is *The Faithful Heart* that I want to focus on, as being the most fully realized of the three and the one which points forward most clearly to later Gainsborough. *Woman to Woman*, like its companion piece *Journey's End* (1930), has some of the weaknesses as well as the strengths of the characteristic early sound theatre adaptation, dialogue-bound and with restricted mobility (both films were Anglo-American co-productions, shot in Hollywood as a form of technical insurance), and the casting of a brattish American as the seven-year-old son of the forgotten wartime liaison is a severe irritation. *Michael and Mary* has a comparable handicap in the whimsical tendency of the play's author, A.A. Milne (father/author of Christopher Robin) – the grown-up son addresses his parents by the pet names of Bubbles (her) and Binkie (him). Yet both films, like *Kitty* and (one guesses) *Tesha*, still exert a strong charge by the direct way they present an 'intensely dramatic story' of family melodrama: that is the phrase used of *Michael and Mary* by an American correspondent of the British trade paper *Bioscope*, welcoming the fact that it had been bought by Universal for general release throughout America.[5]

By the time of *The Faithful Heart*, there were two significant new developments: sound technology was becoming much more flexible, and Gainsborough was building up a form of group production that seems to anticipate what Balcon would establish a few years later at Ealing. Starting with Saville's next film but one, *The Good Companions*, several of the company's films would carry an innovative joint credit for 'production staff: Angus MacPhail, Ian Dalrymple, Louis Levy, George Gunn' – respectively, it seems, the supervisors of script, editing, music and sound. The last three are already in place (separately credited) on *The Faithful Heart*, and some sources also list MacPhail as script supervisor, though the main script credits go to Saville himself and to Robert Stevenson. This suggestion of the coming together of a genuine team of craftsmen, at ease with the synchronized medium, is borne out in the film's distinctive merging of what might be termed theatrical and cinematic strengths – notably in the emotionally devastating finale, which closely echoes the end of the first half of the film.

Figure 2 tabulates, in the left-hand column, the last 21 shots of Section One, and, in the right-hand column, the final 21 shots of the film. Section One, set in around 1900, leads up to the departure from Southampton of Waverly Ango (Herbert Marshall), a young merchant seaman, whose shore leave has been spent in a brief and intense romance with a Southampton barmaid, Blacky (Edna Best). The other characters in the inn scenes are Ginger, who is Blacky's sister and fellow barmaid; their aunt, owner of the inn; and the major, a permanent resident on whom the character of the major in *Fawlty Towers* could well have been modelled.[6]

Waverly plans to make his fortune abroad, but promises to keep in touch; Blacky is less sanguine. Late at night, she looks out from the bay window of the inn parlour as he rejoins his ship. A tinkly tune plays on the inn's old music box. After shot 1, there is no dialogue. The sequence cuts back and forth between inside (parlour) and outside (sea and boats). Soundtrack consists of a music box and the ship's hooter: the volume of both is consistent across interior and exterior shots.

After the fade-out, twenty years have passed. We learn that Waverly has prospered, and distinguished himself in the war: he has been promoted to Lieutenant-Colonel, has won the Victoria Cross, and is about to make an upper-class marriage. Blacky is long forgotten. Suddenly, with electrifying effect, she reappears: Edna Best again, looking not a day older. She is, of course, the child of the liaison, the mother having died in childbirth – the publicity given to the VC ceremony has helped the daughter (also named Blacky) to find her lost father. Waverly gradually remembers, acknowledges her, and wants to help. Before long, however, the fiancée's hostility persuades her to emigrate to Canada to join her Aunt Ginger. Waverly finds out and intercepts her at Southampton. They go to the inn. The fiancée has foreseen this, meets them there, and gives him an ultimatum: it's Blacky or me. He chooses Blacky.

Last 21 shots of Section One	Last 21 shots of the film	
1. Parlour: Blacky, Ginger, aunt. A toast, proposed by the major.	Parlour door. Father and daughter go out.	1
2. Small boat going out to the ship. CU: cutting furrow in water.	Small boat going out to the ship. CU: cutting furrow in water.	2
3. View from boat approaching ship.	View from boat approaching ship.	3
4. LS of boat approaching ship R-L.	LS of boat approaching ship R-L.	4
5. Back view of Waverly as boat comes alongside ship.	Back view of father/daughter as boat comes alongside ship.	5
6. Quick shot of a hand on the tiller.	Parlour: major in, starts music, then shuffles to window.	6
7. From boat: he crosses to ship and climbs up steps to deck.	From boat: both cross to ship and climb up steps.	7
8. Parlour. She enters L, crosses R to start music, goes back L and sits.	Cut closer to 2-shot, smiling.	8
9. Grieving CU of her as music plays.	Back to wider shot.	9
10. Hand turns engine to Full Steam.	Parlour: major shuffles off L.	10
11. LS of boat leaving ship L-R.	CU: hooter sounding.	11
12. CU: hooter sounding.	Parlour, now empty.	12
13. Grieving CU of her (hooter sounds).	LS of boat leaving ship L-R.	13
14. Parlour: back to wide shot, she at L (hooter).	2-shot father/daughter from below.	14
15. LS of boat away from ship (answering hoot).	CU: hooter sounding.	15
16. Parlour, wide shot, she at L (hooter).	Parlour, empty.	16
17. He paces on deck L-R.	Father/daughter.	17
18. CS of receding water.	CS of receding water.	18
19. He paces on deck, back R-L.	Father/daughter.	19
20. CS of receding water.	CS of receding water.	20
21. Parlour, wide shot, she is slumped. Music clicks off. Fade out.	Parlour, empty. Music clicks off. Fade out.	21

Figure 2: The Faithful Heart

This triggers the replaying of the final sequence of Section One, but with the couple now united rather than separated: the use of the same actress for mother and daughter, with no real attempt made to differentiate the two roles visually, clinches the sense of replay, of second chance. And the major is still there to give them a send-off (and to dig out the antique music box and play the same tinkly tune). Some of the shots are identical in both sequences; most others (including those of the parlour) are taken from the same angle. Soundtrack, likewise, closely reproduces the earlier structure.

It is unnecessary to annotate the chart in any detail, the pattern of repetition and variation standing out so clearly: from the close formal parallelism of shots 2-3-4-5 in each series, through a slight divergence matching the respective content, then back to a tight parallelism in the final six shots, the very strength of the repetition serving here to highlight the one momentous change, namely that Blacky and Waverly are now not separate but together. In timing as in ordering of shots, a precise quasi-mathematical structure underlies the editing by Ian Dalrymple, one of whose next credits would be for *Little Friend* (Gaumont-British, 1934), directed by Berthold Viertel and co-scripted by Christopher Isherwood. A few years later, Isherwood would use his experience on that production as the basis for a *roman à clef* about the film industry (*Prater Violet*, 1945): when experienced editor tells callow scriptwriter, impatiently, that 'The movies aren't drama, they aren't literature, they are pure mathematics', we surely hear the voice of the Dalrymple who had edited *The Faithful Heart*. This is the mathematics not of mechanical calculation but of music and poetry, distilling significance and emotion by means of, not in spite of, a precisely ordered structure, via the filmic equivalents of metre and rhyme.

When Paul Schrader wrote, and Brian De Palma directed, *Obsession* (1975), the drama of a man who loses his wife, and much later falls in love with her look-alike and prepares to marry her, only to discover at the last minute that she is his own daughter, their declared model was Hitchcock's *Vertigo* (1958). The connection, underlined by a romantic Bernard Herrmann score, is clear enough, yet it seems at least as close to *The Faithful Heart* in its use of structured repetition, in its casting of the same actress as mother and daughter (Genevieve Bujold), and in the strongly incestuous overtones of the story. *Obsession* makes these explicit, but they are just as inescapable in *The Faithful Heart*. Waverly is told by his fiancée that 'You know in your heart that [mother and daughter] have both become one', and he acknowledges this in telling his daughter at the end that 'I can start all over again, Blacky, from where my life left off all those years ago.' The replayed sequence of shots then enforces this in the purest cinematic form.

It seems unlikely that Schrader and De Palma were familiar with *The Faithful Heart*, though Hitchcock may well have seen it at the time, and if so, perhaps with a certain envy: here was his old associate riding higher (for the moment) in the industry than he was, and creating a delirious Freudian family romance out of another instance of the *Mary Rose* type of story that he was destined never to make. Though a long forgotten film, *The Faithful Heart* was evidently quite a seminal one. Robert Stevenson, its writer, would go on to direct some powerful melodramas of his own, including the nicely titled *Return to Yesterday* (one of Balcon's early productions at Ealing, 1940) and, in Hollywood, *Back Street* (1941), a film which ends in exactly the manner of *The Faithful Heart*, boat and receding water and all: the Margaret Sullavan character, whose life went wrong when she failed to catch a boat that would have taken her to marry Charles Boyer, gets a second chance decades later, when the images and music are reprised and this time she catches it – except that this is her poignant deathbed vision of what might have been.

In terms of Saville's work, the most obvious continuity is with the series of big Gaumont-British musicals he went on to direct in the mid-1930s, notably *Evergreen* (1934). With Dalrymple again as editor, its exuberant musical numbers offer extended scope to play with the mathematics of staging and cutting, while in terms of story and psychology it operates as an extraordinary souped-up résumé of Saville's previous melodramas, structured once again in two parts with a long time-lapse in between them. Part 1, 'Yesterday': musical star Harriet Green retires. Part 2, 'Today': she apparently returns, 25 years older but still youthful, like Barrie's Mary Rose. In fact, Harriet has died in obscurity and this is her daughter, whose existence has been a secret; and naturally, as in *The Faithful Heart*, mother and daughter are played by the same actress (Jessie Matthews). The complication here is that, until the climactic musical number, the public believes her to be the mother, with only a small group of her intimates sharing our knowledge of her real identity. This masquerade becomes the framework for the *playing out* of a rich and strange variety of romantic emotions, ranging from nostalgia and the fear of ageing to more personal ones. In order to maintain the deception about her identity, the male lead (Barry Mackay) finds himself having to pose, both on and off stage, as her son, though they are of the same generation, and are, predictably enough, falling in love: as he says at the end, 'I've been in love with her for weeks and I've had to go about London calling her Mummy.' Though any 'dangers' are all safely recuperated at the end by a standard heterosexual pairing-off (as in Saville's later musical *First a Girl*, with its masquerade based on cross-dressing), the Freudian undercurrents have been thoroughly exploited along the way, and the whole thing deserves the label given by Andy Medhurst to the Dirk Bogarde amnesia drama *Libel* (Anthony Asquith, 1959) – a 'spicy psychoanalytical brew' (Medhurst, 1986).

But *Evergreen* has not lacked for critical and contextual attention (see especially Higson, 1995), and has conventionally marked Saville's first and main claim to serious attention. I want to give equal weight to the biggest of the four films that he directed between *The Faithful Heart* and *Evergreen*: the adaptation of J.B. Priestley's novel *The Good Companions* (1933). Although Robert Stevenson was not involved, it brought together (as noted earlier) its main 'production staff' from *The Faithful Heart*: Dalrymple, Gunn and Levy, along with MacPhail, and also W.P. Lipscomb (who has a script credit on both films). Released a few months before Korda's *The Private Life of Henry VIII* (1933), it had a less spectacular short-term impact but, arguably, a more significant long-term influence. The teamwork of the key collaborators, their individual functions effaced in a joint credit, matches the teamwork celebrated on screen through the 'Good Companions', the theatrical troupe within which a disparate collection of individuals find fulfilment. (Saville's solo director credit can then be seen as matching the special status, both diegetic and extra-diegetic, of Jessie Matthews in the role of Susie Dean, who leaves the troupe to achieve her dream of West End stardom.) This unity is explicitly presented as a national one: the film opens with a map of England, on which it tracks in to locate its protagonists, successively, in the industrial North, the rural West Country, and a private school that could be anywhere but happens to be in the fenlands of the East: they eventually converge upon a symbolic Middle England to discover, and soon to join, the solidarity of the Companions.

If this sounds like a model for the kind of Second World War propaganda film that pulls together individuals from diverse regions and classes, and forges them into an unselfish collaborative unit, it is not surprising, given the personnel behind it. Though not the first film to be based on J.B. Priestley, it is the first to embody the philosophy of 'co-operation, not competition' that would help to make him a key inspirational figure in various wartime media. The two wartime production teams that most directly lived out this philosophy, in terms alike of their internal organization and of the stories they put on screen, were Ealing, run by Michael Balcon, and the Crown Film Unit, run for most of the war by Ian Dalrymple.[7] If the first version of *Woman to Woman* in 1923 was (as argued above) the prototype of the Gainsborough film, by virtue both of its story and of its personnel, then *The Good Companions* in 1933 stands, likewise, as the prototype of the wartime national epic.

The key to the success of *The Good Companions*, and thus to its strength as a prototype, lies in the vigour of narrative and of style that Saville brings to it from his preceding melodramas. It even ends, in an echo as much of *The Faithful Heart* as of the Priestley novel, with the departure of a ship taking a middle-aged father (Edmund Gwenn as Jess Oakroyd) to rejoin his beloved daughter in Canada. This is the climax of a final montage that sketches the fulfilment of a series of personal romantic dreams, in each case the (carefully plotted) result of, and reward for, the individual's commitment to the communal enterprise of the Companions. In a 1930 review of *Murder!*, John Grierson had famously implored Hitchcock to make a film about modern industrial England 'with the personals in their proper place and the life of a community instead of a benighted lady at stake'.[8] *The Good Companions* offers a healthy challenge to this kind of over-neat opposition between personal and social.

A full career article on Victor Saville would go on to explore the diversity of his subsequent output and influence: his association with Alexander Korda (notably on *South Riding*, 1937), his work as producer for MGM British on *The Citadel* (1938) and *Goodbye, Mr Chips* (1939), and his subsequent career in Hollywood, where he achieved more as producer of melodramas by, among others, Borzage, Cukor and Aldrich than as a director. But although he left the Gaumont/Gainsborough set-up in 1936, and left Britain in 1939, his films had helped to establish clear models for certain strong forms of British production that would flourish in the 1940s: not only in the post-Gainsborough work of such collaborators as Balcon, MacPhail, Stevenson and Dalrymple, but at Gainsborough itself. Clearly there are continuities to be traced between his full-blooded theatrical melodramas of the early 1930s and the more famous Gainsborough melodramas of the 1940s (particularly those with narratives featuring amnesia and schizophrenia), and also between the national epic of *The Good Companions* and of Launder and Gilliat's 1943 *Millions Like Us*.

Postscript

Since completing this article, I have had the chance to consult the Alfred Hitchcock papers held at the Academy's Margaret Herrick Library in Los Angeles. These include letters which show that Saville and Hitchcock did stay affectionately in touch right to the end. They exchanged birthday and Christmas flowers in 1978, and Saville and his wife were among the guests at the American Film Institute's tribute to Hitchcock the following March, after which Saville wrote him a heartfelt letter of reminiscence: 'Phoebe and I were so proud to be with you last Wednesday night. Before getting into bed we read through all your credits, and how my thoughts rolled back to those early days' (12 March 1979; Hitchcock Collection, file 1156). Saville died eight weeks later.

Notes

1. *Cinema Europe: The Other Hollywood*. Six-part series made by Photoplay Productions and transmitted on Channel Four, 1995. The material on *Kitty*, and on other early British sound films including *Blackmail*, is in the final programme, 'The End of an Era'.

2. For an account of the greater complexity of the 'hybrid' Hitchcock film, see Barr (1983).

3. From unpublished memoirs by Saville, *Shadows on the Screen*, held in the British Film Institute's library.

4. *Variety,* 13 November 1929.

5. *Bioscope,* 6 January and 13 January 1932.

6. This comparison, casually made, turns out to have some foundation. In a BBC television production of *The Faithful Heart*, transmitted live on 2 July 1950, Waverly was played by none other than Ballard Berkeley, who a quarter of a century later – familiar timespan! – would create the part of the major in the television comedy series *Fawlty Towers*.

7. See Barr (1989), where I discuss Ian Dalrymple's relatively unsung contribution to wartime documentary.

8. John Grierson, *The Clarion*, October 1930, reprinted in Hardy (1981).

5

'A Film League of Nations': Gainsborough, Gaumont-British and 'Film Europe'

Andrew Higson

Among Michael Balcon's earliest production ventures at Gainsborough were Alfred Hitchcock's first directorial assignments. As is well known, Hitchcock made these films in Germany. Jumping ahead a decade, by which time Gainsborough had been absorbed by Gaumont-British, we find that great British musical star of the 1930s, Jessie Matthews, appearing in *First a Girl* (1935), a remake of a German film, with sets designed by the German art director Oscar Werndorff.[1]

European connections such as these were typical of the various Gainsborough and Gaumont films over which Balcon presided between 1924 (when Gainsborough was set up) and 1936 (when he left for MGM British). Indeed, as Philip Kemp and Tim Bergfelder make clear in their contributions to this book, there was a decidedly internationalist streak to Balcon's work in these years. Even as an independent producer at Gainsborough in the mid-1920s, he looked enviously to the American market, while at the same time keeping a close check on the various European markets. In the mid-1930s, when he was working for Gaumont, he was, as I have shown elsewhere, very much caught up in the parent company's vigorous assault on the American market (Higson, 1995, pp. 98ff). That assault depended heavily on acquiring the services of some of the leading film-makers from the German film industry.

These international leanings, and especially the European connections that Balcon and his colleagues C.M. Woolf and the Ostrer brothers made in the 1920s and 1930s, were not unique in the context of the European film industries of the period. By this time, film was very much an international commodity, especially before the conversion to sound, when the primarily visual language of film seemed to allow it to cross borders almost without effort. The American film industry, of course, had been operating on a more or less global stage since the early 1910s. The unrivalled size of its domestic market, and the tight control in which it was held, meant that production costs for American films could be covered at home, so overseas revenues were almost pure profit. These simple economic facts meant that in export markets the American film industry had something more than a head start over its competitors. In particular, this enabled it to establish itself as the major player in most of the European markets. And it did this by routinely producing more expensive, technically accomplished, spectacular and star-laden films than most individual European producers could afford.

The problem for European production companies such as Gainsborough and Gaumont was that domestic markets were too small to support high-budget films that might reasonably compete with American pictures. One possible solution that proved attractive to some of the more ambitious players in the latter half of the 1920s was to collaborate with companies elsewhere in Europe. This strategy had various advantages. Pooling resources by co-producing with other European companies allowed budgets to be expanded, and, potentially, production values to be increased. Distributing each other's films through reciprocal distribution deals in effect enlarged the domestic market, potentially creating a Europe-wide exhibition space of a size comparable with the American domestic market. Potentially too, these strategies would have the effect of increasing the number of European films in circulation in European markets, thereby limiting the space available to American films.

Pan-European co-operation of this order was perceived by many leading industrialists and commentators of the period as the one real means by which the various European film industries might compete effectively with the American film industry, initially by regaining control of their domestic markets. As an article in a British trade paper suggested in 1927:

> The fight with America can only be started if the European countries co-operate among themselves. ... The national field on our Continent is too small for any single country. ... We can only achieve what we want to achieve, if sales to neighbouring countries are secured on the basis of reciprocity under all conditions.[2]

In the German trade press, the phrase 'Film-Europa' was coined to describe such initiatives.[3] More recently, historians such as Kristin Thompson have adopted the Anglicized version, 'Film Europe' (although the activities implied were never the coherent movement they are sometimes presented as, and I have come across no evidence that the English term was ever used in British publications at the time).[4]

A truly pan-European co-operation always existed more as a set of principles than concrete practices, but some of the leading film companies in Germany, France, Italy, Britain and elsewhere did adopt loosely related industrial policies which were designed to be mutually beneficial. These policies included co-productions, reciprocal distribution agreements and other moves in the direction of cartelization (especially around the development of sound film technology).

A key term in the discourse of the more ambitious producers of the period was 'the international picture'.[5] In effect, this meant a film whose production values aspired to Hollywood's best, a film which had the narrational fluency, economy and continuity of the American film and the technical accomplishment and visual style of the German quality cinema. It also crucially meant a film whose stars were big enough to make an impact in the international market-place. To produce the international film required securing the services of creative workers and technicians capable of achieving the highest standards, and casting the necessary star players. To this end, producers set about assembling international production teams and casts for otherwise nationally based productions, and giving their films international settings, themes, and storylines in an effort to create the sort of film that might appeal equally across national boundaries, in the way that so many American films seemed to. And of course, to ensure that the international film reached the right exhibition outlets in the desired markets required setting up appropriate distribution deals.

As Erich Pommer, the influential head of production at the German company Ufa, commented at the time: 'I think that European producers must at last think of establishing a certain co-operation among themselves. It is imperative to create a system of regular trade which will enable the producers to amortise their films rapidly.' He went on in the same interview to say, 'It is necessary to create "European films", which will no longer be French, English, Italian, or German films, but entirely "continental" films.'[6] In another article, Pommer argued that one of the requirements of the international film was that it should be 'absolutely uncomplicated' in order to achieve the universal intelligibility to which the classical Hollywood film aspired.[7] It was usual for executives discussing the international film to add some nationalist ideological gloss to what was primarily an industrial definition:

This does not mean that the picture should be devoid of every national element. On the contrary, if the motion picture is not deeply rooted in the national soil, it loses its solid foundation and, therefore, its convincing and truthful elements.[8]

Even so, it is clear that the international film meant at one level the 'Europeanization' of certain sectors of British, French or German cinema. But if 'Film Europe' was intended as a means of mutually strengthening some of the major European companies in order to challenge the dominance of American distributors, companies such as Gaumont were at the same time aiming at the American market. Success in this market, of course, required some form of co-operation with American companies. So if there was a Europeanization of cinema designed to challenge American cultural expansionism, there was also a much more extensive cultural and industrial internationalization which involved colluding with that institution we have come to know as Hollywood.

The idea of a pan-European trade cartel which might compete more equitably with the American film industry was first mooted seriously around the time that Balcon entered production and set up Gainsborough. Prior to this, in the immediate post-First World War period, competition and trade restriction was the name of the game. Germany, for instance, banned all foreign films until 1920, while exhibitors in both Britain and France had a moratorium on showing German products (Thompson and Bordwell, 1994, pp. 183–4). By 1923, various people began calling for a greater degree of co-operation and collaboration between European film industrialists. The prime mover in this early period was Germany, at a time when there were few British companies strong enough to have their interests taken seriously in the international market-place. It was not until the revival of domestic production in 1926–7 that British companies entered into these negotiations, but they did so then with some vigour,[9] and by 1928 the British trade press was awash with reports of European deals involving British companies.[10]

Gainsborough, one of the more progressive British production companies, had in fact established productive links with Germany as early as 1924, through deals worked out between C.M. Woolf's distribution company W&F and the leading German companies Ufa and, later, Emelka. The Germans part-financed these productions, which were based in their studios, Gainsborough provided production staff and some actors, and W&F distributed the films in English-speaking markets (Low, 1971, p. 166). *The Blackguard* (1925), directed by Graham Cutts at the Ufa studios, was the first film made under these arrangements, with

Balcon and Erich Pommer co-producing, photography by Theodor Sparkuhl, and a cast featuring American and German stars.[11] Sparkuhl was a very experienced German cameraman who later worked in Britain (at British International Pictures, Gaumont's main rival in the late 1920s) and France, before eventually moving to Hollywood. This sort of career structure was typical of many in the 'Film Europe' years.

Hitchcock, of course, had also worked on *The Blackguard* in various capacities, before directing both *The Pleasure Garden* and *The Mountain Eagle* for Balcon at the Emelka studios in Munich in 1926. Once more, the production staff and casts were multinational, the latter including American actors. But if this is evidence of Gainsborough's internationalism, it is worth noting that the movement of personnel was almost all one way, with all but one of Gainsborough's German co-productions up to 1930 being made in Germany, thereby benefiting from their much better-equipped studios and the expertise of their technicians. It was not until the early 1930s that graduates of the German film industry came to work at the Gainsborough and Gaumont studios in London – though several, like Sparkuhl, had worked at Elstree in the late 1920s.

In 1927, in the run-up to the passing of the Quota Act, Gaumont-British was established as a major vertically integrated company. After it absorbed W&F, the distribution of Gainsborough films also came under the Gaumont umbrella, with Gaumont eventually gaining a controlling share in Gainsborough in 1928 (Low, 1985). As part of their expansion, Gaumont announced in 1927 that they would be distributing a number of European productions, including Ufa films. Later that year, Gaumont and Ufa established a reciprocal distribution deal which secured German distribution for British films on an unprecedented scale. This was especially significant given the new German quota (*kontingent*) regulations restricting foreign access to the German market. Reports on the deal noted that: 'It is planned also from time to time to exchange artists, so that British artists may learn German techniques and acquire "box-office" or star value in both countries and vice versa.'[12] In his autobiography, Balcon also recalls (with some distaste) numerous visits with Woolf to Berlin to secure British rights for German films, with Balcon often staying behind as 'production supervisor', advising on the editing of the films for English-speaking markets (Balcon, 1969, p. 52).

Gainsborough's Anglo-German production links continued in this late silent period, with several films being made in Berlin under the supervision of Hermann Fellner and his colleague Josef Somlo, through their Felsom production unit. The first of these films, again made in conjunction with Ufa, was Cutts's Ruritanian *The Queen Was in the Parlour* (1927), based on a Noël Coward play. The next four were made from German scripts (though three of them were adaptations of British plays) by the Hungarian director Geza von Bolvary: *The Ghost Train* (1927), *The Gallant Hussar* (1928), which had to be registered as a foreign film, *Number Seventeen* (1928) and *The Wrecker* (1928), which was the only one of the films made in London. These were all clearly international productions, making the most of the 'Film Europe' idea – though, once more, the scope was not merely European since the casts were again drawn from American as well as British and German talent.

The 'Film Europe' principle gained an additional impetus through a series of international (or at least European) film conferences which took place throughout the 1920s (Higson, 1996a). The first such conference was held in Paris in 1923, at about the time that Balcon's first film was being completed. This was perhaps the first concrete pan-European initiative – but simmering antagonisms and the inflation crisis meant that no German representatives were invited, and there was much bad feeling in the trade press between France, the hosts, and Germany. Even so, the German trade press recognized the importance of international co-ordination for what was pre-eminently an international industry, and looked forward to participating in the next such conference.[13] Three years later, in 1926, a second conference was organized, again in Paris. This time, the trade press was full of reports about the need for co-operation between France and Germany, the two acknowledged market leaders.[14]

The 1923 conference in Paris was in many ways typical of the international film conferences of the 1920s.[15] Most commentators of the time saw it as a major event of potentially enormous significance. This was despite the fact that the conference's internationalism embraced neither German nor American representation, while its industrial scope was restricted to exhibition interests. Thus the central debate of the conference concerned what one delegate described as their 'one common enemy'[16] – not American competition, which seems to have remained implicit at the proceedings, but taxation on box-office receipts. The work of the conference as a whole was justified not in trade terms or on economic grounds, however, but in cultural, political and moral terms. Taxation was improper, it was argued, because cinema was a vital artistic and scientific instrument of modern society, and a vital means of maintaining public morale. Several speeches thus acknowledged how important it was for the trade to champion cinema as a means of education and so raise the status of the film industry.

The conference also resolved to create a permanent consultative and administrative body which might co-ordinate the efforts of the film industry to improve its standing and promote its interests worldwide. While this was officially to be a federation of exhibitors, it was much discussed at the time as a 'Film League of Nations'.[17] This was no doubt an attempt both to uplift the profile of the federation and to link it to production interests. In an editorial under the title 'Internationalising the film', one British trade paper wrote of how the conference might

> set up a standard of production that should so considerably widen the scope of appeal of each individual film as to bestow upon it an international appeal, which must inevitably result in the broadening of the scope of bigger and better pictures, the adopted slogan of every producer, and creating an opening for every picture, no matter what the nationality of its origin, in the markets of the world.[18]

The editorial went on to link economic logic to cultural and political principles, and specifically

> the principle ... that the photoplay, speaking in an universal language, is capable of being made the ambassador of nations, to the advancement of trade, commerce and general security, and the welding into one common brotherhood of the peoples of the whole universe.

In the end, the efforts to establish a pan-European trade federation made little headway. None the less, the reference to the League of Nations, and the appropriation of its discourse, is important, not least because it was this body, through the French National Committee on Intellectual Co-operation, which sponsored the 1926 conference in Paris.[19] The League of Nations, forerunner of the United Nations, had been founded at the Paris Peace Conference in 1919 to promote international co-operation over national concerns. It is worth remembering, however, both that the USA dissociated itself from the League, and that Germany was not admitted until 1926 and subsequently withdrew in 1933.

As with the 1923 conference, the 1926 gathering was decidedly Eurocentric, with very few delegates from outside Europe. From the film trade's point of view, the most poignant omission from the list of countries sending representatives was the USA. The American film trade for its part was extremely wary of the purpose of the conference, and the Hays Office apparently tried to prevent the conference taking place (Seabury, 1929, pp. 148–64). Although the organizers had intended it to be primarily intellectual, moral and educational in its scope, American trade commentators saw the real agenda as, in the words of *Film Daily*, the 'organization of an offensive campaign against the American world "monopoly"', including the implementation in European countries of quota regulations and other restrictions on film imports.[20] In the event, *Film Daily* was right in thinking that the conference would threaten American commercial interests. The proceedings were in the end dominated by trade personnel and trade concerns, and particularly by the effort to establish a pan-European economic policy. In this context, the 'intellectual' concerns of the organizers were more or less sidelined, leading *Film Daily* to conclude that:

> Camouflaging its motives with an altruistic program of the uplift of motion pictures, the first International M[otion] P[icture] Congress is seeking to perfect a combination against the American film 'monopoly'. ... Wholesale attack on American producers featured [in] meetings of the eight congressional committees into which the conference has divided itself. ... But beyond the general idea of a rival combination, there was a lack of any definite proposals for circumventing the 'movie kings of New York and Hollywood'.[21]

Other reports in the European trade press confirm this sense of a cultural and political forum overtaken by trade interests – but also of a lack of concrete developments that might yield tangible results for the European film industry. This was partly because of the ambivalent attitude of European industrialists towards American cinema, embodied in the bi-focalism of Balcon and his colleagues in the British film industry, looking both to Europe and to America. As one German executive put it, 'What's most important [about the conference] is the chance to establish contacts with European industry representatives and their desire to create a far-reaching film policy. But, above all, don't form an anti-American policy.'[22]

If the 'Film Europe' idea was anti-American, it was clear that the European film industry as a whole could not afford to antagonize the American film companies – and there was much dismay, and even anger, among delegates that the American film industry had failed to send representatives, despite its central place in the international film trade. This by the same delegates who were trying to establish a European film alliance designed to increase the market share for European-made films at the expense of American films. As one journalist noted, 'During the film congress, the Europeans waited for the Americans as if they were waiting for a rich uncle.' [23]

It would be difficult to say that this conference, or any of the others, had a really profound impact on the development of European cinema in the period. Pious resolutions about international understanding and the like would have been almost impossible to enforce without a European equivalent of the Hays Office. And while the conference was a place where contacts could be made and deals no doubt struck (and was seen by its participants as vital in this respect), 'Film Europe' as such was never solidly on the agenda. Indeed, it could not have been at Paris in 1926, given the official intellectual discourse of the conference. But clearly this was a forum where the idea of a pan-European cinema alliance came to take on a more solid and extensive understanding. If it were to be taken further, then some sort of permanent commission would have been necessary to co-ordinate the activities and interests of members.

As in 1923, a permanent commission was in fact one of the intended outcomes of the conference, and a resolution was passed calling such a body into being. But once again the efforts produced very little of substance, though a third conference was organized in Berlin in 1928, this time by exhibitors.[24] One of the more concrete proposals discussed at this conference was a plan put forward by the Deutsches Lichtspiel Syndicat to form a European-wide Exhibitors Syndicate, or Trust, with thousands of cinemas – a basis from which they might then move into production of films which would have a guaranteed market. This was envisaged along the same lines as First National in America, and was described in one of the British trade papers as 'one of the most important steps ever initiated in the history of European films'.[25] Inevitably, matters were not this straightforward. Producers and distributors were apparently represented on the proposed council of the new organization. The implication was that this was a production and distribution-led initiative to establish a strong European market within which they could circulate their own wares, a state of affairs which frightened off some of the exhibitors.[26]

At the same 1928 conference, there were renewed efforts to create a Europe-wide trade association for exhibitors. With these two developments afoot, the American trade press once again expressed great anxiety about what *Variety* saw as the launching of 'a formidable opposition to combat American film supremacy'.[27] Once again, however, plans for a pan-European body came to nought. Subsequent conferences were held in 1929 and 1930. For the trade, each congress provided a politically responsible space in which cartelization could be openly negotiated. As one journalist wrote of the 1929 congress, 'It will have served its purpose if it demonstrates to the American industry that there is a definite Pan-European movement with its own aims and interests.'[28]

On paper, the various film congresses seem to have been quite productive, with numerous resolutions directed towards creating a European exhibitors' association, removing local entertainment taxes, ending the practices of blind and block booking, establishing tariff regulations on the same basis in the different European countries, standardizing the use of sound equipment, and generally increasing European production. Likewise, various companies had established productive relations with counterparts in other national markets. But these tendencies towards cartelization were minimal by comparison with developments in the American film industry. There was in the end no international trade body in Europe on a par with the American Motion Picture Producers and Distributors Association which could carry through the proposals. The pan-European idea consequently progressed on a more piecemeal basis, with the strongest companies simply trying to get the most profitable deals for themselves. Reciprocity was thus a means to an end, and did not produce the sort of powerful and permanent cartel that would have been needed to compete equitably with the American companies.

It was no coincidence that national trade barriers to foreign, and especially American, films were introduced during the same period that the pan-European idea was being explored (the German *kontingent* regulations were introduced in 1921, and the British quota regulations in 1927, for instance). Protectionism was a way of consolidating the national base for companies expanding on a multinational front. But while the British and German film trade barriers did indeed reduce the American distributors' share of the market, they also thereby freed up the system for limited exploitation by other European film industries.[29] As a leading German trade journalist commented in 1927 in an article in the British *Kinematograph Weekly*:

> We know full well what the [British Quota] Bill is directed against, and what it stands for, and from the point of view of the Pan-European film idea, we feel in perfect agreement with British opinion on this matter. ... Every strengthening of British production means, viewed from the world market point of view, a strengthening of ourselves.[30]

Likewise, a year later, John Maxwell, head of British International Pictures, one of the two British vertically integrated combines (the other being Gaumont), noted that 'Germany had found it hard to maintain a supply of product which would satisfy their box-offices, and therefore welcomed another source which, while helping to maintain themselves, would not menace their existence.'[31]

The various economic strategies which comprised 'Film Europe' were generally justified in ideological terms which voiced concerns about American cultural imperialism and the erosion of national cultures and of 'the artistic force of the authors, actors and producers of old Europe, the centre of the world's culture'.[32] At the 1929 congress, the president of the French exhibitors' association declared that the purpose of the congress should be to consider how the European film industries could best organize themselves to resist the strength of the American majors:

> We have reached a point in France, in England, Italy, Germany, Spain and Poland when we must ask ourselves if our intellectual patrimony, achieved during two thousand years of civilization, is not passing into other hands, afterwards to be rented back to us by authors of a culture much different to our own. We must consider the means of uniting – defending ourselves on our own territory.[33]

In statements such as these, the economics of cartelization – organizing collectively to protect and improve profit margins – are justified in terms of nationalist ideologies. But it was cartelization which became the central strategy of 'Film Europe', while cultural identities were only really explored in terms of their marketability. In effect, nationalist ideologies were mobilized in the defence of a multinational bid for a greater and more secure control of the most accessible and profitable markets.[34] What is clear from even the briefest look at the production of films designed for the sort of extended market-place that 'Film Europe' sought to establish is that those films are rarely self-consciously national. On the contrary, as we have already noted, a key term in the discourse of the leading industry executives of the period was the international film.

The conversion to synchronized sound, which began in Europe in 1929, forced the internationalists in the film industry on to a new footing. Motion pictures could no longer be understood so carelessly as the outpourings of an international language; they were now, precisely, 'talkies' – and they talked in many different languages. Dialogue seemed potentially to limit the international circulation of films to circulation within language-specific markets – and at the same time to limit pan-European co-operation as well as American penetration of European markets. In fact, of course, the conversion to sound was the occasion for the emergence of by far the strongest European trade cartel, the Tobis–Klangfilm–Kuechenmeister group, which brought together interests in the radio, phonograph, electrical and film industries, with significant stakes in a number of European states. The economic clout of the group posed a real threat to American trade interests in sound film technology, but although the group established several production outlets these were not in the long run particularly successful.[35]

The problem of language was clearly the most pressing one facing producers in the early sound period, especially those interested in developing international co-productions. During the transitional period, and before the development of adequate dubbing techniques, one way in which a number of companies in both Hollywood and Europe attempted to circumvent the language problem was to produce different language versions of the same film. These multilingual versions were generally produced back-to-back on the same sets, using the same narrative structures and continuity and the same production team, but recruiting different casts for each version, including stars known in the market specific to the language being used.[36]

To some extent, the 'Film Europe' project was revitalized by this new strategy which almost inevitably involved co-production arrangements across national borders. The Tobis group was among many which developed multilingual production. The British interests of this group were represented by Associated Sound Film Industries (ASFI), set up by a British-based American entrepreneur, I.W. Schlesinger, and run by a German, Dr Rudolph Becker, former head of the foreign department at Ufa, and a Hungarian, Arnold Pressburger, who had been producing in Germany for many years. ASFI produced two lavish multilinguals in Britain, *City of Song* in 1930 and *The Bells* in 1931.[37]

These were both decidedly international productions and attracted to Britain a number of people active in the German film industry (although ASFI's plans to become a major European producer came to little in the end). *City of Song* was a vehicle for the Polish tenor Jan Kiepura, directed by an Italian Carmine Gallone. The production also brought to London the cinematographer Curt Courant and the designer Oscar Werndorff, who both later returned to work for Balcon. Werndorff also subsequently directed *The Bells*. Balcon, too, became involved in multilingual production, though never in quite such a vigorous fashion as his counterparts at British International Pictures.[38] In April 1929, it was announced that Gainsborough had signed a deal with the German company Greenbaum to make six talkie co-productions, each of them to be bilinguals.[39] Unfortunately, I have no evidence that any of these films were made, and 1929 and 1930 actually seem relatively quiet for Balcon as far as co-productions are concerned.

In 1931, Gaumont-British was reorganized and assumed full control of Gainsborough. Balcon was appointed head of production at both the Gaumont studios at Shepherd's Bush and the Gainsborough studios at Islington. Gaumont continued to import some foreign films for British distribution, among them the spectacular Ufa musical, *The Congress Dances* (*Der Kongress tanzt*, 1931). The film had been made in Germany as a multilingual, with German, French and English versions, the last of which proved a great success at the British box office and paved the way for a renewed Anglo-German co-production arrangement. First of all there was a one-off, Victor Saville's *Sunshine Susie* (1931), an English version of the successful German film *Die Privatsekretärin*, which was also made in French and Italian versions. This was a Viennese-set musical based on a play by Franz Schulz. The German star Renate Müller played the lead part in both German and British versions, and was teamed up with Jack Hulbert in the English version. Although his name does not appear on the credits, Balcon and Low claim that the remake was suggested and arranged by Hermann Fellner, thus continuing his connection with Gainsborough (Balcon, 1969, p. 55; Low, 1985, pp. 130–1). Since *Die Privatsekretärin* was originally made by Wilhelm Thiele for Greenbaum, it is also possible that this was one of the remnants of the deal announced by Gainsborough in 1929.

While Thiele's film had been made as a multilingual, *Sunshine Susie* was a remake, an alternative method of setting up international co-productions in the sound period. It was different from multilingual production in that the versions were not made back-to-back on the same set. Generally, the rights to, say, a German film were bought and the film was remade in an English version in a British studio, with a freer translation, and generally a different crew as well as cast.

The box-office triumph of *Sunshine Susie* and *The Congress Dances* led to Gaumont and Ufa signing an agreement to engage in further co-productions. Thus, in May 1932, it was announced that Gaumont would be making a series of quality versions of selected Ufa super-productions: 'A number of wonderful Ufa productions have been barred to British-speaking [sic] audiences by language difficulties, and the idea is to make English-speaking versions of such pictures.'[40]

The first of these films was *Happy Ever After* (1932). This was actually made at the Ufa studios in Germany under the supervision of Pommer, with the British cast travelling out there *en bloc*, with the exception of Lilian Harvey, who had settled in Germany some years previously and established herself as a major star there (she played the lead role in *The Congress Dances*, for instance). *Happy Ever After* was made as a multilingual, with French, German (*Ein blonder Traum*) and English versions all in production at the same time, with Harvey appearing in all of them. Although the English version had a British cast and was overseen by Robert Stevenson, Gaumont were unable to register it as a British film, which inevitably made it less attractive to exhibitors since it did not qualify for quota purposes.[41]

Other films made under this arrangement with Ufa included *FP1*, directed by Karl Hartl, *The Only Girl*, directed by Friedrich Hollaender, and *Early to Bed*, directed by Ludwig Berger (all 1933), none of which qualified as British – 'nor can they realistically be regarded as products of the British film industry', as Low comments (Low, 1985, p. 94). A later remake of an Ufa film had a slightly different genesis. This was the big-budget Jessie Matthews star vehicle *First a Girl*, made in 1935 by Victor Saville. Where the earlier films had been very much under the control of Pommer at Ufa, *First a Girl* belonged much more to Gaumont. There is thus a clear distinction between the British film and the German and French versions made two years earlier in 1933 by Reinhold Schünzel, *Viktor und Viktoria* (which had starred Renate Müller) and *Georges et Georgette*.

There were plenty of other Gaumont and Gainsborough films with German connections in this period. Following their success in *Sunshine Susie*, both Jack Hulbert and Renate Müller were given further films based on original German scripts. *Love on Wheels* (1932) was a Hulbert vehicle, adapted from a screenplay by Franz Schulz and Ernst Angel. *Marry Me* (1932), starring Müller, was a remake of *Mädchen zum Heiraten*, which had been produced by Fellner and Somlo from another Schulz script. Although *Marry Me* was made in London, it was directed by the successful and experienced German director Wilhelm Thiele, who had also made the German version, but was now on the staff at Gainsborough. Apart from the 1929 version of *The Wrecker*, this was the first of several Gainsborough and Gaumont films directed by émigrés from the German film industry. As such, it was very much a sign of the times.

Further European connections can be found in *There Goes the Bride*, with Jessie Matthews, and *After the Ball*, both 1932, and both remakes of German films. Balcon also set up a couple of French co-productions (*The Battle* and *Temptation*, both 1934), while *First Offence* (1936) was a remake of a French film, and *Car of Dreams* (1935) a remake of a Hungarian film. Franz Schulz's work also proved a fruitful strain, with two further Schulz scripts adapted in 1933 for Anthony Asquith's *The Lucky Number* and Anatole Litvak's *Sleeping Car*.

Arnold Pressburger, who had been in Britain earlier for the two ASFI films, was responsible for a further series of co-productions with Gaumont through Cine-Allianz Tonfilm, which specialized in multilinguals and remakes, generally musicals or operettas. The first Cine-Allianz/Gaumont co-production was the operetta *Tell Me Tonight*, filmed in Germany in 1932. This was a remake of a German film and, like the earlier ASFI films, was very much a multinational production. The producers were Fellner and Somlo, the director Litvak, a Russian, and the cast included Jan Kiepura, for whom the film was a vehicle, and Jessie Matthews's British husband, Sonnie Hale. Two more Cine-Allianz films followed in 1934, *My Song for You*, another Kiepura vehicle, and *Unfinished Symphony*, filmed in Vienna and starring Marta Eggerth. Kiepura and Eggerth were together in *My Heart Is Calling*, directed in 1934 by Carmine Gallone. All three were again versions of German films (the first two were also made in French and Italian versions), and none of them were registered as British films. Later in 1935, in Rome, Gallone directed *The Divine Spark*, another English remake for Pressburger, this time of an Italian film, and again starring Eggerth.

Also made in 1935, *The Tunnel* was another lavish and spectacular big-budget film aimed at the international market. This too was a remake of an earlier German film directed by Kurt Bernhardt (there was a French version as well), but, as with *First a Girl*, Gaumont retained full control over the production, even if they did buy in some shots from the Bernhardt version (Brown, 1977a, p. 67). *The Tunnel* was released more or less at the high point of Gaumont's assault on the American market. In this respect, it is significant that it was no longer a co-production, but was still based on a German model, and used German technicians in cinematographer Günther Krampf and art director Ernö Metzner. The story was perfect for an international film, detailing as it did the building of a transatlantic tunnel. This allowed the space for ideal casting too, with a mixture of American and British stars, including Hollywood-based British expatriates such as C. Aubrey Smith and George Arliss.

The production histories of *First a Girl* and *The Tunnel* are symptomatic of a wider set of issues, for they represent a retreat from the multilingual production. Multilinguals in the end proved far from economic. What was needed to break into world markets was an international picture. But with multilingual production, internationalism was no longer invested in one commodity but was somewhat extravagantly dispersed across the several texts and casts of the multilingual film. Although a few bilingual and trilingual films like the Ufa/Gaumont cycle and the Cine-Allianz films were made later in the decade, multilingual production as a central policy of the European and American film industries was pretty much phased out by 1933.

Ginette Vincendeau argues that economic reasons alone cannot account for the failure of the multilingual mode of production. Such an extreme form of industrial standardization, she suggests, could only in a very small way acknowledge the cultural differences of the various language-specific markets to which such films were addressed. Multilinguals, she writes, were 'too standardized to satisfy the cultural diversity of the target audience, but too expensively differentiated to be profitable' (Vincendeau, 1988, p. 29). To some extent, of course, the multilingual film represented a halfway house between a national cinema grounded in indigenous cultural traditions, and an international cinema whose standards are defined above all by Hollywood and imposed worldwide. But that halfway house was underpinned by the assumption that national identity could be defined solely in terms of language and star image. The eccentricity of the multilingual film was that it spoke the local vernacular but was bound by a stateless blueprint.

'Film Europe' as a coherent and dynamic economic strategy involving businesses in several nation-states virtually died a death with the conversion to a cinema which spoke in tongues and the ultimate failure of the multilingual film. Reciprocal distribution of films no longer made a great deal of sense unless the intended markets for those films spoke the same language, which was patently not true of the pan-European market envisaged in the late 1920s. If we understand 'Film Europe' in terms of the interdependence of markets and international co-productions, then this multinational bid to challenge Hollywood's market supremacy had collapsed by the mid-1930s. If, on the other hand, we understand it in terms of the interdependence of cultures, or of national cinematic traditions – if, in other words, we understand it as a form of international cinema – then 'Film Europe' took on a new form and found a new home in the British film industry in the mid-1930s.

The period from 1932 to 1937 saw a boom in British film production. Several of the more ambitious companies were producing lavish international films designed to compete with Hollywood and break into the American market. Gaumont in particular released a whole string of expensive and spectacular productions, many of them with strong German connections, including *Rome Express* (1932), *Jew Süss* (1934), *The Tunnel*, *First a Girl* and the other Jessie Matthews musicals, and the Hitchcock thriller sextet, from *The Man Who Knew Too Much* (1934) to *The Lady Vanishes* (1938). Almost all these films had leading continental technicians or creative workers in key roles. Again, this was typical of developments in the British film industry at large, and Alexander Korda's London Films and one or two other companies were of course actually run by European émigrés (Higson, 1993).

The cinematographer Mutz Greenbaum, for instance, emigrated to Britain in 1931, where Gaumont put him under contract. One of his first assignments was *Sunshine Susie*, and he filmed numerous pictures for the company in the 1930s. In 1932, the great German art director Alfred Junge joined Greenbaum at Gaumont, and was appointed head of art direction at the Shepherd's Bush studio. The same year, both the cameraman Günther Krampf and the director Wilhelm Thiele joined the Gaumont staff. The next year, Hermann Fellner was at Gaumont as production manager. By 1934, with Junge heading the art department at Shepherd's Bush, Oscar Werndorff was in charge of the art department at Islington. The directors Berthold Viertel and Lothar Mendes were now under contract, as were the art director Ernö Metzner, the cinematographer Curt Courant, the editor Otto Ludwig and the actors Conrad Veidt and Fritz Kortner.[42]

Many of the personnel attracted to Gaumont and other production companies in the mid-1930s were of course refugees from Nazism, but almost all of them had had some connection with the British film industry in the earlier phases of 'Film Europe' – arranging co-production deals, working on British co-productions made in German studios, working on multilingual films, and so on. A number of them had already worked on films in Britain. In other words, they were employed not for political reasons but because they were both known quantities and high-quality professional film-makers whose previous work guaranteed a certain standard of production and who could therefore be expected to bring the sort of polish to films that the internationalist policy required. At the same time, the presence of so many talented technicians and production staff under Balcon's supervision in the mid-1930s was an indication of the relative strength and aspirations of the Gaumont-British combine in this period. In a sense, co-production was no longer a necessary strategy since so many senior colleagues from the major German studios were now working at Gaumont and other British companies.

But the European and the American always went in tandem. Thus, of the eight cameramen who worked on more than four films each for Balcon at Gaumont or Gainsborough between 1933 and 1937, two were British (Bernard Knowles and Leslie Rowson), three had worked in the German film industry (Krampf, Greenbaum and Courant) and three had long experience in Hollywood (Glen MacWilliams, Phil Tannura and Charles van Enger). Out of a total of 94 films, 27 were shot by Krampf, Greenbaum and Courant, and 29 by the Hollywood-trained cinematographers.[43] And while Balcon used several actors from the German studios, he also used Hollywood stars like Sylvia Sidney, Robert Young and Walter Huston.

Rome Express is a good example of the sort of cosmopolitan production designed to secure access to international markets that typified these years: a train journey across Europe (or at least a little bit of it: France and Italy), accumulating on the way various ethnic character types (the upper-middle-class English golf addict, the French police chief, the central European villain ...), foreign stars (Conrad Veidt ...), and foreign technicians (the Austrian cinematographer, Günther Krampf ...). But alongside Veidt we find an American star, Esther Ralston, and alongside Krampf, an American editor, Frederick Y. Smith. This hybrid internationalism, combining what one reviewer saw as 'the fine imagination and clever psychology of the Germans, the showmanship of the Americans, and the clear-cut fresh narrative skill of the British',[44] might be seen as a recipe for disaster. But the film was in fact a great success at the box office, and admired by critics on both sides of the Atlantic. Caroline Lejeune, for instance, believed that, 'For the first time in the history of British films we have a production that can be judged by international and not by British standards, and can present its case in a form as efficient and persuasive as Hollywood's own.'[45]

'Film Europe' in the 1920s was a series of strategies designed to expand and consolidate markets and spread production costs. The international aspirations of the British film industry in the mid-1930s, and its absorption of so many European film-makers who had earlier collaborated on co-productions, were in effect a reworking of the 'Film Europe' idea, an attempt to create in London the sort of multicultural space that was (and is) Hollywood. But it was never really on a scale that might seriously challenge the world's film capital.

When the British production sector, including Gaumont, collapsed in 1937, there was less incentive for top film-makers to stay in Britain, and fewer places where they could work. Gaumont was by now in severe financial difficulties and had already cut back drastically on production and staffing. The onset of war and internment only exacerbated the problems. Inevitably, several moved on to Hollywood, including British directors and producers such as Alfred Hitchcock, Herbert Wilcox and Victor Saville. At the same time, several of the graduates of the German film industry (they were not by any means all German) stayed on in Britain and had a lasting impact on studios such as Gainsborough.

The developments charted above and referred to collectively as 'Film Europe' represent a vital moment in the international cultural and economic development of cinema. The part played in these developments by Gainsborough and Gaumont-British was clearly of some importance, both within the confines of the British film industry and on the wider European stage. The differences between the small independent production company of the mid-1920s and the large, vertically integrated combine are also clear. In the mid-1920s, Gainsborough maximized its film-making potential by its involvement in co-productions in German studios. By 1928, Gainsborough was no longer an independent but was simply one of the production arms of a much larger enterprise, for which distribution deals were as important as co-productions. Probably the most telling difference is that in the 1920s, Gainsborough sent a few of its staff to Germany, but in the 1930s, while some Gaumont staff continued to travel to Germany, movement in the other direction was more prominent. For both political and economic reasons, it was now London that was the Mecca, not Berlin. Or perhaps it was just a resting-place on the way to the real Mecca, Hollywood. Even if that was the case for many of the people involved, the European influence, and specifically the German influence, was of long-term importance, not just for Gainsborough but for the British production sector as a whole.

Notes

1. Parts of this chapter have appeared elsewhere in a different form, in German translation in Higson, 1996a, and as a conference paper, '"Film Europe": an Historical Perspective', presented at *Turbulent Europe: Conflict, Identity and Culture*, EFTSC, London, 19–22 July 1994.

2. *Kinematograph Weekly*, 21 July 1927, p. 29.

3. See, for instance, 'Film-Europa – Keine Theorie mehr', *Film Kurier*, 7 August 1928.

4. See, for instance, Thompson (1985, 1987); Thompson and Bordwell (1994); also Staiger and Gomery (1979); Higson (1992, 1993, 1996a); Higson and Maltby (1998).

5. This is the title of an article by Erich Pommer in *Kinematograph Weekly*, 8 November 1928, p. 41.

6. C. de Danilowicz, 'Chez Eric Pommer', *Cinemagazine* 4 (27), 4 July 1928, p. 11, quoted in Thompson and Bordwell (1994), p. 184.

7. *Kinematograph Weekly*, 8 November 1928, p. 41.

8. Ibid.

9. See, for example, *Kinematograph Weekly*, 8 July 1926, p. 34; 21 July 1927, p. 29; and *Bioscope*, 5 August 1926, p. 19.

10. For details of some of the more ambitious deals of the period, see Higson (1992).

11. Details of films and personnel have been gleaned from a variety of sources. Denis Gifford and Simon Davies's filmography elsewhere in this book has proved invaluable, but I have also consulted contemporary trade papers, as well as Brown and Low (1984); Low (1971 and 1985); Wood (1986); and Schöning (1993).

12. *Bioscope*, 15 December 1927, p. 21; see also *Kinematograph Weekly*, 12 May 1927, p. 39; and *Bioscope*, 12 May 1927, p. 39.

13. See, for example, *Film Kurier*, 22 October 1923 and 2 November 1923.
14. See, for example, *La Cinématographie Française*, 29 September 1926 and 1 October 1926.
15. For contemporary reports of the conference, see issues of *Film Kurier*, *Bioscope* and *Kinematograph Weekly* for September, October and November 1923.
16. Quoted in *Bioscope*, 1 November 1923, p. 29.
17. See, for example, *Bioscope*, 1 November 1923.
18. *Bioscope*, 25 October 1923.
19. For details of the 1926 conference, see Seabury (1929); also issues of *Film Daily*, *Film Kurier*, *La Cinématographie Française*, *Bioscope* and *Kinematograph Weekly* for September and October 1926.
20. 27 September 1926.
21. 30 September 1926.
22. Herr Correll of Phoebus Films, quoted in *La Cinématographie Française*, 1 October 1926. Thanks to Sonia Paternoster for help with French translations.
23. *Film Kurier*, 5 October 1926. Thanks to Nick Riddle and Uwe Brunssen for help with German translations.
24. For details of the 1928 conference, see issues of *Variety*, *Film Daily*, *La Cinématographie Française*, *Film Kurier*, *Bioscope* and *Kinematograph Weekly* for July, August and September 1928; also Krazsna Kransz (1928).
25. *Bioscope*, 29 August 1928, p. 24.
26. See *Kinematograph Weekly*, 30 August 1928, p. 33, and *Variety*, 22 August 1928, p. 8.
27. 22 August 1928, p. 8.

28. *Kinematograph Weekly*, 6 June 1929, p. 25; see also 13 June 1929, pp. 34–5.
29. See Staiger and Gomery (1979), p. 41, and Thompson (1985), pp. 124–5, who both give statistics to this effect.
30. A. Rosenthal, 21 July 1927, p. 29.
31. Quoted in *Kinematograph Weekly*, 29 March 1928, p. 29.
32. Herr Scheer, leader of the German delegation to the 1929 congress, quoted in *Kinematograph Weekly*, 13 June 1929, p. 34.
33. Quoted in *Kinematograph Weekly*, 13 June 1929, p. 34.
34. Cf. Staiger and Gomery (1979).
35. See Kieswetter (1930); Gomery (1976); Staiger and Gomery (1979); Gomery (1980); Murphy (1984); Thompson (1985); Dibbets (1988).
36. See Thompson (1985); Vincendeau (1988); Higson (1992); Ďurovičová (1992); Higson and Maltby (1998).
37. *Kinematograph Weekly*, 14 November 1929, p. 23, 16 January 1930, p. 41, and 16 October 1930, p. 32.
38. On BIP's activities, see Higson (1992).
39. *Bioscope*, 17 April 1929, p. 21.
40. *Kinematograph Weekly*, 5 April 1932, p. 29.
41. See *Kinematograph Weekly*, 5 April 1932, p. 29, and 19 April 1932, p. 19.
42. See *Kinematograph Year Book*, 1933, 1934, 1935, 1936, 1937; also Schöning (1993).
43. Statistics based on Brown and Low (1984).
44. *Kinematograph Weekly*, 24 November 1932.
45. *Observer*, 20 November 1932.

6

'Nothing to Beat the Hay Diet': Comedy at Gaumont and Gainsborough

Sue Harper

Three-tenths of the 271 films produced between 1924 and 1950 by Gainsborough and its parent company Gaumont-British were designed to make audiences laugh. During the 1930s and '40s, comedy films were Gainsborough's staple output. They offered cinema audiences a consistent product, featuring familiar comics who would keep them coming to Gaumont cinemas. Between 1932 and 1936, Gainsborough's creative decisions were intimately involved with those of Gaumont-British, and cannot really be studied without reference to its policies (see chapters by Higson and Kemp in this volume).

Gainsborough was founded in 1924 by Michael Balcon, using the old Paramount studios in Islington, London. Eventually, it became formally associated with the Gaumont-British Picture Corporation, which was set up by the Ostrer brothers in 1927. Balcon became director of production for both companies, and also had overall responsibility for Gainsborough films.[1] Gaumont, the mother company based at Shepherd's Bush, normally produced quality productions, while Gainsborough's studios at Islington were usually dedicated to more low-status fare. Balcon was fortunate in the official support his companies received. The British Board of Film Censors favoured his films, particularly the comedies, which it thought 'clean and light throughout'.[2] More importantly, the Foreign Office actively supported Gaumont during the first half of the decade. Balcon had assembled an unparalleled ensemble of foreign designers and cameramen, and the Foreign Office felt that he could make films which would express the best of British culture, since they were artistically acceptable by international standards. The Foreign Office even sent photographs and scholarly information to Balcon to help him select appropriate workers and aesthetic styles for export.[3] Although Balcon made a modest mark on the international market, it was his ability to successfully export British comedy which drew praise from American distributors.[4]

The Gainsborough comedies fall broadly into six groups. During the first half of the 1930s, two different cycles of comedies were produced, which were in competition with each other. These were the 'Jack' comedies, starring Jack Hulbert, and the film versions of the Aldwych stage farces, featuring Ralph Lynn. In the second half of the decade, these were replaced by the more down-market comedies of Will Hay and the Crazy Gang, which had their roots in variety. During the Second World War, Gainsborough exploited the popular radio comedians Tommy Handley and Arthur Askey. Each cycle of comedies usually had its own producer, its own scriptwriters, individual art director or director, lending it a degree of thematic and visual consistency.

Jack Hulbert, 1932–5

Between 1932 and 1936, comedies accounted for a third of the total output from Gainsborough and Gaumont-British.[5] Balcon was the only producer in the 1930s to accord high production values to comedy, and to deploy top-notch workers in the genre. Most of the films had started life as West End hits. They were sophisticated, verbally adept and culturally up-market. Balcon particularly favoured Jack Hulbert, whom he chose to star in the 1931 *Sunshine Susie* (Balcon, 1969, p. 55). In Balcon's films the gangling Hulbert, with his monolithic chin, was transformed from a light musical comedian into a social and sexual entrepreneur. In *Jack's the Boy* (1932, reissued 1940) the focus of the comedy was the relationship between the father and son, and the way the father frustrated the son's professional ambitions. *Jack's the Boy* was a Gainsborough film made at Islington; it was technically pedestrian, and the art direction by Alex Vetchinsky was lacklustre. It contrasts interestingly with two of Hulbert's other films, which were Gaumont vehicles made at Shepherd's Bush. *Jack Ahoy!* (1934) had the same director, Walter Forde, but a different production team. The hero of *Jack Ahoy!* is a matelot descendant of Lord Nelson who aims to replicate the heroics of his ancestor ('I glory in the past'), and at the end he magically dons the uniform of the battle of Trafalgar. Forde's treatment of the naval/historical theme was reverential, and the film had considerable support from the Admiralty.[6] The script made fun of the class mobility of the hero,[7] but is dominated by the art direction of Alfred Junge. At this stage in his career, German expatriate Junge was able to stamp his signature on even the most intractable material, and for *Jack Ahoy!* he devised some extraordinary effects. The Chinese scenes, including the opium den, are remarkably lush and 'busy', and they are not entirely integrated into the narrative.[8] The complex camerawork and fluid editing, including many circular wipes, are overbalanced by the rather contrived sets (Brown, 1977b, p. 32). The same pattern is true of *Bulldog Jack* (1935), also directed by Forde, where Junge's sets, rather than Jack Hulbert, are the hero of the text. Hulbert again plays a character who is upwardly mobile and who imitates quasi-aristocratic models of behaviour (Brown, 1977b, pp. 7–8, 33–4).

According to Balcon, Hulbert's films were popular at the box office.[9] Hubert Cole argued in *Film Weekly* that Hulbert's charm lay in his ordinariness:

> It is his great virtue that he can conjure up in the heart of his unseen audience the feeling that he is just one of them ... he's just an ordinary sort of bloke with whom we could have a drink without feeling in the least patronized or overawed.[10]

Hulbert himself agreed with this populism.[11] Essentially, the Hulbert comedies demonstrated the ease with which ordinary people might transform themselves into their social betters.

The Aldwych farces, 1933–5

Hulbert and Balcon were close friends, and the 'Jack' films were made with Balcon's full support (Hulbert, 1975, p. 187). This was not the case with the adaptations of the Ben Travers/Aldwych farces. Initially these had been produced by Herbert Wilcox and only distributed by Gaumont-British, for whom they had been extremely profitable.[12] When Wilcox went to work for United Artists, it was C.M. Woolf, the joint managing director of Gaumont-British, who insisted that the Aldwych ensemble players be taken wholesale into the Gaumont stable. Balcon opposed this, but Woolf forced Balcon to produce the films. Balcon objected to the autonomy given to Aldwych playwright Ben Travers and actor/director Tom Walls.[13] Their star, Ralph Lynn, was able to negotiate a contract with Gaumont for £6000 a year, reputed at the time to be the highest salary paid to a British film actor.

The Aldwych film farces were divided between the two studios. *A Cuckoo in the Nest* (1933), *Turkey Time* (1933, reissued 1942), *Lady in Danger* (1934, reissued in 1943), *A Cup of Kindness* (1934) and *Dirty Work* (1934) were made at Shepherd's Bush and were all designed by

Alfred Junge. *Fighting Stock* (1935), *Foreign Affairs* (1935) and *Pot Luck* (1936) were made at Islington and were designed by Oscar Werndorff, Alex Vetchinsky and Walter Murton respectively.

To Balcon's chagrin, the Aldwych farces were extremely popular, both at the domestic and international box office. Tom Walls appeared as the second favourite director in the Sidney Bernstein Questionnaire of 1933, and the films made a great deal of money.[14] In general, the films themselves received more positive than negative responses from the critics, although there was churlish sniping about the 'cotton wool snow' in *Turkey Time*.[15] However, there was some controversy about Tom Walls's style of direction, which was condemned by critics for its theatricality and lack of cinematic flair. The *Observer* unfairly noted that 'This is a director whose idea in making films is to line his stage players against a wall and shoot them at close range.'[16] The studio took such views seriously enough to rebut them in its press books.[17] Walls defended himself stoutly, arguing that good dialogue was more important than fancy camera angles: 'Who, except a handful of people, wants art in the cinema? The masses go there for entertainment. I break them [the filmed farces] up as much as I can. ... I don't *want* things to look static. But I won't sacrifice good dialogue.'[18]

Ralph Lynn and others developed the controversy into an important debate about comic style. Lynn argued that the Aldwych films were deeply rooted in comic tradition, in that they relied on typecasting and caricature.[19] He described in detail the spontaneity still available within the filming process, and the necessity of leaving space for 'extra business' or 'building up': those little, technically unnecessary gags and gestures which, by their very redundancy, defer, prolong and intensify pleasure.[20] In his key article on comedy and national identity, Hubert Cole used these aspects of the Aldwych films as the basis of his argument.[21] The Aldwych films functioned as an important stimulus for both critics and audiences, intensifying the debate about cinematic comedy. But they also offered very specific pleasures: the films made at Shepherd's Bush contained Junge's beautiful and complex sets which, unlike those of the Hulbert films, were integrated into the narrative – the carol-singing sets in *Turkey Time* and the pub exteriors in *A Cuckoo in the Nest* are especially impressive. But even the sets for the Islington films are richly evocative: Werndorff's rural idyll in *Fighting Stock*, and Murton's mean streets in *Pot Luck* are especially eye-catching.

All the films exhibit a swingeing cynicism about human nature, which is conveyed by the acting style of the stars as well as by the scripts. For example, *A Cuckoo in the Nest* deals with a supposed adulterous liaison. The young wife's mother asks her husband how he can be so sure that their son-in-law has committed the deed, to which he replies, 'Just an ordinary public school education.' The dénouement is thoroughly amoral. The erring wife shows her supposed lover to her husband: 'Go on! Look at him!' The husband replies, 'You're right. It's impossible.' By implication, adultery is avoided simply because the prospective lover is unprepossessing. The Aldwych comedies present a world in which women brutally exert power over their menfolk, either by wheedling or by bullying; indeed, Rachael Low suggests that the films are misogynistic.[22] The men keep a weather eye on the sexual main chance; the older man in *Fighting Stock* complains that 'I started off with the mother, before I knew I could better myself with the daughter!' But the films display their cynicism with a quality gloss, so that the audience's guilt at witnessing such betrayal is vitiated. It is the world of the Donald MacGill postcard, but made genteel.

The films demand considerable verbal sophistication from their viewers. The irascible hero of *Foreign Affairs* vows to placate the Goddess Fortune: 'I'll humour the trollop, ere long.' The scripts abound in *non sequiturs*. The old husband in *A Cuckoo in the Nest* remarks, 'I was dreaming I was a Christian among the lions,' to which the rejoinder is, 'But Sir, this is Piddock!' Linguistic precision is also deployed to vent social spleen. One character in *A Cup of Kindness* is described as 'an Old Testament prophet with the staggers', and another is 'a walking weather report in a bowler hat'. The films are an agreeable threnody of spite, which ratify the expression of social bile. Their amorality and sexual cynicism are matched by a profound mistrust of the social system.

These Aldwych films contained a late and significant manifestation of two key comic characters in British culture: the wily Autolycus figure ('the snapper-up of unconsidered trifles', according to Shakespeare), and the foolish Dandy, played by Walls and Lynn respectively. The comic roots of these figures were recognized by Frank Reynolds, when he described the classic Walls role as 'a blackguard who, fortified with enough port, is equal to any occasion, never dismayed, entirely without self-criticism', and the Lynn role as 'the Silly Ass to perfection'.[23] The Autolycus and Silly-Ass/Dandy figures appeared in the novels of Dorothy L. Sayers, P.G. Wodehouse and E.F. Benson, and had a long literary pedigree by way of Oscar Wilde and Arthur Conan Doyle to Lytton and the 'silver-fork' novelists of the 1820s (see Adburgham, 1983). Both Autolycus and the Dandy were always stylish and competent protagonists with social flexibility and compromised morality. After the mid-'30s they continued to appear in cinematic culture, but in a decayed or parodic form. The comic figures who replaced them displayed incompetence, awkwardness and lack of *savoir-faire*. This shift is exemplified in Gainsborough's production of Will Hay's *Boys Will Be Boys* in 1935.

Will Hay, 1935–9

It seems clear that Balcon had begun to downgrade Gainsborough as a centre for the production of quality comedies long before late 1936 when he left Gaumont-British and joined MGM. He had moved first-class personnel, such as Werndorff, away from Islington by mid-1935. Balcon brought in Will Hay and director William Beaudine from British International Pictures to Gainsborough, where they made *Boys Will Be Boys* (1935), *Where There's a Will* (1936) and *Windbag the Sailor* (1936). When Balcon left, Gaumont-British closed down the Shepherd's Bush studio, and Islington became the sole production arm. Five more Hay films were made under the leadership of Maurice Ostrer and Ted Black: *Good Morning, Boys* (1937, reissued 1948), *Oh Mr Porter!* (1937, reissued 1947), *Convict 99* (1938), *Hey! Hey! USA* (1938), *Old Bones of the River* (1938). *Ask a Policeman* (1939, reissued 1942) was made for MGM at Gainsborough, and *Where's That Fire?* was made for 20th Century Fox in the same year (Gifford, 1986). The Hay films were not liked by the censors as Balcon's other films had been, because they were perceived as disrespectful to the authorities.[24]

Hay had his roots deep in vaudeville.[25] He worked on the scripts of the films, and had a healthy disrespect for highbrow approaches: 'Of all the words the film critics use in "slating" a film, I like that word "episodic" the best.'[26] Hay saw his protagonist as a pathetic fellow, a hopelessly inefficient man blundering through a job he knows nothing about. For the audience, laughter was a relief from the threat of identification: 'The real reason why we laugh is because we are *relieved*. Because we are released from a sense of fear. You laugh with relief because it isn't *you* ... it is another character who is made a fool of.'[27] His films are not intended to augment social or humane sympathy, but to disrupt it; they encourage a kind of cheerful, brutal individualism.

Hay's Gainsborough comedies are about venal and incompetent ne'er-do-wells who despise the social system but manage to survive within it. His heroes all masquerade in their roles: schoolteacher, ship's captain, stationmaster, colonial administrator, fireman, police sergeant. The sidekicks in the films, Graham Moffatt and Moore Marriott, are there in order to augment the sense that difficulties can be fudged, that the authorities are fools, and that being portly or toothless is no impediment to getting one's own pleasurable way. The message is that society is irreparably ramshackle and that *sauve qui peut* is the only solution. The hilarious scene in *Oh Mr Porter!* when the trio are pinioned on the sails of the windmill is a perfect metaphor for the human condition. The hapless victims are whirled round in an absurd process which separates them from each other. The Hay films exemplify a different world-view from the Aldwych or Hulbert films, in that they carefully avoid a class-based explanation of the world. Hay may play characters of *parvenu* status, but that is never stressed.

From the 1936 *Windbag the Sailor*, the Hay comedies express an interest in the mass media. In this film, the protagonists are shipwrecked and they use their radio to subdue the natives. The bakelite set instigates a classic cargo cult, in which 'Big Chief Radio Luxemburg' is evoked.[28] The commercial radio network features prominently in *Hey! Hey! USA*. *Ask a Policeman* begins with a broadcast which goes wrong, and listeners are assured that 'The BBC always fades out the best items.' Other aspects of mass culture are parodied, too. Both *Convict 99* and *Hey! Hey! USA* refer to American films. The former quotes Warner Bros' 1932 *I Am a Fugitive from a Chain Gang*, and the latter refers to such gangster classics as Warners' 1931 *The Public Enemy*. The crooks explain away their criminal activities in *Where's That Fire?* by saying that they are 'making an historical film'. *Old Bones of the River* is a sustained meditation on, but not a reworking of, *Sanders of the River* (including an aside from the villain that Bosambo is only a 'bloody nigger').

The Hay films do not transform these references with subversive intent; the deadpan manner merely delivers them, with studied neutrality, for scrutiny. The films work by evoking mild surrealism. For example, the double-decker bus is entirely out of place on the speedway in *Ask a Policeman*, and that provides the humour. More importantly, the Hay films work by establishing a comforting locale where the central myths of the culture can be rehearsed and recognized. These dominant forms of explanation are always presented in a confident and unproblematic manner. In *Old Bones of the River*, Hay attempts to lull a bawling infant by telling a story which is an amalgam of *Cinderella*, *Jack and the Beanstalk*, *Goldilocks and the Three Bears* and the story of George Washington. It works.[29] Certainly the Hay films worked for audiences too, according to the *Kinematograph Weekly* listings.[30] And for critics, there was 'Nothing to Beat the Hay Diet'.[31] The films' anarchic attitudes appealed particularly to the young, and the *Daily Mail* bewailed the imposition of an 'A' certificate on *Boys Will Be Boys*: 'Perhaps it was thought that unless some restraining adult influence were imposed on juvenile beholders of the film, regrettable incidents might ensue in the schools.'[32]

Made in Berlin: Walter Rilla (right) duels Robert Scholtz in *The Blackguard* (1925).

Foreign parts: Ivor Novello (centre) in *A South Sea Bubble* (1928).

Imported lustre: Lili Damita in
The Queen Was in the Parlour
(1927).

Thoroughly modern: Jessie
Matthews in *There Goes the
Bride* (1932).

Remaking gender: Griffith Jones and Jessie Matthews in *First a Girl* (1935).

Victor Saville (left), Edna Best and Herbert Marshall on the set of *The Faithful Heart* (1932).

Obsession: Herbert Marshall and Edna Best in *The Faithful Heart* (1932).

Revisiting the past: Victor Saville at the 1974 National Film Theatre retrospective of his work.

Future design: Ernö
Metzner's set for *The
Tunnel* (1935).

International exotica: Lili
Damita in *The Queen
Was in the Parlour*
(1927).

Eye-catching: Alfred Junge's set design for *A Cuckoo in the Nest* (1933).

Back to the future: Tommy Handley in *Time Flies* (1944).

Star attractions: Ivor Novello and Mabel Poulton in *The Constant Nymph* (1928).

Pushing back the boundaries: the innovative glass ceiling shot in *The Lodger* (1926).

Dark desires: 'expressionist' lighting in *Madonna of the Seven Moons* (1944).

Star stable: (Left to right) Sydney Box with Patricia Roc, James Mason, Pamela Kellino, Stewart Granger and Richard Attenborough.

After Balcon's departure, Marcel Varnel directed all the Hay films, beginning with *Good Morning, Boys* (1937). Arthur Crabtree photographed them, and Vetchinsky was art director. The results were workmanlike but visually unremarkable; the films' lightness of touch comes from rapid camerawork.[33] In all cases except *Boys Will Be Boys*, Marriott Edgar had a major input into the Gainsborough scenarios. Edgar was a playwright who wrote most of the wonderful monologues performed by Stanley Holloway, such as *The Lion and Albert* (1932) and *Marksman Sam* (1934), which demonstrated his penchant for spicing the vernacular with cynicism.[34] This quality disappears from the films after Edgar ceased to collaborate with Hay.

The Crazy Gang, 1937–40

Maurice Ostrer and Ted Black had quite a different philosophy of film comedy from that espoused by Balcon in the early 1930s. Their comedies addressed different social needs; they tend to encourage social consolidation rather than express social isolation. The Crazy Gang films at Gainsborough illustrate the extent of the change. *Okay for Sound* (1937, reissued 1942), *Alf's Button Afloat* (1938, reissued 1943), *The Frozen Limits* (1939) and *Gasbags* (1940) were all reasonably popular.[35] They had the same production team as the Hay films (Varnel, Crabtree, Vetchinsky, Edgar), and their players, like Hay, had a solid vaudeville reputation. But the Crazy Gang films were culturally more eclectic and more up to date. The Hay films were deliberately timeless and, as I have argued, classless. The Crazy Gang films, on the other hand, were more opportunistic and entrepreneurial in the way they exploited contemporary events, and their target audience was more clearly working class, if the preoccupation with 'wallop and birds' (in *Alf's Button Afloat*) can be adduced as evidence.

The Crazy Gang was ensemble playing *par excellence*. Each of the three pairs (Flanagan and Allen, Nervo and Knox, Naughton and Gold) insisted on having equal screen time. This inhibited narrative flow, since Varnel was obliged to use a cumbersome 'trucking' technique and to avoid close-ups.[36] The films were also extremely self-referential. *Okay for Sound*, in particular, is so firmly located within British film culture that it could be interpreted as a cinematic *roman à clef*. It contains a German Jewish producer, Mr Goldberger, who must be interpreted as one of the Ostrers, C.M. Woolf or Alexander Korda; there is a bluff northern financier, who even looks like J. Arthur Rank, and there is a charismatic German director muttering 'Verrückte Kerl!' ('crazy fellow'), who must signify Berthold Viertel or one of the other well-known continental directors working in Britain at the time. The Crazy Gang themselves play film extras, are mistaken for movie moguls and proceed to bring mayhem into the filming process.

All the Crazy Gang films celebrate popular culture. In *The Frozen Limits*, Moore Marriott plays a crazed gold prospector in the Yukon who puts on a music hall show and acts as box-office clerk, stage manager and general messenger boy, rather like an amalgam of all the Ostrers. In the music hall scene, the staircase is clearly a painted backcloth, and the melodrama is recognized by the rowdy audience as 'a phoney from start to finish'. Even so, it is presented as a powerful experience, with the usual components of bad squire and outraged virgin. The performers' disclaimer – 'We're only acting!' – reinforces the vitality of the melodrama, and prompted Graham Greene to comment that the Gang possessed 'an appalling vigour'.[37] The vigour of popular culture is also roundly endorsed in *Okay for Sound*. The Gang supervise a film scene in which a couple, in seventeenth-century dress, dance a conventional ballet. The Gang disrupts this high-art form, and a mutual (and salacious) striptease takes place. Members of the Gang further subvert the film scene by dressing up themselves and performing the ballet in drag. This is much more satisfying than the original dance, which of course is made to seem vapid by contrast.

The Crazy Gang films locate events firmly within the historical process. For example, the whole narrative of *Alf's Button Afloat* is set in motion by the past. In a remarkable opening sequence, we see the transformation of Aladdin's lamp into a treasure trove, accidentally unearthed by the plough. It is bought by a matelot, sold to a rag-and-bone man and melted down into buttons for naval uniforms. Only then does the tale of Bud Flanagan and the magic button begin. *Gasbags*, too, is placed precisely within context. The Gang are accidentally conveyed to Germany on a rudely flatulent barrage balloon. In a series of energetic and tasteless scenes, they enter a concentration camp (where their main punishment is confiscation of their fly buttons), attend a Nazi rally, encourage 50 Hitler lookalikes to go on strike and masquerade as a clump of luckless trees visited by dogs.

Why were the Crazy Gang films so precisely historically situated? This cannot be attributed to the Gang themselves, whose clowning, though inspired, is not exactly cerebral. Varnel never showed any particular historical bent. Edgar's monologues and plays tend to conflate past and present. It seems likely therefore that the impetus came from Ted Black and Maurice Ostrer, and that this aspect of the Crazy Gang films was a sort of rehearsal for the uses of history which they would later ratify with the costume melodramas such as *The Man in Grey* (1943) and *The Wicked Lady* (1945). In effect, the Crazy Gang films signal the beginnings of a change of policy at Gainsborough. They contain the germ of notions about history which would inform Gainsborough's practice during the war, when the past was used as the site of pleasure and stimulus. There is also a clear continuity between the Crazy Gang's use of history, and that of the Tommy Handley films made at Gainsborough.

Wartime comedy

By February 1939 Gainsborough was so successful that it could expand back into Gaumont's old studios at Shepherd's Bush. Indeed, *Gasbags*, the last of the Crazy Gang films, was made there. However, the studio suffered during the bombing of London, and *The Ghost Train* (1941, reissued 1947) was made under extreme difficulties at the height of the Blitz (Askey, 1975, p. 112). During the war Gainsborough was heavily committed to propaganda and camouflage work; Maurice Carter commented to me that 'that was the justification of keeping the studio going'.[38] By the start of the war, as I have argued in detail elsewhere, Gainsborough was structured in a classic Taylorist manner and the producers enforced tight commodity control (Harper, 1994, pp. 119–35). Ostrer and Black were unique in the period in the rigorous way they targeted their films at the mass audience. Wartime costume melodramas were constructed primarily for female audiences. The comedies, too, were intended to fit the needs of wartime, and Gainsborough producers minimized financial risk by investing in stars who had already made successful careers in other media: Bebe Daniels and Ben Lyon and Tommy Handley in radio comedy, and Arthur Askey in vaudeville.

In his overview of wartime comedy, Anthony Aldgate convincingly argues that there was a 'need for a sustained measure of comic relief among the population at large, in order to offset the periodic bouts of depression which inevitably ensue, not least in moments of great crisis'.[39] Aldgate surveys Mass-Observation reports on humour, and concludes that topical references to the war had an intense but short-lived popularity, but that the topics which tickled people's fancy in the long term were ill health, sex and domestic affairs. My own more cursory reading of the same material suggests that there were no significant differences between the sexes in matters of humour.

The wartime Gainsborough comedies had varying degrees of box-office success. *Hi, Gang!* (starring Bebe Daniels and Ben Lyon), released in 1941, had the usual production team (Ostrer, Black, Varnel, Edgar) and the usual Gainsborough comic preoccupations (the mass media, topical references). But it was a flop.[40] This was probably because of the *manner* in which the references were handled. *Hi, Gang!*, based on the weekly BBC programme of the same name, is set in America and deals with the internecine battles between commercial American radio stations. These were not inherently interesting to British audiences, nor did they make any impact abroad. The USA is represented in an unimaginative way by Walter Murton's sets. The film only takes off when the *louche* Graham Moffatt is imported as a child refugee from England. Since he is alarmingly priapic (he leeringly describes his adopted mother as 'a bit of all right'), there are some piquant scenes when he outrages the shibboleths of good taste. His snorts in the song 'Susanna's a funniful man' are truly epic.

During the war, British audiences were resistant to obvious propaganda, but they also seemed to dislike mockery of those things they held most dear (Harper, 1994, pp. 136–46). The social cynicism which obtained in early 1930s comedy was no longer appropriate in wartime. Any sneering references to that social system for which the population was fighting and dying were received badly. The definition of democracy in *Hi, Gang!* as a system where 'people can say anything they like and we don't have to listen to them' is flippant and ill conceived.

Tommy Handley, 1943–4

Although the Tommy Handley films made at Gainsborough were also produced by Black and Ostrer, they did not appear in the *Kine Weekly* listings. However, Handley's radio programme *ITMA (It's That Man Again)* had a phenomenal following during the war: Tom Harrison of Mass-Observation suggested in 1942 that Handley had 'contributed more than any cabinet minister towards keeping up morale, without ever mentioning the war'.[41] Handley's premature death in 1949 evoked intense and widespread grief.[42]

The *ITMA* radio programmes were fast, anarchic and surreal, and were anchored by catchphrases such as 'Can I do you now, sir?', 'I go – I come back', and 'Don't forget the diver.'[43] Francis Worsley, producer of the programmes, was reluctant to allow Gainsborough to film them, as he felt that *ITMA* combined situation comedy, topical reference and puns, which were lacking in visual interest, and anyway 'Listeners form their own picture of places like Foaming-at-the-Mouth ... and all the wiles of the art director cannot take that image away.'[44] The film of *ITMA*, which was released in 1943, was directed by Walter Forde and scripted by radio writer Ted Kavanagh, who had no experience with scenario work. Forde himself complained about the script, and about the fact that the producers insisted on a three-week shoot (Brown, 1977b, pp. 47–8).

Gainsborough's *ITMA* was, like the Crazy Gang films, full of references to contemporary culture. Roy Rogers and his horse appear in parody form, as do Carmen Miranda, Ruritania and G. B. Shaw ('I never attend first nights except my own'). But the quotes are not as confidently delivered as in the Crazy Gang films. There are some delights – Cat Whittington and his Dick, for example – but on the whole the film lacks the consistency of the radio programmes; its tone lacks coherence. No such problems are evident in Handley's 1944 *Time Flies*, which is a fascinating text. A mixture of genres (science fiction, comedy, musical), it was probably too innovatory to succeed at the box office. It is set in America and features wide boy Handley, who persuades American friends to invest in a time machine invented by an eccentric scientist. They are all transported to Elizabethan London, meet Shakespeare (and tell him how to complete the balcony scene in *Romeo and Juliet*), and prompt Sir Walter Raleigh to use his cloak as a royal jiffy-cloth. Elizabethan music is performed alongside modern American swing; they are, after all, doing the same job of providing pleasure for the masses. In this film, anachronism is deployed in an amusing and inventive way: 'Here be the news, and this be Septimus Wadell a-crying it.'

The script is unusual in the way it renders complex philosophical ideas about time in a palatable form.[45] One speech, by the eccentric inventor (played by Felix Aylmer), is particularly revealing:

> The river of time is a river of consciousness and we are travellers for a brief lifetime in that boat. Normally we drift with the current and travel downstream. But if we equip our little boat with a motor, we can beat our passage downstream into the future – or, breasting the upstream, view again those self-same scenes that we were part of ... all that ever existed, still exists; all that will ever happen, has already happened.

This takes well-assimilated ideas from H.G. Wells's *The Time Machine* (1895) and J.W. Dunne's *An Experiment with Time* (1927) and combines them with philosophical aspects of Einstein's theory of relativity. It demonstrates a surprisingly eclectic and intellectually ambitious side of film comedy of the period, as well as providing us with an invaluable insight into the thinking of the studio, which was embarking on the cycle of costume melodramas already mentioned. There was clearly cross-fertilization between the comedy and costume genres at Gainsborough during this period. The Gainsborough combination of history with comedy was quite different from Ealing's, whose 1944 *Fiddlers Three* can be compared with *Time Flies*. *Fiddlers Three* is also about time travel, but its anachronisms are leaden (Stonehenge is 'another government housing scheme'), and visually it is pedestrian.

The art direction of *Time Flies* is extraordinary. The film was designed by John Bryan, who rarely worked in comedy. He was an art director of remarkable talent, whose visual style contributed to the success of *Fanny by Gaslight* (1944), *The Wicked Lady* (1945) and *Caravan* (1946) (Harper, 1994, pp. 127–9). He also designed *Caesar and Cleopatra* (1946), *Great Expectations* (1946) and *Oliver Twist* (1948). Bryan's work always aimed to raise the emotional temperature of the viewer by challenging the canons of realism. He had two contrasting styles. On the one hand, he constructed stark sets that focused attention on one symbolic object (the trees in the openings of both *Great Expectations* and *Oliver Twist*, for example); on the other hand, he would fill the screen with a cornucopia of rich objects so as to stimulate the audience's eye to maximum creativity, and almost to confusion (*The Wicked Lady* or *Caesar and Cleopatra*).

Bryan's representations of contemporary New York in *Time Flies* are a distinct improvement on those of Walter Murton in *Hi, Gang!* Bryan's sets are stylish and atmospheric, with mysterious perspectives, complex planes and new 'inventions' such as video cameras. His sets for Elizabethan London present the past as a place full of recesses, unexpected corners and surprising objects. But perhaps the most interesting object of all is the time-ship. It is spherical, and thus immeasurably suggestive: perfect, symmetrical, with a massive interior, able to hover at will, and its doors are invisible. It is the egg of time.

Arthur Askey, 1940–4

With *Time Flies*, the Gainsborough producers played a wild card. Although it was innovatory and audacious, it was not particularly profitable at the box office; it never appeared in the *Kine Weekly* listings. The Arthur Askey comedies, however, did very well indeed.[46] They now appear very dated, and present a severe challenge to the cultural historian. Askey, who had been a singer and comedian on the northern music halls, on radio and at the Palladium, was enormously popular. Indeed, at the peak of his career, music hall programmes would bill other comics (such as Max Wall) as playing 'Askey'.[47] In this case, Gainsborough was making a safe bet.

The Askey films were all produced by Ted Black and Maurice Ostrer; Marriott Edgar had a hand in all the scripts, and the camerawork was by either Arthur Crabtree or Jack Cox. The films had a range of directors and designers. *Band Waggon* was released in 1940, directed by Marcel Varnel with art direction by Vetchinsky; *Charley's (Big-Hearted) Aunt* in 1940, by

Walter Forde and Vetchinsky; *I Thank You* in 1941, by Varnel and Vetchinsky; *The Ghost Train* in 1941, by Forde and Vetchinsky; *Back Room Boy* in 1942, by Herbert Mason and Walter Murton; *King Arthur Was a Gentleman* in 1942, by Varnel and John Bryan; *Miss London Ltd* in 1943, by Val Guest and Maurice Carter; and *Bees in Paradise* in 1944, again by Guest and Carter (Gifford, 1986).

The cycle featured a number of common themes. The films evoke a community in which everyone shares not only the same needs, but the same beliefs. In *The Ghost Train*, for example, the refugees say, 'We might as well share what we've got.' In *King Arthur*, the protagonists note that, 'There's a lot of us nothings, but put together, we make a something.' The unlikely figurehead of this utopian system is Askey, whose indefatigable good cheer makes the narrative bowl along. The songs he encourages the community to sing are worth considering. In *I Thank You*, Askey conducts the following ditty:

Men and women in this community,
You and I are one big family,
Men and women, there's one thing we should do
Here and now I put it up to you:
Let's get hold of Hitler and string him up on high,
Anyone in favour? Aye! Aye! Aye!

This is sung with gusto by the crowd.

The community evoked and symbolized by Askey (whose function is rather like that of Gracie Fields in her '30s films) is one which uses humour as a means of exercising control over social dissidents, and of conferring approval on those who conform to the consensus. The jokes are at the expense of those who feign ignorance of the unwritten rule that those too old or too ugly to inspire desire should cease to experience it. Those who attempt to be extraordinary in any way are expelled beyond the boundaries of the community. The humour in these films is far less permissive than that in the Will Hay or Crazy Gang films.

The Askey films are firmly anchored to the context of contemporary Britain, which perhaps explains why none of them were re-released at a later date. *Band Waggon*, for example, is full of references to the condition of the BBC and its propaganda difficulties. In *The Ghost Train*, Askey wonders 'if I can teach the parrot to say Heil Hitler. Blimey! Not with a beak like that!' The blackout scenes in *Miss London Ltd* are an opportunity for fun. The girls' singing group in *Bees in Paradise* is called the MoI (Ministry of Information) Quartet. When history *does* appear, it functions in a very literal manner. In *King Arthur Was a Gentleman*, Arthur King is convinced that he has discovered King Arthur's sword Excalibur. He thinks it will confer courage on him as it did on 'the goodliest fellowship of famous knights'. Because he believes it is the historical sword, he can capture Nazis with it. Once he knows it is merely a stage prop, he loses his nerve. History has a straightforwardly propagandist function.

The Askey comedies express extreme anxiety about women. *Back Room Boy* is about a man in headlong flight from them; he takes a job in a lighthouse just to get away from the hated species. In *Miss London Ltd*, Askey runs an escort agency providing female friends for lonely officers, and his prurient manner suggests that the business is prostitution. But the most significant film in this respect is *Bees in Paradise*, which is set on an uncharted island where women are in charge; men are required to commit suicide three months after the wedding, which inevitably inhibits their libido. The island is populated by female bricklayers, potters and rugby players, who utter phrases such as, 'It is the law of the beehive that woman is paramount in all things', and 'He's got an A1 body and an F4 mind.' This dystopia causes the utmost panic among the male castaways, particularly Askey, whose minuscule stature makes him vulnerable to female assault. In one scene, wearing frilly knickers and Bo-Peep shoes, he scuttles off squealing, 'Don't touch me, I can't bear it! Even a husband must have some privacy.' His buxom wife then breaks down the bedroom door. It is tempting to interpret Askey's role here and elsewhere as a means of assuaging male anxieties about size, both of the penis and of the body as a whole. Askey is irritating, graceless and childish, and above all he is small. Yet he survives, because he tries harder.

The misogyny and size-anxiety of the Askey films cannot, perhaps, be ascribed to the Gainsborough producers who, we must remember, were responsible for those costume melodramas which celebrated female desire. There were too many different directors and scriptwriters to ascribe it to their authorship either. Rather, we must suggest that Askey developed his fictional persona in that way as an unconscious response to the sexual fears of the male audience. That audience was depleted in wartime, and the male population in any case was subject to extreme exigencies and dangers.

Comedy at Gainsborough ended in a minor key. Ted Black left in late 1943. Maurice Ostrer concentrated more and more on the melodramas. From making up over half the studio's total output, comedies were practically non-existent by late 1945, and director Val Guest, who had specialized in so many comedies, left too. The Rank Organization was firmly in the saddle. Maurice Ostrer's contract came to an end in late 1946, and Sydney Box took over. His penchant had never been comedy; his real interest was contemporary melodrama. To be sure, there were comic *elements* in some Box films: for example, the sexually voracious victim in *Holiday Camp* (1947). *It's Not Cricket* (1949) has an extraordinarily jokey opening, in which Basil Radford and Naunton Wayne (as themselves) reveal that they have been invited to make a film with 'some chap Sydney Box'. But otherwise the film is a routine detective tale. The Huggett cycle was categorized as comic by *Kine Weekly*, but *Here Come the Huggetts* (1948), *Vote for Huggett* (1949) and *The Huggetts Abroad* (1949) show that they are motivated more by a desire to analyse the post-war settlement from a wry and uncommitted perspective than to make audiences laugh. Interestingly, *The Happy Family* (1952), produced by Sydney Box and directed by Muriel Box after Gainsborough closed, uses the Huggetts as a source of fantasy rather than humour; the final shot is of a psychic who has finally achieved levitation.

Gaumont-British and Gainsborough comedies have much to teach us about how a popular genre can change dramatically over a short period of time. Clearly, two important determining factors are the degree of control exerted by the producers, and the degree of co-operation existing between the star and the scriptwriter. Balcon favoured the Hulbert comedies, and their social message was thoroughly consonant with the praise of social mobility contained in *The Good Companions* (1933), *Rhodes of Africa* (1936) and his later productions at Ealing. The Tom Walls/Ralph Lynn comedies were made in the teeth of Balcon's opposition, and they exemplified a sophisticated milieu which handled residual and old-fashioned aspects of the culture with great confidence. The key break came when Ted Black and the Ostrers took over production: they opened up a space where more individualistic and anarchic notions of the social (Hay, the Crazy Gang) could be expressed through comedy.

Another key factor in Gainsborough comedy is the *manner* in which popular culture is dealt with. In the Hay films, the materials of mass culture were delivered in an impassive manner, without comment or nuance. In a sense, both the Hay and the Crazy Gang films provided a sense of cultural security for their audiences; the materials of the culture – its myths, its certainties – were laid out in front of them, as it were, and audiences were not expected to get it wrong. The films put the audience in a position of confidence and competence. All that changed during the wartime comedies at Gainsborough. With the Askey and Handley films, the composition of the culture is thrown into doubt. The ordinary components of society's sustaining mythologies – the accepted definitions of gender and history – are thrown into disarray. Because the old certainties are problematized, a chronic rearrangement takes place before our very eyes, which produces intense anxiety within the texts. This is displaced and symbolically transformed into a more simple one which can be more readily addressed. Hence the size-anxiety in the Askey films.

The significant factor in Gainsborough film comedy, then, is that of history. It is nuanced in very different ways. In the Aldwych film farces, the old order is brought into play, satirized and ultimately validated. In the Hay films, the present is confidently presented as equal to the protagonists' expectations, because they are firmly grounded in a sense of the coherence of the culture. History as such is foregrounded more acutely after the rise of Black and Ostrer. For the Crazy Gang, events are firmly located in the historical process, and *Time Flies* and some of the Askey films deploy the past as a means of heightening emotion and stimulating thought. It seems as though, as the war progressed, the producers of comedy at Gainsborough were increasingly exploring the viability of the past as a site where emotional intensity could be exploited at the expense of everyday reality. Those ideas were to resurface, not in later Gainsborough comedies, but in the historical melodramas.

Notes

I should like to acknowledge the help given to me in this project by three colleagues: Laurie Ede, of the University of Portsmouth, generously provided me with material on the Travers farces; Andrew Spicer, of the University of the West of England, chased up rare films for me; and Vincent Porter, of the University of Westminster, gave invaluable advice on the final draft.

1. Balcon (1969), p. 57. See also Oakley (1964), pp. 104–5, and Murphy, R., 'A Brief Studio History', in Aspinall and Murphy (1983).
2. The BBFC Scenario Reports (in the British Film Institute library) are generally tolerant, particularly of the comedies. See, for example, the treatment of *Jack's the Boy*, 2 February 1932; *The Midshipmaid*, 21 September 1932; and *Foreign Affairs*, 26 July 1935 (this contains the 'clean light comedy throughout' remark).
3. Public Record Office, Kew, FO 395/487, FO memo 16 September

1933. For further information, see Harper (1994), pp. 16–17.
4. *Kinematograph Weekly*, 10 April 1930. This was Nick Schenck of MGM.
5. The proportion of comedies at Gaumont and Gainsborough in the period 1924–31 was 18 per cent, according to figures taken from Gifford (1986).
6. The credit sequence states that 'Certain facilities have been given by the Admiralty but the Admiralty are in no way responsible for the treatment of the situations.'
7. The script was by Sidney Gilliat and Leslie Arliss.
8. It is possible that the deletions demanded by the censor were partially responsible for this. See BBFC Scenario Reports (in BFI library), 14 September 1933, where the meaning of the scene cannot be clarified because 'opium pipes must not be showed'.

9. Balcon (1969), pp. 72–3. See *Film Weekly*, 20 May 1933, where Hulbert is fourth favourite for *Jack's the Boy*. See Courtneidge (1953), and Hulbert (1975).

10. *Film Weekly*, 6 April 1934.

11. See Hulbert (1975), p. 187: here he argues that 'The audience should always be made to feel sorry for him [the comic hero] and laugh at the things he does to get out of a jam when because of sheer bad luck they go wrong.'

12. Wilcox (1967). Wilcox had produced Travers's *Rookery Nook* very cheaply and profitably – it was made for £14,000 and yielded £150,000 in its first year alone (see p. 88). He viewed Walls as 'the greatest farceur of the century' (p. 89).

13. Balcon (1969), p. 91. See also Low (1985), p. 140.

14. See Low (1985), p. 140. Contemporary journalism refers frequently to the popularity of the films, and often alludes to the plays: see *Film Weekly*, 11 July 1931 and 6 April 1934; *The Sunday Referee*, 24 December 1933, and *Evening News*, 29 July 1934 ('the films made a lot of money for Tom's bosses').

15. Doyle (1936), p. 255. See the BFI microfiches on the films, particularly the excellent reviews of *A Cup of Kindness* and *Lady in Danger*. An interesting remark about *Turkey Time* in the *Evening Express* (27 December 1933) was that it was 'on the masculine side of light screen entertainment'.

16. *Observer*, 29 October 1933. See also *Evening News*, 17 March 1933; *The Times*, 23 December 1933; *The Saturday Review*, 18 January 1935. *The Sketch* noted on 1 August 1935 that 'Tom Walls's direction is on the usual Christie Minstrel lines.'

17. See the Press Book for *Lady in Danger*, BFI library.

18. *Evening News*, 18 December 1933. See also *Glasgow Herald*, 28 December 1933, and Walls's letter to *The Sunday Referee*, 3 November 1933.

19. *Picturegoer*, 27 May 1933. See an interesting piece on the 'silly-ass' type in *Film Weekly*, 23 November 1934.

20. Lynn's most interesting article is in *Film Weekly*, 7 December 1934. See also his piece in the same, 13 April 1934 and 16 January 1937. See Hare (1956), p. 72.

21. Hubert Cole, 'The Triumph of British Screen Humour', *Film Weekly*, 6 April 1934.

22. Low (1985), p. 144. Here she describes the films as having 'Stockbroker Tudor surroundings, where gay bachelors and men-about-town in faultless English tailoring, pretty girls, horrible mothers-in-law and henpecked husbands were involved in frantic muddles over sex and property.' She suggests that the older women are presented 'with undisguised dislike'.

23. Reynolds (1937), pp. 27–8. On p. 29 he suggests that the Aldwych film farces were successful because they deal 'with an aspect of life which we know and understand, and which does not make the mistake of competing with that which the Americans do so much better – the "rough stuff".'

24. BBFC Scenario Reports, op. cit., 5 April 1935.

25. Seaton and Martin (1978).

26. Will Hay Papers, BFI library, Item 2, 'I Enjoyed Every Minute'. See also an interesting article by Hay, 'The Stories I Like', in Lee (1937). Here he describes his taste for 'the good-natured villain' (pp. 173–4).

27. Undated essay by Hay in Hay Papers, op. cit. See interview with Hay in *Film Weekly*, 10 May 1935.

28. A cargo cult is a mainly Polynesian phenomenon, in which shipwrecked cargo is converted by local tribes into an object of veneration.

29. For other accounts of the films, see Allen Eyles, 'Will Hay and Co.', *Focus on Film*, December 1979. See also Midwinter (1979). This contains a nice remark on p. 54 that Hay embodies 'dismay, greed, foxiness'.

30. For example, in *Kinematograph Weekly*, 13 January 1938, *Windbag the Sailor* and *Good Morning, Boys* appear as big successes; so do *Oh Mr Porter!* and *Hey! Hey! USA* on 12 January 1939; so does *Old Bones of the River* on 11 January 1940.

31. *The Era*, 18 January 1936. For other extremely positive reviews, see the cuttings collection in the Will Hay papers, op. cit. See also microfiches in BFI library. The only negative critical reviews are of Hay's post-Gainsborough films.

32. *Daily Mail*, 17 August 1935. See also *The Cinema*, 4 January 1936, for an account of the besieging of a Hull cinema by young people: 'the management just don't know what to do about it, so anxious are the local lads and lasses to see it'.

33. Interestingly, the only thing which *The Cinetechnician* can find to say about Varnel in September/October 1947 is that he was 'a technician of the highest order' who knew how to organize a very fast shoot.

34. See Edgar (1937 and 1938). See Marshall (1979).

35. *Kinematograph Weekly* notes that *Alf's Button Afloat* was a hit on 12 January 1939, and *The Frozen Limits* on 9 January 1941. See also Flanagan, B. (1961) *My Crazy Life*, p. 160. See material on *The Frozen Limits* in Richards and Sheridan (1987), pp. 163, 175, 178, 192, 197, 198.

36. *Film Weekly*, 16 July 1938: Varnel says, 'I mean that the camera shows two of them at a time, then trucks to another two, and so on, and then trucks back for a long shot.'

37. *Spectator*, 17 November 1939. He was reviewing *The Frozen Limits*.

38. Interview with Maurice Carter by Sue Harper, in Aspinall and Murphy (1983), p. 55. Askey starred in a 1942 MoI short directed by Val Guest about sneezing called *The Nose Has It*.

39. Aldgate and Richards (1986), p. 77.

40. See Aldgate and Richards (1986), p. 91. It did not appear in *Kine Weekly* listings but, according to the *Kine Weekly* reviewer (in the BFI microfiche on the film), it was potentially 'box office because of its title and star values'.

41. Quoted in Aldgate and Richards (1986), p. 92.

42. See 'Poor Yorick' in *Mass-Observation Bulletin*, no. 32, February 1950. This was based on a directive of January 1949. See also material in Mass-Observation Archive, TC Radio 1939–49, Box 4, *The Death of Tommy Handley*. See also File Report 3026 (August 1948) on the British sense of humour.

43. See Kavanagh (1949 and 1974). See also Handley (1938). There is a BBC Radio Collection edition of four of the wartime shows.

44. Worsley (1949), p. 71. See also pp. 79–80.

45. The script was by Ted Kavanagh, the radio *ITMA* scriptwriter, by old Crazy Gang hand J.O.C. Orton, and by novelist Howard Irving Young.

46. For example, *Band Waggon* and *Charley's (Big-Hearted) Aunt* appeared in the *Kine Weekly* listings of 9 January 1941. *The Ghost Train* and *I Thank You* appeared in the lists of 8 January 1942.

47. William K. Everson, 'Arthur Askey', *Films in Review*, March 1986, p. 175.

7

Looking for Lustre:
Stars at Gainsborough

Geoffrey Macnab

Like most film studios, Gainsborough was built on stars. Even before the formation of the company in 1924, its boss-to-be Michael Balcon insisted that big names were crucial as a cynosure with which to lure British filmgoers to British pictures. He was equally certain that there were no British stars with the necessary lustre. When he hired American actress Betty Compson to appear opposite rising young British actor Clive Brook in *Woman to Woman* (1923), he was setting a trend which Gainsborough would follow. 'We needed a star,' he recalls in his autobiography, 'a name the public would know, which at that time meant it had to be a Hollywood name' (Balcon, 1969, p. 15). He wanted to compete with Hollywood, but recruiting Compson only served to underline the gulf between the robust American star system and its fledgling British counterpart. According to trade papers of the time, she was paid £1000 a week for the ten weeks of shooting, an astonishing sum compared with the tiny fees generally offered to British actors.

No prints of the film survive. Nevertheless, from the stills and synopsis, it is apparent that this was a melodrama every bit as flamboyant as those baroque Maurice Ostrer efforts of the 1940s in which Margaret Lockwood flaunted her cleavage while James Mason scowled in the background. The story concerns a handsome young Englishman (Clive Brook decked out in a variety of smoking jackets, dinner jackets and military uniforms) who falls recklessly in love with a beautiful Moulin Rouge dancer (Compson in slinky gown and peacock-plumed head-dress). The two have a child, but war comes between them. Brook is wounded at the front, loses his memory, and ends up marrying another woman (Josephine Earle), 'an English woman from his own somewhat upper-crust social circle' (Balcon, 1969, p. 15). Many years pass before he meets the dancer again (see Barr in this volume).

Brook, the 'strong, silent man of the screen' as he was described by the *Dundee Evening Telegraph*,[1] was blessed with a beautiful profile. Reputedly, he went to bed with a strap round his neck to keep his chin up.[2] He also had a phlegmatic, impassive quality not at all typical of British screen actors of his generation, many of whom, as producer George Pearson witheringly observed, resorted to 'over-acted pantomimic gesture and frozen facial expression suggesting emotion at its strongest' (Pearson, 1957, p. 183).

Reviewers praised Brook's 'essentially British masculinity',[3] his 'fine appearance and carriage'[4] and his ability to 'look sinister or fascinating, good or evil, by the moving of an eyebrow'.[5] This may have been weary stoicism rather than technique. Like many subsequent Gainsborough male leads, Brook had a very British aversion to being objectified as a film star. He wished, he stated in his unpublished autobiography, 'to be thought of as an actor and not as a well-known brand of goods such as Bovril, Lucky Strikes or General Foods cake mix'.[6] Not that this stopped him from going to Hollywood for twenty years to play stiff, handsome Englishmen in films such as *Shanghai Express* (1932) and *The Return of Sherlock Holmes* (1929). Brook has a fair claim as the earliest home-grown Gainsborough star: shortly before being lured to the USA, he appeared opposite Alice Joyce and Marjorie Daw in *The Passionate Adventure* (1924). Scripted by Alfred Hitchcock, this was among the first pictures Balcon and company made under the Gainsborough banner at the tiny Islington studios they had just acquired from Paramount. It was already apparent that Balcon faced a struggle to hold on to his leading names: not only Brook, but also his rambunctious co-star Victor McLaglen headed off to Hollywood not long after the film's completion.

Perhaps Gainsborough's most important find during its fledgling years was matinée idol Ivor Novello. Welsh-born (original name Ivor Davies), with lambent skin, brilliantined hair and a profile to match Brook's, Novello was as close as British cinema has come, before or since, to its own Valentino or Ramón Novarro. Whereas Brook was stoical, manly and quintessentially English, Novello was of altogether more exotic stock. His most famous role (in *The Rat*, 1925) was as a Frenchman. He had an androgynous appeal, 'luscious eyes, oliveness, glistening black hair, Romeo, Romeo',[7] far removed from the stiff formality of most British male leads of the time. The fact that he was a mannered, limited actor who did little but strike intense, dreamy poses in front of the camera did not matter in the slightest to his fans, of whom there were many thousands.

His first screen role was in Louis Mercanton's *Call of the Blood* (*L'Appel du sang*, 1919) as a philandering husband who cheats on his wife with a Sicilian girl. With his usual becoming modesty, he described the film as 'one of extreme beauty'.[8] Venerable, one-legged stage legend Sarah Bernhardt, who saw the film at a private viewing in Paris, agreed with this estimation. 'She found the emotional scenes deeply affecting and said it was the finest screen romance she had ever seen, Phyllis Nielson-Terry and Ivor Novello coming in for a generous measure of her appreciation.'[9]

Before appearing in his first Gainsborough film in 1925, Novello had already made an unsuccessful foray to Hollywood to co-star in D.W. Griffith's *The White Rose* (1923). Although described in the American press as 'the British Adonis' and 'the Valentino of England' (Noble, 1951, p. 96), his role for Griffith did not allow him to shine. 'I had a very stupid part,' he later wrote, 'that of a sanctimonious clergyman utterly devoid of humour.'[10] The great American director had once boasted 'he could make even monkeys act',[11] but none the less failed to renew his option on Novello.

Back in Britain, Novello redeemed his reputation with the play *The Rat*, which he co-wrote with actress Constance Collier. It is the story of Pierre Boucheron, the 'swaggering, ultra-romantic hero of the Gallic underworld' (Wilson, 1975, p. 65). According to his creators, Boucheron was 'a character without one redeeming feature in his make-up'.[12] Nevertheless, Novello went on to play him more than 600 times on stage and three times on screen. The original screen adaptation of *The Rat* was his first film for Gainsborough. Directed with verve by Graham Cutts, it is full of fights, exhilarating chases (at one point, Boucheron disappears down a manhole to escape the police), and boasts its own sultry tango sequence, all too clearly based on Valentino's tango in *The Four Horsemen of the Apocalypse* (1921). (To help his partner dance more easily, Boucheron rips her skirt at the hip.) Most of the action unfolds in the White Coffin, a *demi-monde* bar populated by Bohemians and ruffians. The story, which involves Boucheron seducing a wealthy, bored aristocrat whose jewels he covets, is far-fetched enough to accommodate Novello's *louche*, anti-naturalistic style without undue embarrassment. After all, Boucheron is more pantomime hero than fully hewn character.

Balcon was so impressed with his new star that he put Novello under contract in 1926. Even if they fall short of Hollywood standards, the actor's terms seem generous. Novello undertook to appear in three films for Gainsborough Pictures Limited between January and September 1927. In return, he was to receive £100 a day while actually working, and 'those days were not to exceed four in each week when he was fulfilling a stage engagement'. When he was not engaged for stage work, he was obliged, if required, to work six days a week, for which he would receive a flat fee of £500.[13] He was guaranteed a minimum of £3000 as total salary for the three films combined – small change by Hollywood standards (even a minor American star such as Mary Miles Minter earned £20,000 a year) but a bonanza in British terms. (Producer Cecil Hepworth, who set up his own mini-stable of stars at his studios by Walton-on-Thames, was notoriously frugal with wages, while Charles Rock, an important British star of a few years before, was rumoured to earn only £25 a week.)[14] There was a clause in Novello's contract which bound him 'to comport himself with both dignity and decency in private and professional life, and not to commit or permit any act or thing which would bring him into notoriety, or contempt, or disgrace'. (This may have seemed academic, but Novello led a colourful private life and had occasional scrapes with the law. Some years later, during the Second World War, he served a stint in prison at Wormwood Scrubs for breaking government fuel regulations.) Such a clause hints at British film-makers' anxiety in the face of moral reformers,[15] but it also suggests a disappointing discretion in British stars. As Kenneth Anger's *Hollywood Babylon* books (Anger, 1975 and 1986) make clear, scandal and celebrity used to go hand in hand in Tinseltown. Britain, it seems, was short on both.

Novello was certainly, as Michael Balcon put it, 'a star of the first magnitude' (Balcon, 1969, p. 36). He regularly topped readers' favourites polls in *Picturegoer* and was nominated the most popular male star by women participants in Sidney Bernstein's 1928 audience poll.[16] His appeal was always strongest with women fans. Unlike the more conventional male lead Ronald Colman, who was voted second in both men's and women's lists, he does not even register on the male participants' 'Top 10' list. (One can only presume his expressive style was not to male tastes of the time.) Sometimes, Novello's sheer popularity caused the studio problems. During the mid-1920s, Gainsborough had developed links with the prestigious Ufa studios in Berlin. Hitchcock, in particular, was influenced by German lighting techniques and approaches to set design. Oblique camera angles and looming shadows were not necessarily well suited to showing off Gainsborough's main asset of the period, namely Novello.

The tension between Hitchcock's will to artistry and his need to show his star in the best possible light is at its most pronounced in *The Lodger* (1926), his first film in England. (His two earlier directorial efforts, *The Pleasure Garden* (1926) and *The Mountain Eagle* (1926), had both been shot in Germany.) Novello plays the lodger of the title, a pale, intense young man who takes up residence in the spare room of a lower-middle-class family. While he paces to and fro across his room like a lost soul, the family huddle in the parlour below, trying to work out whether or not he is the Jack-the-Ripper-style murderer who has been prowling London's mist-shrouded streets, terrorizing blonde chorus girls. All the evidence points to Novello's guilt. From the very first moment he appears at their front door with the bottom half of his face hidden by a scarf and a suspicious, febrile look on his face, he goes out of his way to behave furtively. In the closing reel, the mob chase him across London and look set to lynch him. Only at the very last moment is the martyr's innocence established.

> Novello's performance [Lindsay Anderson wrote] is throughout extremely crude (and often, now, very funny); this is partly due to his own limitations as an actor, but partly also to script and direction which, with a quite unscrupulous dishonesty, require him to behave in a blatantly 'guilty' manner in order deliberately to mislead his audience.[17]

Anderson's criticisms imply that Hitchcock is being wilfully cynical and manipulative. However, as the director told Truffaut, he was beholden to Novello, one of the few British stars more important to the film-making process than anybody behind the camera.

> That was the difficulty. The leading man was a matinée idol in England. He was a very big name at the time. ... Very often the storyline is jeopardised because the star cannot be a villain. ... I might have liked him to go off in the night, so that we would never really know for sure. But with the hero played by a big star, one can't do that. You have to spell it out in big letters – HE IS INNOCENT.[18]

There was never any real doubt about Novello's heroism in his next collaboration with Hitchcock, *Downhill* (1927). He plays Roddy Berwick, a public-school rugby hero who sacrifices his name and career for his friend, Tom Wakely, son of an upstanding clergyman. Tom is faced with expulsion after getting up to no good with a girl from the local village, but Roddy takes the blame on his own shoulders, even if it means that he 'won't be able to play for the old boys'. In disgrace, he sneaks away to Paris, briefly becomes a professional motor racing driver, reaches his lowest ebb in a Marseilles doss-house, but lives to see his reputation restored. Long-suffering, masochistic Roddy Berwick was a part tailor-made for Novello, scarcely surprising since he wrote the play himself.

Ivor Montagu, who was entrusted with doctoring the script, was not impressed.

> The more I studied it, the less I liked it. It was a drama of subjective action, expressed almost wholly in terms of extravagant and occasionally erotic emotion. ... There was no effort to present a constructive story and there was no plot worth mentioning. ... I have worked in two strong feminine parts. I have also endeavoured to preserve the hero's character. If he is to marry a clean girl, we must keep him as clean as possible. He can be foolish and Quixotic, but not unmanly.[19]

Ironically, these are just the kind of criticisms levelled in later years at Gainsborough melodramas. It was precisely the 'extravagant and erotic emotion' that Novello brought to his parts which made him such a star in the first place. Montagu's patronizing dismissal of the actor hints at a tension which has always existed between the intellectuals of British cinema,[20] and those who set out to make popular, accessible films.

Novello was offered two subsequent, improved contracts by Gainsborough in 1928 and 1929; he left the company for another abortive trip to Hollywood, where he played second lead opposite Ruth Chatterton in *Once a Lady* (1931) and wrote dialogue for Irving Thalberg's first Tarzan film, *Tarzan, the Ape Man* (1932), but was somewhat chastened to discover that his reputation as Gainsborough's leading matinée idol counted for nothing in the USA.

> Someone said I was too English. This quite staggered me; it seemed such an absurd remark to make until it was explained. I was told there were at least 5000 picture houses in America whose audiences had never heard an Englishman speak. English was like a foreign language to them![21]

In silent movies, Novello, sensual and expressive, was far from the typical English leading man. In the sound era, it seemed, his clipped West End vowels spoiled the impression.

Back in Britain, Novello made one or two forgettable talkies before abandoning cinema for good in 1934 to concentrate on writing and acting in West End musical romances. He was certainly Gainsborough's most bankable star of the late 1920s. All his films prior to the coming of sound, Michael Balcon observed, were 'outstandingly successful in commercial terms' (Balcon, 1969, p. 36). Nevertheless, when Novello died in March 1951, his movie career seemed all but forgotten. His funeral at Golders Green Crematorium was mobbed ('elderly women struggled with police and trampled over flowerbeds in their efforts to get a glimpse of the funeral rites'[22]), but every newspaper tribute hailed him as a man of the theatre, quite an irony considering his acting career started in films, not on the stage. Novello's *Times* obituary did not even deign to mention that he had once been British cinema's most popular star.

> Novello [it proclaimed] was one of those exceptional people for whom the phrase 'a man of the theatre' acquires meaning and virtue. He really was a man of the theatre. As actor, playwright and composer he occupied a position with the public in general which even Mr Noël Coward, his friend and rival, could scarcely challenge. ... It is probably by the spectacular musical romances of the later period that Novello will be popularly remembered. *Glamorous Night, Careless Rapture, Crest of the Wave, The Dancing Years, Arc de Triomphe, Perchance to Dream, King's Rhapsody* – their very titles cunningly suggest the succession of spacious and highly coloured scenes which their author found for the great stages of Drury Lane and similar theatres.[23]

The Lodger, The Rat and his other films have been conveniently forgotten.

Throughout the 1920s, Balcon continued the policy, first established with *Woman to Woman*, of importing foreign stars. Virginia Valli, Paul Richter, Renate Müller and Lili Damita were among the international names lured over to appear in Gainsborough pictures. But the range of films made by the studios was not always as ambitious as it might have been. There was occasionally an undue reliance on stage plays and smart, sophisticated comedies. 'We were not over-exercising our intellectual powers in the choice of subjects' (Balcon, 1969, p. 37), Balcon later wrote in his autobiography. In 1928, when Gainsborough was taken over by Gaumont-British, the three projects on the slate were *Downhill, The Vortex* (1927) and *The Constant Nymph* (1928). All of them were originally stage plays and each, as Balcon acknowledged, 'relied almost exclusively on dialogue and verbal images rather than visual action'. Even a director with as much visual flair as Hitchcock was hard-pressed to animate such intractable material as *Easy Virtue* (1927), a Noël Coward adaptation, and *Downhill*. Nor was he impressed with the stars on offer. In 'Have We the Talent?', a *Picturegoer* article commissioned in the wake of the 1927 Cinematograph Films Act, he made a familiar complaint. 'We have often been forced to employ stage actors who, in too many instances, regard film work as a fill-in for pocket money. Film acting has never been taken sufficiently seriously and discipline has often been lacking.' By comparison with American stars, who clocked on 'just as though they were studio staff', he believed British screen actors were dilettantish amateurs.[24]

Not that all Gainsborough recruits were West End stars on sabbatical from the stage. One of the most popular, Mabel Poulton, started her career working as a typist at the Alhambra Theatre in Leicester Square. Her first teetering steps into the film industry were made when her boss, convinced she was the spitting image of Lillian Gish, recruited her to dress in a kimono and lie in front of the screen three times a day during showings of D.W. Griffith's *Broken Blossoms* (1919).[25] She was 'spotted' as she posed by producer George Pearson, who offered her a part in his sentimental drama about a gone-to-seed music hall star, *Nothing Else Matters* (1920). She was paid £20 a week when she worked, but times were hard and Pearson could not afford to keep her under contract. She very nearly landed a role in Abel Gance's *Napoléon* (1926), but although that fell through she was offered a part in Germaine Dulac's *Ame d'artiste* (1925).

Back in England, she finally established herself opposite Ivor Novello's mercurial composer in Gainsborough's *The Constant Nymph*. Likened to Lillian Gish at the start of her career, she was now compared to America's sweetheart: 'Mabel Poulton may, without fulsome flattery, be described as Britain's answer to Mary Pickford.'[26] Quicksilver and vivacious, she was heralded by Balcon as having 'that inner something which enabled a few silent screen actresses to convey emotion without the power of speech' (Balcon, 1969, p. 37). A few years later, a nostalgic John Betjeman, enchanted by her performance, wrote:

> Men will understand me when I say how one suddenly notices in the tube or tram or bus a girl with a pathetic face, pathetically beautiful, who seems to stand for all the thousands of people who only come out of their offices during the rush hour to go back to their little furnished rooms. Mabel Poulton stands for these.[27]

She was not a vamp like her co-star in *The Constant Nymph*, Benita Hume, Gainsborough's glamour queen of the late 1920s who went on to marry first Ronald Colman and then George Sanders. ('There's none that's sweeter than Benita', as Hume's cigarette card put it.) Nor did she have the icy hauteur of Madeleine Carroll, another in the long line of Gainsborough stars who decamped to Hollywood. But Poulton approached her roles with an emotional intensity few of her contemporaries could match.

Not long after the release of *The Constant Nymph*, Poulton caused a stir in the fan magazines by insuring her eyes, 'Those precious orbs which irradiate the screen',[28] for £30,000. (This was not simply vanity. The unshielded carbon lights often used by 1920s film-makers were potentially damaging to sight and could cause conjunctivitis.) Her future in British cinema seemed assured. Sadly, like *The Constant Nymph* itself (the film went missing, presumed lost, for many years before a print turned up unexpectedly in a Sussex house in 1995), Poulton herself soon vanished from British screens. As Poulton's fellow actress Chilli Bouchier recalls, the arrival of sound caught Gainsborough on the hop. Bouchier played a trapeze artist in Gainsborough's *City of Play* (1929), which was half-silent, half-talkie. 'Nobody had considered the rather odd assortment of sounds which would issue from the mouths of the leading players. There was the stage-trained dark brown bass of Lawson Butt, the regional accent of the leading man, and my Minnie Mouse squeak' (Bouchier, 1995, p. 62). With microphones swathed in blankets and hanging over actors' heads like magnets, it was little wonder British films now seemed more static than ever.

As in Hollywood, talkies put an end to several careers. 'So many actors fell by the wayside at that time,' Bouchier remembers; 'The most regretted was little Mabel Poulton, a silent star who had the face of a lovely flower but a cockney accent which no amount of elocution lessons could eradicate' (Bouchier, 1995, p. 52). In the class-confined world of the early British talkies, this meant Poulton could play only character parts. When it came to leading roles, 'The lamentable preference was for the English of the drama schools and of South Kensington' (Balcon, 1969, p. 37). Such snobbery seems all the more baffling when one remembers that far and away the most popular British star of the silent era was Betty Balfour. British cinema's Queen of Happiness, as she was nicknamed, Balfour started her career alongside Poulton in Pearson's *Nothing Else Matters*, and had risen to prominence on the back of her performance as *Squibs* (1921), an Eliza Doolittle-like cockney flower seller. She appeared in a similar role in her one Gainsborough film, *The Sea Urchin* (1926). But her career in the early sound era largely bears out Balcon's dictum that stars who did not speak 'proper' were only allowed to play character parts. Although she starred in a sound remake of *Squibs* (1935), her main roles in the early 1930s were as Jessie Matthews's sidekick in *Evergreen* (1934) and as John Mills's long-suffering mother in the creaking, jingoistic adaptation of a C.S. Forester novel, *Forever England* (1935).

Matthews herself, far and away Gaumont-British's biggest star of the decade, ruthlessly suppressed any hint of the vernacular in her own voice (she was the daughter of a Soho fruit and veg trader), adopting the most rarefied, plummy accent this side of Edith Evans. This did not diminish her popularity in the slightest. Her voice may have sounded stilted, but her performances never were: with her dark hair, limpid eyes, tight-fitting costumes, macaw-like singing voice and rubbery dancing style, the Jessie of *Evergreen* seems like a live-action version of cartoon siren Betty Boop. 'I was convinced we had the biggest international star in the country,' Michael Balcon, who discovered her, later wrote; 'She had everything. ... She is the grandest person to work with, although very highly strung. ... I have more admiration for her than for any other person I have worked with.'[29] She was even popular in America. Balcon's strategy was to play her in two lavish musicals every year rather than to exploit her appeal in a series of low-budget fillers.[30] Her Gainsborough films, made before the peak of her popularity, were *The Man from Toronto* (1933), *There Goes the Bride* (1932) and *Friday the Thirteenth* (1933).

Balcon's jeremiads about the rampant snobbery of 1930s British cinema are belied by what happened over the decade at Gainsborough. Even as Poulton's career went into John Gilbert-like decline, irreverent music hall stars and comedians, many of them with regional accents, were becoming the mainstay of the studios. George Robey, the bushy-eyebrowed 'prime minister of mirth', played Ali Baba in Gainsborough's lavish musical comedy of 1934, *Chu-Chin-Chow*. (Again, a Hollywood star, Anna May Wong, was hired to lend the picture a little lustre: music hall stars such as Robey may have been popular, but they were hardly exotic.) Husband and wife team Jack Hulbert and Cicely Courtneidge appeared together in a string of musical comedies: they were passengers on *The Ghost Train* (1931), and lovesick journalists in *Falling for You* (1933). Tom Walls, Ralph Lynn and Robertson Hare, mainstays of the Ben Travers Aldwych farces, made several movies at Gainsborough in the mid-1930s (see Harper in this volume). Walls, who directed as well as acted in most of them, believed that British teamwork and variety could counter the Hollywood star system: 'The weight of the whole film never lies on the shoulders of any one man. You never get tired of seeing one face gazing at you in long shots, mid-shots and close-ups.'[31] As he correctly surmised, the British star system often relied more on a repertory company of studio actors than on glamorous individuals.[32] Gordon Harker, who specialized in cheeky cockney character parts, graduated to principal star status in various Edgar Wallace adaptations, sports dramas and comedies at Gainsborough in the early 1930s.

Although Balcon's successor as studio boss, Ted Black, is generally credited with steering Gainsborough away from West End adaptations towards more popular material (see Murphy in this volume), the studio was already turning out cheerful, undemanding comedies before he took over in 1936. At times, it seemed as if Gainsborough had abandoned its attempts at emulating Hollywood-style glamour, and was turning into a small family concern where character actors mattered as much as stars. In his study of Hollywood, *The Genius of the System*, Thomas Schatz writes about the moment in *The Public Enemy* (1931) in which James Cagney staggers down a street, wounded, muttering, and falls face down in the gutter. He describes this as 'a narrative-cinematic epiphany when star and genre and technique coalesced into an ideal expression of studio style' (Schatz, 1989, p. 6). In its own unlikely fashion, Will Hay in railwayman's outfit, waving down a passing locomotive at Buggleskelly Station in *Oh Mr Porter!* (1937), achieves something similar. 'The interplay of budget, star and genre was crucial to studio film-making,' Schatz argues; 'The three were, in effect, the holy trinity of the studio system' (Schatz, 1989, p. 79).

The Will Hay vehicles, like many of Gainsborough's other comedies of the period, may have been formulaic, but there was no denying that this particular marriage between star, budget and genre worked. Just as Cagney played hoodlums, Hay played endless variations of his trademark bumbling schoolteacher: whether a fireman (*Where's That Fire?*, 1939), a colonialist (*Old Bones of the River*, 1938), or a policeman (*Ask a Policeman*, 1939), he was always the same pettifogging, incompetent figure of fun. Just as the Warner Bros gangster cycle featured the same repertory of character actors, Hay was invariably supported by the antic duo Moore Marriott and Graham Moffatt. The former owned five sets of false teeth and specialized in playing wizened, cantankerous geriatrics, none more famous than his Harbottle. The latter was like the fat boy in Dickens's *Pickwick Papers*, gormless, sleepy and prodigiously lazy.

In his classic account of the British music hall tradition, *A Funny Way to Be a Hero* (1973), John Fisher suggests that the team of Hay, Marriott and Moffatt was 'the nearest British approximation in the thirties to the Marx Brothers' (p. 43). The Crazy Gang's humour, Fisher believes, was in the seaside-postcard tradition, whereas Hay and his two stooges were genuinely anarchic. However, most of Gainsborough's comedies of the period, whether they featured Hay, the Crazy Gang or even the diminutive, charmless Arthur Askey, were similar in tone. Their self-deprecating, knockabout brand of humour was essentially British. It is no surprise that they did not travel well.[33] Unfortunately, Gainsborough's more ambitious efforts fared little better on the international market, where their home-grown stars were all but unknown. Robert Stevenson's *Tudor Rose* (1936), a lavish costume drama charting the brief, tragic reign as queen of Lady Jane Grey, is a case in point. On the face of it, there seemed to be a market for this kind of prestige picture: a few years before, Alexander Korda's *The Private Life of Henry VIII* (1933) had won Oscars and broken box-office records in the USA. A rambunctious historical soap opera, it provided clear evidence that Korda's attempts at nurturing a star system were working.[34]

However, there was to be no such welcome for Stevenson's film. Despite a sturdy British cast (led by Nova Pilbeam, John Mills, Cedric Hardwicke and Sybil Thorndike) and impressive production values, it was lambasted by American critics. 'An historical costume piece, this British film is sombre, slow and inclined to be dull,' declaimed *Variety*; 'There are no names to help even slightly at the B/O on this side of the Atlantic, and the dialogue is clipped and muffled in the British manner so irritating to American audiences. Some of it is so slurred as not to be decipherable in the US.'[35] The reviewer was especially harsh about Pilbeam, the teenager in the lead role who only a year or two before had been appearing as a child actress. 'She should be a fine actress when she grows up. Expecting her to handle this emotional, mature assignment is unfair.' Lady Jane Grey, the Tudor rose of the title, lasted nine days on the throne. The film, it can safely be assumed, disappeared even more quickly from American screens.

Despite such reversals, Black was determined to build up Gainsborough's very own stable of stars. 'It seemed to me,' he observed, 'that there was a great dearth of British stars, especially as the best of them usually found a permanent home in Hollywood as soon as they were successful enough. So I set out to create some new stars by putting fresh talent into well-made pictures' (Tims, 1989, p. 70). His trick was to play the same actors again and again in eye-catching roles while building them up off screen: he put their faces on bus shelters, newspapers and hoardings. There was nothing especially original about this. For years, British stars had been used to advertise everything from Lux Soap ('Nine out of ten film stars use Lux Toilet Soap. In the Hollywood and English studios there are 714 important actresses, including all stars – 98 per cent of them care for their skin this way! And Lux Toilet Soap is the official soap in the dressing-rooms of all the big studios. Order Lux Toilet Soap from your grocer today. That instant foamy lather will delight you!'[36]) to Ovaltine; from Ponds Vanishing Cream to Kia-Ora Lemon Squash.[37] Black, though, was far more aggressive in bringing his new faces to public attention than any of his predecessors since Alexander Korda, who promoted Merle Oberon and Robert Donat with similar *élan* in the early 1930s.

Once he had placed young actors under contract, Black tried to ensure that they behaved like stars off screen as well as on. With Margaret

Lockwood, who he signed up in 1937, this initially proved a struggle. 'Around the *Dr Syn* time it was a great trouble to get her to dress up and look presentable at premières and parties. Her idea of dress seemed confined to a raincoat and beret. I had to reason with her, explaining that the public expected glamour from their favourites' (Tims, 1989, p. 77). Another hindrance to Black's star-making schemes was the relative shortage of suitable vehicles.[38] While it was possible for the big Hollywood studios to play young actors in near identical roles time and again, British producers were invariably obliged to cast them across genres in a range of very different parts simply because so few films were being made. Lockwood may be best remembered these days for her gallery of wicked ladies, but during her career at Gainsborough, she also played consumptive pianists (*Love Story*, 1944), sensitive *ingénues* (*A Place of One's Own*, 1945) and turn-of-the-century music hall stars (*I'll Be Your Sweetheart*, 1945). Black intended to capitalize on the success of *The Lady Vanishes* (1938) by casting her opposite Michael Redgrave in a series of comedy-thrillers along the lines of MGM's Myrna Loy/William Powell 'Thin Man' films. These plans were defeated by the war: the only other film in which Lockwood and Redgrave appeared together was the mining drama, *The Stars Look Down* (1939), which was not even made under the Gainsborough banner. Meanwhile, she, like other Gainsborough stars, took any roles which came her way. As James Mason put it, 'A star who is not constantly thrusting his face at the public very soon finds he is no longer in demand.'[39]

In some ways, Black placed himself in an invidious position. While trying to build up Gainsborough's roster of stars, he also determined to make the studio embrace an earthier, more demotic style of film-making that would 'appeal to audiences in the Midlands and North' (Seaton and Martin, May 1982, p. 11). Films such as *Bank Holiday* (1938) and *Millions Like Us* (1943), about the romances and disappointments of ordinary people, hint at the new kind of populist realism that Black was striving for. However, they were not the kind of pictures in which stars were easily foregrounded. It is a bizarre irony that many of the actors whose careers Black nurtured, and whose faces he guided into the fan magazines, heartily loathed their work at Gainsborough. James Mason, who signed a six-film contract with the studio, attributed his success as the sadistic eighteenth-century aristocrat Lord Rohan in *The Man in Grey* (1943) to his inveterate dislike of the role. 'I have to conclude,' he later wrote, 'that my sheer bad temper gave the character colour.'[40] He was even more cantankerous as the caddish husband in *They Were Sisters* (1945), a part he played with a well-nigh permanent hangover (Morley,

1989, p. 60). Stewart Granger described his Gainsborough films as 'junk' (Granger, 1981, p. 90). Even Phyllis Calvert seemed less than enthused about the pictures which made her famous. 'I hate the word, "film star". ... I've never been a dedicated film actress' (Aspinall and Murphy, 1983, p. 60).

Despite this cacophony of grumbling, the baroque historical melodramas which the studios started making from 1942 onwards were, above all, star vehicles. Maurice Ostrer, the executive in charge of production at Gainsborough, believed that wartime audiences wanted escapism, not realism, and was determined to provide it.[41] Under his guidance, Leslie Arliss, writer/director of *The Man in Grey*, *Love Story* and *The Wicked Lady* (1945), offered Granger, Mason, Lockwood, Patricia Roc and Phyllis Calvert the kind of torrid emotional roles which could not fail to make an impression on audiences. Arliss had a special theory about his heroines. 'Yes, I like wicked women – on the screen,' he told *Picturegoer*, 'They are so much more interesting than the average heroine type. They've got more colour and fire – and they're more human.'[42]

In return for the chance to swagger, swordfight, wield pokers, wear Elizabeth Haffenden's elaborate costumes and parade their feelings in big close-ups, accompanied all the while by swirling orchestral music, the stars began behaving every bit as petulantly as their Hollywood counterparts. There was the famous occasion on the first day of production of *The Wicked Lady* when Mason walloped Arliss on the nose, and almost provoked a full-blown technicians' strike in the process.[43] Mason's excuse for such aggressive behaviour was that he had been kept waiting around on set and never used. (The technicians' union, the ACT, pointing out that he was being paid, could not see why he was complaining.) Then there was the time that Stewart Granger shared a railway compartment with Arliss on the way to Cornwall for location shooting on *Love Story*. 'He asked me,' Granger recalled in his autobiography, 'what I thought of the script. Not knowing he'd written it, I told him it was the biggest load of crap I'd ever read' (Granger, 1981, p. 75). In a series of letters and articles in *Picturegoer* magazine, Mason continued to complain about the state of the industry. He expressed the opinion that, 'There was precious little glamour in British films', let fans into the secret that a certain actor in a Gainsborough film 'had to be photographed only from the waist up because he had fallen out of a window in a drunken stupor and injured his leg', and threatened to emigrate to Hollywood forthwith.[44]

While Mason and Granger's behaviour was not exactly encouraged, it tallied with the roles they were playing. They were supposed to be rakes and bounders. Lockwood, too, joined in the dissent, and ended up suspended when she refused to accept a role in the comedy *Roses for her Pillow*, which was eventually made by Triton as *Once upon a Dream* (1949), with Googie Withers. Whatever tantrums the various stars threw, they still invariably topped fans' popularity polls. In hindsight, the costume melodramas seem the quintessential Gainsborough films. The studio's famous trademark, the mock miniature of the 'Gainsborough Lady' in ruffled eighteenth-century dress and feathered hat smiling at the cinema audience, certainly has more in common with Margaret Lockwood as a highwaywoman than with Will Hay as a railway porter. However, the melodramas represent only a tiny part of the studio's overall output. Each decade, or regime, seems to have produced different star types. But it was never possible to erase memories of the old favourites entirely. After all, Novello's Pierre Boucheron in *The Rat* is not so far removed from the dashing cads played by Granger and Mason twenty years later.

Ted Black left Gainsborough in 1945. Historians Seaton and Martin (1982) suggest that the rift between him and his boss, Maurice Ostrer, has been exaggerated: *The Man in Grey* and *The Wicked Lady* may have been a long way removed from the popular, realistic dramas Black wanted to make, they argue, but he was too much of a showman to turn up his nose at them. He was certainly involved in key decisions about hairdressing. As Granger recalls in his autobiography, it was Black who made him bleach his locks for his role in *The Man in Grey* (Granger, 1981, p. 62). Nevertheless, the friction between Black and Ostrer was apparent to all, and their shared distrust of Rank, who owned the studios, boded ill. Despite the box-office success of the costume melodramas, all of which were made on modest budgets, Rank felt that Gainsborough was being inefficiently run. Not long after Black's departure, he eased out Ostrer too.

Sydney Box was drafted in as their replacement (see Murphy in this volume). He took over in the spring of 1946 with instructions from Rank to make twelve pictures a year. This was a huge increase in productivity, and inevitably changed both the style of films made and the way the studio's actors were treated. Instead of showcasing a handful of volatile, top-rank stars, Box drew on what amounted to a small repertory company of lesser lights. If ever Gainsborough needed to cast a lawyer, Eric Portman was the man. Mai Zetterling and Greta Gynt provided a whiff of exoticism in such films as *Portrait from Life* (1948) and *Dear Murderer*

(1947). Cecil Parker and Jack Warner played the sturdy character roles. Diana Dors was often cast as the buxom young coquette. Maxwell Reed and Dennis Price were the juvenile leads. Googie Withers furnished the earthy glamour. It is difficult to think of any of the above as Gainsborough stars. All also appeared in films at Rank's other studios.

In his days as an independent producer at Riverside Studios in Hammersmith, Box had set up the Company of Youth. His aim was less to unearth new stars than to enable good young actors to see how films were made.

> They could come whenever they liked to the studios and watch what was happening. We'd give them any parts we could find for them. They were in their late teens or early twenties. They got paid every week and any clothes that were provided for them they were allowed to keep, and that sort of thing. And they were given lifts to the studio. It was very small-scale by present-day standards.[45]

When Box moved to Gainsborough, the Company of Youth was absorbed by the Rank Organization and eventually mutated into the Rank Charm School, which had very different aims. Still, Susan Shaw (born Patsy Sloots), Jane Hylton and Bill Owen, all Company of Youth alumni, went on to appear in Gainsborough pictures.

Box's background was in documentary, theatre and journalism. He was not a natural-born showman. 'Sydney and I never much liked the *Wicked Lady*-style films,' Betty Box, who was put in charge of the tiny, two-stage Islington studio while her brother ran Shepherd's Bush, recalls. 'We thought they were very unreal. We never had the Gainsborough identity – the lady in the hat. We used it because we were making Gainsborough films, but we never really took over that identity.'[46] Under the new regime, one further Arliss-style melodrama, *Jassy* (1947), was completed. It is the only one in the series shot in Technicolor. (Later historical dramas such as *The Bad Lord Byron* (1949) and *So Long at the Fair* (1950) were very different in tone.) Box, who had inherited the project, did not conceal his disdain for it. Even before it was complete, he confided to the diary he and his wife kept that: 'The shooting has been a disappointment to us and so have Maggie [Lockwood] and Basil Sydney. There is no subtlety in their work at all. We hope the colour of sets and costumes will help sell the picture, which seems mediocre to us at this stage.'[47]

Despite being hindered by obsolescent equipment, Box succeeded in his ambition of turning out 'a series of middle-budget pictures at an average cost of well under £200,000'.[48] But they varied hugely in tone and quality. Low-budget thrillers such as *Dear Murderer*, popular comedies such as

Holiday Camp (1947), the Huggett series, and stilted literary biopics such as *The Bad Lord Byron*, were all made at Gainsborough during the Box era. Arguably, such heterogeneity did not help the star system: there was no longer a consistent Gainsborough style, as there had been with the costume melodramas in the early 1940s and the comedies in the 1930s. For obvious reasons, stars were generally paid less at Gainsborough than at Pinewood, Denham or even Ealing: schedules were shorter (an average of five or six weeks' shooting) and budgets much smaller. This meant that really big names were rarely to be found in front of the cameras at Islington or Shepherd's Bush. Box carried on in the old Gainsborough tradition by hiring an American star, Fredric March, to star in *Christopher Columbus* (1949), but it proved an expensive flop.

Betty Box, busy turning out potboilers at Islington, reacts testily to the suggestion that late 1940s Gainsborough pictures were short on glamour. 'I did make a film at Islington which I thought was very glamorous, the one with Glynis Johns as a mermaid – *Miranda* [1948].'⁴⁹ Several important names (Jean Simmons, Trevor Howard) passed through the studios during the Box interregnum, but they were never Gainsborough stars in the way Lockwood, Mason, Granger and even Novello had been. Still, this late phase in the studio's history seems in hindsight to have paved the way for the emergence of a new kind of star system at Pinewood in the 1950s. During that decade, the Rank Organization's biggest names under contract included Dirk Bogarde and Diana Dors, both ex-Gainsborough, as well as a host of unpretentious character actors and comedians who would not have looked out of place under Ted Black in the 1930s.

Notes

1. *Dundee Evening Telegraph*, 20 March 1923.
2. The details about Brook's sleeping arrangements are taken from the author's interview in March 1996 with producer Betty Box. She knew Brook in the 1940s. Her brother Sydney worked with him on *The Flemish Farm* (1943).
3. *Motion Picture Studio*, 17 November 1923.
4. *The Impartial Film Report*, 13 November 1933.
5. This quote is taken from a clipping in *The Clive Brook Press Book*, British Film Institute Special Collections.
6. Brook, C. *The Eighty-four Ages*, p. 146.
7. *London Calling*, 19 January 1929.
8. *News of the World*, 8 October 1933.
9. This quote is taken from a cutting in the Ivor Novello 'Personal File' kept in the Theatre Museum Library, Covent Garden, London.
10. *News of the World*, 8 October 1933.
11. *London Calling*, 19 January 1929.
12. *News of the World*, 8 October 1933.

13. These details about Novello's contractual arrangements with Gainsborough are taken from MacQueen-Pope (1952), pp. 217–18. MacQueen-Pope was formerly Novello's business manager.

14. The details about Rock's salary and Minter's earnings are taken from Low (1971), p. 59.

15. See, for instance, Burnett (1932). This is probably the most virulent of the many indictments of cinema published in the late 1920s and early 1930s.

16. See *Picturegoer*, January 1928.

17. This quote is taken from the BFI microfiche cuttings on *The Lodger*.

18. Ibid.

19. Taken from a memo on *Downhill* submitted by Ivor Montagu to C.M. Woolf (1927), The Ivor Montagu Collection, BFI Special Collections.

20. Ivor Montagu was co-founder of the Film Society (1925), a club devoted to the presentation of avant-garde and politically challenging films. He worked with Eisenstein, and made documentaries in Spain during the Spanish Civil War. As a critic and polemicist, he advocated realism, not glamour. A zoologist, ping-pong enthusiast and committed Communist, he was not likely to champion a British star system.

21. *News of the World*, 15 October 1933.

22. *Daily Telegraph*, 13 March 1951.

23. *The Times*, March 1951.

24. *Picturegoer*, June 1927, p. 9.

25. Mabel Poulton may not have been a West End actress but she had studied at drama school. Despite the criticisms voiced by Hitchcock and others about mannered British screen acting, film producers still remained reluctant to take risks with newcomers who had no stage experience whatsoever.

26. *The Weekly Dispatch*, 26 February 1928.

27. *Evening Standard*, 18 July 1934.

28. The information about Poulton's eye insurance is taken from an unsourced 1920s cutting included in the BFI microfiche of the actress's career.

29. These quotes are taken from *Rough Notes* by Michael Balcon, 26 February 1937, kept in the Michael Balcon files, BFI Special Collections.

30. Balcon, ibid.

31. *Film Pictorial*, 29 February 1936, p. 13.

32. Ealing during the 1940s, Hammer during the late 1950s and early 1960s, the *Carry On* films from the 1950s onwards and the Gainsborough comedies in the 1930s all preferred to rely on their own, home-grown character actors rather than big-name outsider stars.

33. See the US trade paper *Motion Picture Herald*, 18 November 1939, for a dismissive review of *The Frozen Limits*: 'The Palladium Crazy Gang, British equivalent of the Marx Brothers, have a following mainly metropolitan in Great Britain, built on the strength of their stage appearances. Provincially, notably in the less adult sectors of the wildwoods, their brand of twentieth-century fooling still needs to be sold. Like comment might be made of the Gang's potential appeal outside these shores.'

34. Charles Laughton won a Best Actor Oscar for *The Private Life of Henry VIII* while two of Korda's newcomers, Merle Oberon and Robert Donat, were effectively launched as stars as a result of the film's international success.

35. *Variety*, October 1936.

36. This effusive Lever Brothers advertisement on behalf of Lux Soap can be found in the Betty Balfour press book, BFI Special Collections.

37. A brief survey of advertisements in any 1920s editions of *Kinematograph*

Weekly will quickly reveal the frequency with which British stars were used to endorse household products.

38. See *Picturegoer*, 2 September 1944, p. 11, for a discussion of Lockwood's baffling range of roles, 'What Are They Doing to Margaret Lockwood', and the same magazine, 9 December 1944, for Lockwood's reply in which she describes why she was obliged to take such a range of parts.

39. *Picturegoer*, 22 July 1944.

40. *Sunday Times Magazine*, 1 November 1970.

41. See an unpublished memo on *Production Facilities (Films) – Piffle* by F.L. Gilbert, managing director of the outfit, for a discussion of Maurice Ostrer's aims. BFI Special Collections.

42. *Picturegoer*, 10 November 1945, p. 70.

43. For a full account of the Mason/Arliss spat, see Sydney and Muriel Box's diaries, 16 March 1945, BFI Special Collections.

44. 'I May Find Myself Obliged to Emigrate', *Picturegoer*, 3 December 1945; 'Letters from Our Readers', *Picturegoer*, 19 January 1946.

45. Interview with Betty Box, op. cit.

46. Box, ibid.

47. Sydney and Muriel Box, op. cit., 27 December 1946.

48. This quote is taken from *A Report on Production and Future Planning at Gainsborough Studios* drawn up by Sydney Box for J. Arthur Rank in 1947, BFI Special Collections.

49. Betty Box interview, op. cit.

8

Innovation and Economy: The Contribution of the Gainsborough Cinematographer

Duncan Petrie

The label 'A Gainsborough Picture' has come to be associated with a relatively small number of costume melodramas produced during the 1940s. Until recently almost unanimously derided by critics and ignored by scholars, these productions have much to recommend them in aesthetic terms, not least their vivid sense of visual style. Indeed, the resurgence of critical interest in Gainsborough melodrama has been spearheaded by some inspired analysis of the function of, and pleasures offered by, costume and set design in these films (Harper, 1987; Cook, 1996a). Somewhat less explored is the part played by creative cinematography in the Gainsborough studio aesthetics. Yet it is precisely the deployment of lighting and camera movement which sets off the other visual elements within the frame, including the all-important sets and costumes.

I shall consider in some detail the contribution of the cinematographer to the film-making process at Gainsborough. Despite the significance of the 1940s melodramas, they represent only a fraction of the films made under the Gainsborough banner between 1924 and 1950. Consequently, I shall examine the development of cinematography at the studio from the late silent period, through the introduction of sound and the rationalization of British production, to the box-office triumphs of the 1940s and the subsequent decline which led to the closure of the company at the beginning of the 1950s. While certain cinematographers warrant particular attention, my primary concern will be the changing context of production, the technological and institutional conditions that effectively circumscribed the creative space within which these individuals operated. Above all, from its inception Gainsborough was a wholeheartedly commercial operation, churning out product designed to be popular – and therefore profitable – at the British box office. In the history of such an enterprise the dictates of economics are as important as those of aesthetics.

The silent years: Michael Balcon and the international influence

Michael Balcon's contribution to the revival of British cinema in the 1920s is covered elsewhere in this volume (see Kemp). Balcon, like his contemporary Herbert Wilcox, understood implicitly that if British films were to have any chance of competing with Hollywood product both at home and abroad, then a drastic improvement in production values was necessary. He set out to make high-quality modern films, starting in 1923 with the production of *Woman to Woman*.[1] Directed by Graham Cutts, *Woman to Woman* was made as an independent production at the Famous Players–Lasky (later Paramount) studios in Islington. As a short-term tenant, Balcon was afforded the services of the studio's staff, including experienced British cameraman Claude McDonnell, who was thoroughly immersed in modern (that is, Hollywood) film-making practices (Balcon, 1969). The film was commercially successful and extensively praised for its production values and modern technique, including relatively lavish and expressive studio lighting and photography which set it apart from the flat illumination and rather static style which dominated British cinematography at the time.[2] According to Rachael Low, this success enabled Balcon to make a further three independent films at Islington, *The White Shadow* (1924), *The Passionate Adventure* (1924) and *The Prude's Fall* (1924), before taking over the studio as a permanent production base for his new production company, Gainsborough Pictures (see Low, 1971, pp. 135–6).

It was during the teens that Hollywood had begun its major expansion into international markets. In Britain, where cinema-going had been steadily increasing, American studios began setting up subsidiary companies to distribute their product in the UK market. In 1919 Famous Players–Lasky went one stage further by establishing their own London production facility on the site of a former power station in Poole Street, Islington. From the outset Islington had an advantage over most of the other British studios in that it was equipped with the latest American technology, including modern lighting equipment, and staffed by experienced technicians. The location had certain implications for cinematographic style, as Jesse Lasky recalls in his memoirs:

We picked a location for the Islington studios where heavy fog would collect even when the rest of London was in bright sunshine. ... Some of the artistic soft-focus photography admired by critics in this country was simply fog that eluded the fans (Lasky, 1957, p. 132).

The visual style referred to by Lasky was particularly popular in the German cinema of the 1920s, with the skilful use of gauzes and smoke to produce a soft, diffuse quality to the image becoming a stock in trade of many cinematographers. The real impact of these techniques in Britain did not occur until the late 1920s, when several top continental technicians began working regularly in British studios.

Among the cinematographers employed by Lasky's at Islington were Claude McDonnell, who had previously worked for Ideal, and experienced Hollywood cameramen, including the British-born Hal Young and the American Roy Overbaugh. Arthur Miller, who would later become one of Hollywood's greatest cameramen with credits such as the Oscar-winning *How Green Was My Valley* (1941) and *The Song of Bernadette* (1943), photographed two films for George Fitzmaurice at the studio during this period – *Three Live Ghosts* (1922) and *The Man from Home* (1922) – and recalls that when he arrived at Islington he found the studio to be 'modern in all respects' (Balshofer and Miller, 1967).

The presence of such talented technicians and a state of the art studio facility could not fail to have an impact, given the rather unsophisticated and depressed state of the British production sector. Rachael Low notes that 'The new company concentrated on good lighting in which England now lagged far behind America' (Low, 1971, p. 142), while the 1921 edition of the *Kinematograph Year Book* reported a drastic alteration in studio lighting practices in British studios during 1920. Hollywood-trained cinematographers found the enclosed long arcs used in British studios primitive and inflexible, and consequently modern American white flame studio arcs, including Wohl 'broadsides', Kleigl spot lamps and Sun arcs, slowly became more commonplace. Similarly, Cooper-Hewitt mercury vapour lamps, popular for many years in Hollywood but hardly used in Britain, also became more common with the presence of technicians experienced in their use.[3] For the better-equipped studios like Islington, this allowed cinematographers to be versatile in terms of the range of lighting effects they could create and to exert a great deal of control over that lighting.

It was around the same time that the first Bell & Howell professional cameras also began arriving in Britain (Bennett, 1921, p. 84). These were the most technically advanced cameras in the world, far superior to the cameras used in Britain at that time, which included both the cumbersome 'Box Cameras' made by the Prestwich, Williamson, Darling and Moy companies, and the French Pathé and Debrie models. Expense was a major factor: a new Bell & Howell cost as much as five times the price of a Pathé camera.[4] In the 1920s most cameramen owned their own equipment, and this put such sophisticated modern machines beyond the reach of the average British technician (Low, 1950, p. 224). However, Hollywood-trained technicians tended to be more highly paid, which in turn contributed to the increase in the number of Bell & Howells being used on British productions. The benefits afforded by the Bell & Howell included superior registration, producing a steadier image in the gate, a revolutionary and highly efficient focusing system which saved on shooting time, and a crank handle which minimized friction and made a steady cranking rate easier to obtain.[5] The cumulative benefits of the new technology facilitated more efficient and flexible camera operating and helped to pave the way for a more fluid camera style. In purchasing the lease for Islington studios from Lasky's at the bargain price of £14,000, Balcon not only acquired a modern-equipped production facility – he also inherited some of Lasky's key personnel. As well as McDonnell and Young, there was chief electrician George Gunn, who would later manage British Technicolor, and a young art director and scriptwriter named Alfred Hitchcock (Balcon, 1969, p. 18).

Another key element of Balcon's strategy to raise the standard of production values was to enter into co-production with European partners, particularly those with more advanced facilities and film-making expertise. In the mid-1920s the obvious place to look for such qualities was Germany, due to the advanced nature of an industry which had enjoyed considerable support from the Weimar government, and in 1925 Balcon embarked on his first Anglo-German co-production. *The Blackguard* was directed by Graham Cutts at the Ufa studios in Berlin, with the collaboration of top German technicians including cinematographer Theodor Sparkuhl, who had photographed several of Ernst Lubitsch's internationally successful costume dramas. Cutts's assistant director on *The Blackguard* was Alfred Hitchcock, who absorbed a great deal during his time at the studio (Taylor, 1978, p. 35).

The following year Hitchcock was given his first films to direct by Balcon. *The Pleasure Garden* (1926) and *The Mountain Eagle* (1926) were both co-productions made at the Emelka studios near Munich.

Hitchcock's cameraman was an Italian of considerable international experience, Baron Ventimiglia, who in 1924 had worked on an independent production at Islington, *The Money Habit*, directed by Walter Niebuhr. His skill and resourcefulness as a cinematographer was to be much more dramatically apparent on Hitchcock's next film, produced back in London at Islington. *The Lodger* (1926), hailed by *Bioscope* as 'the finest British production ever made',[6] is certainly one of the first be distinguished by its use of lighting and camera techniques.

The film is a testament to Hitchcock's German influences. The expressionist impulse is evident in the use of looming shadows and forced camera angles to generate atmosphere and suspense, while the central motif of the staircase (frequently photographed from overhead in a manner which links the film with sequences in *Psycho*, directed by Hitchcock 34 years later) not only provides a subliminal layer of meaning but also physically structures much of the action and set-ups. The use of blue tints for the night exteriors adds a further expressive layer. Among the many memorable visual moments in the film are the sinister shadow falling on the door signifying the arrival of the mysterious 'lodger', played by Ivor Novello; his subsequent emergence out of the London fog recalling the image of Conrad Veidt's somnambulist stepping out of his 'coffin' in Robert Weine's expressionist classic *The Cabinet of Dr Caligari* (1919); the reflection of the window-frame on his face, eerily forming the shape of a cross; the subjective image of feet pacing back and forth across a glass ceiling; the high overhead shots of the staircase, which Tom Ryall suggests may have been influenced by René Clair's experimental 1924 film *Entr'acte* (Ryall, 1986); and in the climactic chase sequence, the chilling moment when Novello, handcuffed and hanging helplessly from railings, is attacked by the mob who believe him to be guilty of a series of murders.

As a cameraman Ventimiglia served Hitchcock well on *The Lodger*, but it was to be their last collaboration. The Italian continued to work in Britain, mainly at the Gaumont-British studio at Shepherd's Bush on a series of less distinguished productions. The young Englishman, on the other hand, set about consolidating his career as the most innovative director working in Britain. His imaginative approach to the craft of film-making, and his total commitment to telling stories visually, provided cinematographers with the opportunity to push themselves to new heights of creative achievement on a Hitchcock production. For example, Claude McDonnell photographed Hitchcock's next two productions at Gainsborough, including *Downhill* (1927), which afforded him some opportunities for expressive Germanic lighting, unusual angles (including an overhead shot in a taxi) and effective camera movement. Hitchcock was then invited to join British International Pictures (BIP) at their large new studio complex at Elstree, and McDonnell was set to accompany him on to the production of *The Ring*. However, there was disagreement over the financial terms being offered and McDonnell was replaced by Jack Cox. Balcon's first cameraman was to remain at Islington until the end of the silent period, his last two films for Gainsborough being *City of Play* (1929) and *The Crooked Billet* (1929).

The studio's other chief cinematographer during the 1920s was Hal Young, who had first worked for Balcon on *The Prude's Fall*. A skilled technician, Young proved to be adept at both location and studio cinematography. His best outdoor work includes his picturesque but subtle images of the English countryside, lending distinction to the independent production *The Fox Farm* (1922). Later, at Islington, Young excelled himself on the 1925 studio-bound production *The Rat*, directed by Cutts and featuring Ivor Novello as an exotic but roguish Parisian apache dancer. Next to Hitchcock's work, the film features some of the most impressive lighting and camerawork achieved at the studio during the period. The most memorable sequences are those set in the seedy 'coffin club' where Novello carouses with women and engages in knife fights. The lighting is effectively low key, while the camera wanders restlessly around the set dollying towards and away from the action as the Rat is observed at play by a group of bourgeois thrill-seekers from a private booth. Young continued to work regularly with Cutts on productions such as *The Triumph of the Rat* (1926), *The Sea Urchin* (1926) and *The Rolling Road* (1927) before leaving the studio in 1927.

By the end of the decade Gainsborough had been overtaken as a premier production facility by larger, more modern studios that had been built, including BIP at Elstree. However, films such as *The Lodger*, *The Rat* and *Hindle Wakes* (1927) stand as landmarks in the development of British cinematography during the late silent period. The last is notable for some impressive location cinematography in Blackpool by William Shenton and Jack Cox, including some exhilarating shots taken from a camera mounted on the big dipper at the pleasure beach, recalling the visual thrill of the 'unchained camera' associated with German films such as *The Last Laugh* (1924) and *Varieté* (1925). While not quite up to the achievements of the American and German cinemas, lighting and camera techniques in Britain had absorbed a great deal from studio practice in Hollywood and Berlin and had consequently improved dramatically from the static and unimaginatively lit pictures of the teens and early 1920s.

This was a process to which Gainsborough cinematographers had made a significant contribution.

Sound comes to Islington

The sound revolution transformed the British film industry between 1929 and 1930. Gainsborough was relatively slow to respond and consequently its first 'sound' films were silent productions such as *The Wrecker* (1928) and *The Return of the Rat* (1929), revamped with a synchronized soundtrack. The studio was subsequently refurbished in the summer of 1929 with RCA sound equipment at the cost of £70,000. According to Rachael Low, the first all-talking picture produced at Islington appeared the following year, the musical *Just for a Song*, directed by V. Gareth Gundrey and photographed by Jimmy Wilson. While this delayed reaction to the challenge of sound allowed others to capture the high ground, Balcon was carefully assembling quality technicians and creating the environment for 'a stable and creative production unit' (Low, 1985, pp. 126–7).

As elsewhere, the coming of sound had a dramatic impact on cinematographic style in Britain. The new technology had implications at both the level of technology (type of lighting and film stock) and technique (see Petrie, 1996, pp. 20–4). The general trend towards more meticulous, expressive lighting and fluid camera mobility was arrested, with the cameras temporarily confined to soundproofed booths and lighting simplified to facilitate multi-camera shooting and to minimize the risk of shadows being cast by the sound boom. These setbacks were slowly overcome, however, with the development of camera 'blimps' and more portable and sophisticated sound-recording equipment.

Balcon continued to look to Europe and America for the talent he believed necessary to maintain high production standards. Among the continental cameramen to arrive at Gainsborough during this period was the Czech Otto Kanturek, who photographed *The Wrecker* before moving on to BIP, where he became the studio's foremost cinematographer during the 1930s. The German Mutz Greenbaum (later Max Greene) made a far more significant contribution to the studio, shooting more than twenty productions for Balcon at Islington and Shepherd's Bush between 1931 and 1936. A consummate craftsman, Greenbaum is described by his former camera assistant Lionel Banes as 'the greatest cinematographer I ever worked with. He could cope with anything, from a low key to a Sahara desert scene' (BECTU Oral History Project, 28 July 1988).

Greenbaum's more notable work for Gainsborough includes several successful collaborations with director Victor Saville (see Barr in this volume), such as the atmospheric 1931 remake of *Hindle Wakes*, the popular musicals *Sunshine Susie* (1931) and *Love on Wheels* (1932), and the romantic melodrama *The Faithful Heart* (1932). Greenbaum also aided the work of several of Balcon's most talented directors, including the American Tim Whelan on *It's a Boy* (1933), Walter Forde on the oriental extravaganza *Chu-Chin-Chow* (1934) and Robert Stevenson on *Tudor Rose* (1936), a historical drama based on the story of Lady Jane Grey which featured impressive sets designed by Alex Vetchinsky. What Greenbaum brings to this diverse set of films is a visual imagination and a solidity which allows them to transcend the physical and budgetary limitations of (in comparison with newer, more modern studios such as Elstree, Denham or Pinewood) Islington productions.

In addition to the continentals, Balcon also continued to attract American technicians to Gainsborough. Adrian Brunel's 1928 production *The Constant Nymph*, one of the studio's most successful late silent films starring Ivor Novello and Mabel Poulton, had featured some impressive Austrian location photography by Dave Gobbett. Even more passed through the studio during the 1930s, including Glen MacWilliams (best known for his work on the Jessie Matthews musicals produced at Shepherd's Bush, including *Evergreen* (1934) and *First a Girl* (1935)), Phil Tannura and Charles van Enger. With the exception of MacWilliams, these technicians were solid commercial cinematographers rather than artists, associated with perfunctory high-key, flat illumination rather than atmospheric chiaroscuro and careful modelling. Enger (whose work in Hollywood had included the 1925 Rupert Julian/Lon Chaney version of *The Phantom of the Opera*) increasingly found himself shooting low-budget comedies and musicals, including *Aunt Sally* (1933), *Boys Will Be Boys* (1935), *Jack of All Trades* (1936) and *Where There's a Will* (1936) starring the likes of Jack Hulbert, Cicely Courtneidge and Will Hay. Clearly, in both genres visible action was deemed more important than 'atmosphere', which suited Enger's rather functional lighting style.

A new regime: Ted Black and Maurice Ostrer

In 1936 Michael Balcon moved to MGM British, making way for the new management team of production executive Maurice Ostrer and his associate producer Ted Black (see Murphy in this volume). During Black's reign from 1936 to 1943, Gainsborough concentrated on a mixed production programme of popular comedy vehicles featuring Will Hay,

Arthur Askey and the Crazy Gang, thrillers and low-budget musicals. Like Balcon before him, Black understood the importance of stars in popular cinema.

Unlike Balcon, Black put his faith in British technicians and, during the seven years he was in charge at Gainsborough, the bulk of the studio's films were photographed by either Arthur Crabtree or Jack Cox. Crabtree had operated for Glen MacWilliams at Shepherd's Bush, before being given his break on *First Offence* (1936), directed at Islington by Herbert Mason. MacWilliams is credited by Crabtree as effecting a shift away from the dominant Germanic style at Shepherd's Bush, associated with the likes of Günther Krampf and Mutz Greenbaum, towards a more American style of lighting. The difference, as described by Crabtree, was that the Germans tended to light the set while the Americans concentrated on lighting the star (Sainsbury, 1941–2). In reality, the development of cinematographic style in Hollywood and on the Continent had many parallels. For example, so-called 'expressionistic' low-key lighting had been used by director Cecil B. DeMille and his cameraman Alvin Wycoff in the teens, while German cinematographers learned a great deal from Hollywood about lighting their leading actors and actresses (Louise Brooks in *Pandora's Box*, Marlene Dietrich in *The Blue Angel*). However, the Hollywood studio system did invest a great deal in the appeal of stars, and the imperative of 'putting the light on the money' had an added importance in this context. It also proved to be a major influence on Crabtree's own development as a cameraman, chiming with Black's championing of British stars. It is probably more accurate to describe the dominant lighting style at Gainsborough by this time as a synthesis or hybrid form of Hollywood 'gloss' and German 'expression', the subject-matter – whether serious or light – tending to direct the emphasis towards one pole or the other.

Crabtree subsequently photographed many of the comedies directed by Marcel Varnel at Islington, including the Will Hay vehicles *Oh Mr Porter!* (1937) and *Old Bones of the River* (1938). Varnel was an extremely fast director who also used a large number of set-ups and so the tendency was, as with other comedies, to adopt an overall high-key lighting design. (Sainsbury, 1941–2). In comedy the emphasis is on visual as well as verbal gags, and Crabtree's lighting preferences stood him in good stead. In addition to comedies, Crabtree worked with the young Carol Reed on more sophisticated and challenging productions such as *Bank Holiday* (1938), which, despite rather unremarkable studio scenes, does feature more interesting locations shot in Margate which have a lively documentary quality, and the prestigious period film *Kipps* (1941), a glossy and solidly photographed adaptation of the novel by H.G. Wells starring Michael Redgrave and Phyllis Calvert.

Black's other senior cameraman was the more experienced Jack Cox, who had photographed his first features back in 1921. Cox had briefly passed through Islington in 1927, shooting *Hindle Wakes* for Maurice Elvey and the First World War drama *Blighty* (1927) for Adrian Brunel, before becoming Hitchcock's regular cinematographer at BIP, where he collaborated with the director on ten features including *Blackmail* (1929), the first British talkie. Cox subsequently returned to Islington in 1936, and while, like Crabtree, he was assigned his fair share of comedies and musicals, he also demonstrated a flair for atmospheric and imaginative cinematography on the horror vehicle *The Man Who Changed His Mind* (1936), starring Boris Karloff; *Dr Syn* (1937), a ghostly tale of smugglers featuring George Arliss; and *The Lady Vanishes* (1938), a reunion with Hitchcock on a modest production set primarily on a train. The latter was probably the most dramatically effective British film set on a train since *Rome Express*, which was directed at Gaumont-British by Walter Forde and featured photography by Günther Krampf. Cox and Hitchcock successfully disguise the limitations of shooting on a cramped, 90-foot-long set (Truffaut, 1968) and a single mock-up of a train carriage by careful staging of ensemble playing and skilful use of transparencies and miniatures.

After striking a distribution deal with 20th Century Fox, Gainsborough expanded into the larger and better-equipped Gaumont-British studios at Shepherd's Bush in 1940. When war broke out in 1939, many British studios were requisitioned and production was massively curtailed. However, Gainsborough remained open, concentrating on a mixture of comedies, war films and the occasional prestige production for 20th Century Fox, including the Carol Reed films *Night Train to Munich* (1940), *The Girl in the News* (1940), both photographed by Otto Kanturek, and *The Young Mr Pitt* (1942), shot in a similarly polished style by the distinguished British cameraman Freddie Young. Young had been Herbert Wilcox's chief cameraman during the 1930s and his credits included *Victoria the Great* (1937), *Sixty Glorious Years* (1938) in Technicolor, *Goodbye, Mr Chips* (1939) and *49th Parallel* (1941) – the latter featuring extensive location work in Canada. In 1941 the Gaumont-British empire was taken over by J. Arthur Rank but, more interested in his 'prestige' productions at Denham, he left Gainsborough more or less to its own devices.

It was during the war that British cinema became strongly associated with a documentary–realist aesthetic, championed by critics who regarded this as a sign of the development of a mature and distinctive national cinema (Ellis, 1978, 1996; Higson, 1986). Among the films cited as central to this breakthrough is the Gainsborough production *Millions Like Us* (1943), written and directed by Frank Launder and Sidney Gilliat. A documentary-inspired vision of life on the home front, the film was photographed by Jack Cox and Roy Fogwell. The most memorable scenes from a photographic point of view are those which take place in the large armaments factory where a disparate group of women are posted to serve on 'the home front'. These convey a palpable image of industrial activity which not only provides an effectively realistic backdrop to the action, but also serves to situate the film clearly in the visual tradition of the 1930s documentary movement. Cox was also responsible for a further two of the studio's war films: Anthony Asquith's claustrophobic submarine drama *We Dive at Dawn* (1943) and Launder and Gilliat's 1944 prisoner of war story *2000 Women*. However, the contemporary naturalism associated with Launder and Gilliat – their third and final wartime production for the studio being *Waterloo Road* (1945) – and promoted by Edward Black did not find favour with Maurice Ostrer, and it was under the latter's guiding influence that the studio assumed a new identity, as far removed from the acclaimed naturalism as seemed possible in the mid-1940s.

Cinematographic style and the costume melodramas

The costume cycle of the mid-1940s arguably provided Gainsborough with the studio's most visually distinguished phase since the achievements of the late silent period. The visual conception of the melodramas was profoundly studio-bound and anti-naturalistic, with much of the distinctive Gainsborough look attributable to the centrality of design. Sue Harper claims that the art department of the studio was dominated by four designers, Maurice Carter, Alex Vetchinsky, Andrew Mazzei and John Bryan, who were influenced by an anti-realist, 'expressionistic' style initially associated with continental art directors such as Vincent Korda and Alfred Junge (Harper, 1987, p. 180). Harper suggests that the Gainsborough designers viewed history as a source of sensual pleasure rather than in terms of historical accuracy or verisimilitude, an approach complemented by the costume designs of Elizabeth Haffenden. The centrality of production design influenced the cinematography, in that lighting and framing arrangements were guided by the designer's drawings. As Maurice Carter noted, 'The master sketch was the long master shot, and it had to be lit and photographed that way' (Aspinall and

Murphy, 1983, p. 59). In addition, designers were closely consulted on the planning of tracking shots and other long takes.

The first two melodramas, *The Man in Grey* (1943) and *Fanny by Gaslight* (1944), were both photographed by Arthur Crabtree. He subsequently became a director (the studio had a relatively small number of permanent creative staff during Ostrer's reign, and it was easier to promote 'insiders' than to go looking for new directors from outside) and was responsible for a further two, *Madonna of the Seven Moons* (1944) and *Caravan* (1946). Economy continued to be one of the major considerations at the studio, with implications for the ways in which technicians could express their creativity. As Robert Murphy argues, 'The sets and the way they were lit in most of the Gainsborough melodramas are indicative more of imagination and ingenuity in the use of the cramped Shepherd's Bush studio than of lavish expenditure' (Aspinall and Murphy, 1983, p. 6).

This is confirmed by cameraman Paul Wilson, who began his career at Shepherd's Bush as a clapperboy on *The Man in Grey*. Wilson worked with most of the studio's cinematographers, including Crabtree and Cox, noting that the main lesson he learned from them 'was to be economical with light. That way you had more control over it.'[7] While such a strategy ran the risk of producing rather flat and uninteresting lighting, the thematic ambiguities which were often central to the plot allowed for a certain expressionistic play of light and shadow. But studio policy also dictated the importance of displaying the Gainsborough stars, costumes and sets to their best advantage. This meant that in order to see as much detail as possible, while keeping lighting costs down, films tended to be shot at maximum aperture[8] – f.2 on Cooke Speed Panchro lenses – rather than adopting a low-key approach, similar to that of the American film noirs, which plunged substantial sections of the set into shadow. It was considered highly irregular when Mutz Greenbaum, who replaced Crabtree on *The Man in Grey* when the latter fell ill, insisted on using a stop of f.4. While this provided a greater depth of field, it also meant doubling the amount of light.

Crabtree's cinematographic approach to *The Man in Grey* was consistent with his favoured style, placing the emphasis very much on lighting the four leading players – James Mason, Margaret Lockwood, Stewart Granger and Phyllis Calvert. The camera moves fluidly around the sets, designed by Walter Murton, which are lit for maximum display. The most dramatic photographic and lighting effects occur at key moments in the plot: the simulated candle and firelight which illuminate Clarissa's (Calvert) wedding chamber, producing a soft romantic veneer which is subsequently destroyed by the cruelty and indifference of her husband, Lord Rohan (Mason); while the horrific climax, in which Rohan beats the duplicitous Hester (Lockwood) to death, is also bathed in low-key firelight, but this time the ambience created is one of malevolence and terror.

The trend set by Crabtree on *The Man in Grey* and *Fanny by Gaslight* was developed and refined by Jack Cox on *Madonna of the Seven Moons* (1944) and *The Wicked Lady* (1945). *Madonna* effectively utilizes two visual styles, each corresponding to an aspect of the fractured psyche of the leading character Maddalena/Rosanna (Phyllis Calvert). The meek and demure Maddalena inhabits brightly lit bourgeois interiors while her *alter ego*, the fiery and sensual Rosanna, exists in a world of excitement, romance and danger at the Inn of the Seven Moons in a shabby district of Florence. These sets are lit in a much more expressionist manner, with strong shadows and imaginative use of the interplay of light and shade. In one bedroom sequence featuring Calvert and Stewart Granger, all we can see are their eyes and the glowing tips of cigarettes.

The Wicked Lady features a similar mix of a generally high-key lighting design with lower-key effects signifying moments of passion or danger: Lady Barbara's (Margaret Lockwood) secret room is dark and shadowy, and it is from here that she slips out into the night dressed as a highwayman, while the sequence in the inn when she is first seduced by Captain Jackson (James Mason) is lit with simulated firelight. Both *Madonna* and *The Wicked Lady* employ bolder visual touches at moments of narrative crisis. There are extreme close-ups: for example, Rosanna's distressed face in *Madonna* rendered all the more effective by the reflected crucifix in her eyes, or Lady Barbara's baleful triumph as she smothers the old family retainer Hogarth with a pillow in *The Wicked Lady*, and expressive camera movement, most notably the crane shot which begins on the back of Barbara's head before pulling back and up and out of the window as she falls and dies, alone and isolated.

Gainsborough enters its final phase

While Maurice Ostrer undoubtedly had an instinct for the popular, his overreliance on costume melodramas led to a significant reduction in output at the studio. In 1946 control at Gainsborough changed hands once again with the appointment of Sydney Box as production chief with a brief to treble the studio's output to sixteen films a year. To assist him in this task, he brought his own cinematographers with him to Gainsborough. Reginald Wyer had worked with Box on documentaries during the war, before moving into feature production. A competent rather than an outstanding technician, he had photographed Box's successful independent production *The Seventh Veil* (1945), and his subsequent feature credits include *Daybreak* (1946), *The Upturned Glass* (1947), both made for Box's own production company Triton at Riverside, and several productions directed by Ken Annakin, including the portmanteau productions *Quartet* (1948) and *Trio* (1950), and the comedy trilogy *Here Come the Huggetts* (1948), *Vote for Huggett* (1949) and *The Huggetts Abroad* (1949). More interesting is the costume film *So Long at the Fair* (1950), set in Paris and starring the young Dirk Bogarde and Jean Simmons. The production features a great deal of camera mobility – tracking and craning around the hotel sets, which conveys a strong sense of three dimensional space – and some very effective and dramatic use of close-up.

Jack Cox remained at the studio until its closure in 1950. He photographed one of the last costume melodramas instigated by Maurice Ostrer, *The Magic Bow* (1946), directed by Bernard Knowles who had been a top cameraman at Shepherd's Bush during the 1930s, where he photographed several films for Alfred Hitchcock, including *The 39 Steps* (1935) and *Sabotage* (1936). But under the new regime Cox's assignments, which included *Holiday Camp* (1947), *Broken Journey* (1948) and *Traveller's Joy* (1949), proved less rewarding and he was gradually usurped as the studio's costume drama specialist by newcomer Stephen Dade, who had made his own début as a cinematographer on *A Place of One's Own*, directed by Knowles in 1945. Dade quickly established himself as a skilled technician on films such as *Caravan* (1946) and *The Brothers* (1947).

The former, set largely in a studio-bound Spain, is one of the most atmospheric of the costume melodramas. Its more memorable moments include the appearance of Jean Kent as the gypsy dancer Rosal, her seductive dance augmented by soft and delicate lighting which is reflected off the bells which adorn her costume, creating a sensuous shimmering effect. The low-key lighting in the cave where she nurses the injured Richard (Stewart Granger) creates an erotically charged space (not unlike the Inn of the Seven Moons in *Madonna*) which contrasts with the furnished, brightly lit and more straight-laced English interiors. The climactic scene, when Richard forces the villainous Sir Francis (Dennis Price) into a swamp, is underscored by a brooding studio sky, smoke and eerie lighting which combine to produce one of the film's most dramatic moments. *The Brothers*, on the other hand, is notable for the poetic and evocative use of its Hebridean locations, the shimmering lochs and the ominously dark Cuillin Hills, powerfully setting off this tale of passion and tragedy set in an isolated community on the Isle of Skye at the turn of the century.

Several of the costume films made at Gainsborough under Box were much more lavish than those produced by Black and Ostrer. It was Box who produced the studio's first two films in Technicolor, *The Man Within* and *Jassy*, both directed in 1947 by Bernard Knowles, who had photographed one of the first British Technicolor features, *The Mikado*, in 1939. His cameraman on both productions was Geoffrey Unsworth, a technician highly experienced in colour, having previously worked as an assistant and operator on many Technicolor films of the late 1930s and early 1940s, including *The Drum*, *The Four Feathers*, *The Thief of Bagdad*, *The Great Mr Handel*, *The Life and Death of Colonel Blimp* and *A Matter of Life and Death*. Unsworth signed a contract with the Rank Organization in 1946 and was assigned to Gainsborough.

The Man Within, a tale of eighteenth-century smugglers, was also the first production made after Sydney Box had taken over the studio. Robert Murphy remarks that Unsworth's colour cinematography gives the film 'a completely different atmosphere' from the earlier Gainsborough melodramas (Murphy, 1989, p. 126). *Jassy*, on the other hand, was a direct attempt to imitate the past successes of films such as *The Wicked Lady*. Unsworth consequently used plenty of light to show off the lavish sets, designed by Maurice Carter, and Elizabeth Haffenden's brightly coloured ballgowns worn by Margaret Lockwood and Patricia Roc. The expressionist undertones are retained, as shadows begin to creep in when the fortunes of the huge country house at the centre of the drama fall into decay, and the odd low camera angle and lighting effect point up the menace of certain scenes, such as the poisoning of the tyrant by the mute servant girl.

While *Jassy* may have been somewhat more sumptuous than the black and white melodramas, it still betrays the marks of a cost-conscious production policy. An instructive comparison can be made with the Cineguild production *Blanche Fury* (1947), directed by Marc Allegret at Pinewood. The cameraman, Guy Green, photographing his first Technicolor production, approached the lighting of *Blanche Fury* in a similar manner to his celebrated black and white work, utilizing a meticulous low-key, high-contrast style. The result is a very atmospheric film, full of dark, brooding sequences. Paradoxically, the 'high-art' pretensions of the film allowed Green to plunge huge areas of the set into darkness. The more cost-conscious Gainsborough aesthetic was concerned with making the budget – the stars and the sets – as visible as possible.

The respective court scenes in the films demonstrate this. In *Blanche Fury*, as the trial scene progresses, the set darkens considerably and is almost devoid of colour at the point when the jury deliver their verdict. *Jassy*, on the other hand, displays a brightly lit courtroom, featuring a large window with visible blue sky.

Stephen Dade photographed his first colour feature in 1949, *Christopher Columbus*, directed by David MacDonald and starring American actor Fredric March as the fifteenth-century explorer. One American critic described the film as 'a succession of extremely-well-photographed but intrinsically lifeless tableaux' (Quirk, 1971, p. 199). The location work in the West Indies (supervised by Cyril Knowles, brother of Bernard) is particularly noteworthy, characterized by vivid and suitably exotic blues and greens which contrast well with the browns and beiges of the Spanish court. But the handsome mounting provided scant compensation for what was a rather pedestrian drama. Dade was also responsible for one of the last big-budget costume films made by the Boxes at Gainsborough. In marked contrast to the earlier melodramas, *The Bad Lord Byron* (1949) invested a great deal in authenticity, particularly in terms of design and location, but once again the results were pedestrian and the film proved to be a commercial failure. Some of the more memorable sequences in what is otherwise a rather unremarkable-looking film, are those shot on location in Venice by Gordon Lang. But even these images seem old-fashioned when compared with Jack Hildyard's radiant Technicolor rendition of the city six years later in David Lean's *Summer Madness*.

While *The Bad Lord Byron* displays little of the visual resourcefulness and aesthetic power of its more modest predecessors, including Dade's own work on *Caravan*, it does display certain technical improvements, particularly in terms of back projection, the quality of which is demonstrably higher than the rather obvious use of the technique in earlier Gainsborough productions, including *The Wicked Lady* and *The Brothers*. The Rank Organization had become very interested in the technology of film production in the late 1940s. One of the major projects instigated was the independent frame system, a revolutionary approach to film-making designed to reduce costs and speed up the production process. Independent frame relied a great deal on pre-planning and prefabrication (Poole, 1980). While the experiment ultimately failed due to a combination of financial and aesthetic reasons (including the lack of flexibility imposed by using back projection in conjunction with interlocking sets constructed on vast mobile rostrums), the research and development had led to major improvements in back projection facilities within the Rank Organization (Macnab, 1993).

A mere seven films were made with independent frame techniques, including two Gainsborough productions. The first of these, the borstal drama *Boys in Brown* (1949), employed the process quite extensively (see Dixon, 1994), but despite a strong cast including Jack Warner, Richard Attenborough and Dirk Bogarde, is cinematically rather stilted and unimaginative. The second, *So Long at the Fair*, as Julian Poole notes, owes little to the process in visual terms (Poole, 1980, p. 110). There is some back projection – including a plate of the Eiffel Tower which also featured in the Two Cities production *Prelude to Fame* (1950) – but the main hotel set is utilized in a more conventional manner.

British cinematography: the Gainsborough legacy

Gainsborough studios closed in 1950, bringing yet another chapter in the history of British film-making to a (premature) end. But the legacy of Gainsborough in terms of the development of British cinematography remains an important one. The approach to film-making pioneered by Michael Balcon in the 1920s, a central strand of which was the employment of top-class technicians from overseas, revolutionized domestic product. The cutting edge of British cinema technique may have subsequently shifted to the new studios of Elstree and then Denham, the latter built by Alexander Korda in 1936, but Gainsborough continued to make a modest but significant contribution. From the naturalistic impulse of *Bank Holiday* and *Millions Like Us* to the low-budget expressionistic qualities of *Madonna of the Seven Moons*, *The Wicked Lady* and *Caravan*, the studio's cinematography displayed the kind of inventive and resourceful approach to the craft which remains a hallmark of British film-making.

As far as individual reputations are concerned, the claims on behalf of Gainsborough cameramen would be modest. In Jack Cox the studio certainly had one of the most experienced British technicians of his generation, arguably one of only three (along with Freddie Young and Bernard Knowles) who could stand alongside the continental and American cinematographers who dominated British production in the 1930s. Gainsborough proved to be Cox's creative swansong – he ended his long, distinguished career shooting a series of visually uninteresting Norman Wisdom comedies. The visual qualities of the melodramas were also enhanced by the fact that directors Arthur Crabtree and Bernard Knowles had been cameramen, and Knowles a particularly distinguished one at that.

Stephen Dade's most impressive post-Gainsborough work was on Cy Endfield's 1963 feature *Zulu*, while Reg Wyer faded into relative obscurity. Geoffrey Unsworth did become a top international cinematographer with credits for *2001: A Space Odyssey* (1968) and the Oscar-winning *Cabaret* (1972), but he had been under contract to Rank rather than Gainsborough. Other technicians of similar stature who began their careers at the studio, albeit in its twilight period, include John Alcott, who photographed *A Clockwork Orange* (1971), *Barry Lyndon* (1975) and *The Shining* (1980); and Ronnie Taylor, whose credits include Richard Attenborough's multi-Oscar-winner *Gandhi* (1982). But perhaps the most interesting legacy of the Gainsborough camera department is that associated with Jack Asher. Asher had operated for Unsworth on *Jassy* before being given his break as a lighting cameraman in 1948, and his work included two films with director Terence Fisher, *Portrait from Life* (1948) and *The Astonished Heart* (1950). The two were to be reunited almost a decade later at Hammer Films, where they developed the studio's distinctive approach to horror on productions such as *The Curse of Frankenstein* (1957), *Dracula* (1958) and *The Mummy* (1959). The Hammer aesthetic, expressive but economical in its use of colour, period settings and costumes, owes more to the look and spirit of the Gainsborough melodramas than to any precursor in the annals of cinematic horror.

The history of cinematographic style at Gainsborough, like Hammer's, may be a modest one, lacking the ambition or resources of the films made for Korda in the 1930s or Rank in the 1940s. Yet it is important to recognize the (sometimes remarkable) creative achievements of technicians working within the constraints of tight schedules and restricted budgets on commercial product which was just as much a vibrant part of the lifeblood, and the history, of British cinema as the more 'respectable' offerings.

Notes

1. The film is unfortunately lost.
2. For a fuller discussion of the British cinematographic style of the period, see Petrie (1996), Chapter 1.
3. Other Hollywood-trained technicians working in Britain at this time include the Frenchman René Guissart, who shot *Flames of Passion* (1922) and *Paddy the Next Best Thing* (1923) for Herbert Wilcox at Islington, and Nicholas Musuraca, who worked with J. Stuart Blackton at Cricklewood studios and would later make his reputation for low-key, atmospheric cinematography on the series of low-budget horror films produced by Val Lewton for RKO in the 1940s.
4. Baynham Honri notes that the Pathé professional cine camera cost £70, while Colin Bennett quotes £350 as the price of a new Bell & Howell in

1920. See Honri, 'Appendix 1', in Low (1950), *The History of the British Film 1914–1918*, p. 244; Bennett, 'Technical Survey of 1920', *Kinematograph Year Book 1921*, pp. 84–5.

5. These features are explored in relation to the introduction of the Bell & Howell in America by Kristin Thompson in Bordwell, Staiger and Thompson (1985), Chapter 20.

6. *Bioscope*, 16 July 1926, p. 39.

7. Letter to the author, 12 August 1993.

8. Barry Salt (1992), p. 229, notes a similar tendency by the Hollywood studios to adopt a uniform light level in the early 1940s, with all the studios (except Fox) working at maximum aperture.

9

Gainsborough after Balcon

Robert Murphy

It was tremendous fun, that studio, because – I didn't realise it at the time – how *available* Maurice Ostrer and Ted Black were, you just walked into their office when anything was wrong. When I went to Hollywood ... you had to give memos and five days would elapse and you'd see somebody and they'd pass it on and after about three weeks you'd get a 'No' back from the main office. That I didn't understand because I'd always worked at Gainsborough, which was so lovely and so easy. But I hated the films (Phyllis Calvert).[1]

Exploring Britain's 'unknown cinema' in 1969, Alan Lovell pointed out that, 'Unlike other European countries, Britain quickly developed a highly organized industry, which in structure was closer to the American industry than to the French or Italian industries' (Lovell, 1969, p. 4). In Britain, as in America, a studio system evolved and producers exercised a vital role. But whereas the Hollywood moguls have become household names, British producers (with the exception of Alexander Korda, Michael Balcon and, more recently, David Puttnam) have remained anonymous figures. Basil Dean, the founder of Ealing studios, Norman Loudon of Shepperton's Sound City, John Maxwell of Elstree, Julius Hagen of Twickenham, for example, remain shrouded in obscurity. Balcon has received his share of attention for his work at Ealing, but until now his Gainsborough period has been given little consideration, while his successors at Gainsborough (Ted Black, Maurice Ostrer and Sydney Box) have been virtually ignored. Balcon is covered elsewhere in this volume (see chapters by Kemp and Higson in this volume). Here, I focus on these lesser-known Gainsborough producers, Black, Ostrer and Box.

Ted Black

Ted Black appears to be one of the most highly regarded and least well known of British producers. James Mason considered his period at Gainsborough to be its most creative and productive (Mason, 1981, p. 181). Sidney Gilliat, who worked with Black as scriptwriter and director, pointed out that he had 'the longest and most financially successful run that *any* producer in Britain has ever had' (Brown, 1977a, p. 112). And for Alan Wood he 'unquestionably ranks as one of the greatest figures in British film history, the maker of stars like Margaret Lockwood, James Mason, John Mills and Stewart Granger' (Wood, 1952, p. 145). Ted Black was born in Birmingham in 1900, the third son of George Black, property master at the Theatre Royal, Birmingham, whose entrepreneurial tendencies led him to branch out on his own, first with a touring waxworks show and then with a travelling cinema using one of Robert Paul's Animatograph projectors. In 1905 he decided that the supply of film was now so prolific that it would be feasible to stay in one place, and returned to his home town of Sunderland to set up the Monkwearmouth Picture Hall, one of the first permanent cinemas in Britain.

The cinema prospered and he bought two more before he died in 1910. Ted and his brothers George and Alfred carried on where their father left off, building up a circuit of thirteen cinemas in the Tyneside area. In 1919 they sold them and set about establishing another circuit. In 1928 this too was sold, to Sir Walter Gibbons's conglomerate, the General Theatre Corporation. When GTC was taken over by Gaumont-British, George, the oldest brother, was put in charge of the corporation's non-cinema interests, a string of important provincial music halls and the London Palladium.[2] Ted was employed as a cinema circuit manager but in 1930 he switched to the production side of Gaumont-British, which by this time had absorbed Gainsborough, and he became assistant production manager at Shepherd's Bush and then studio manager at Islington. In 1935 he and Sidney Gilliat were appointed associate producers with responsibility for Gainsborough's uncharacteristically lavish *Tudor Rose*. Gilliat soon returned to scriptwriting and Black took over the running of Islington studios.

In December 1936, Balcon left Gaumont-British for MGM. At the end of March 1937, Shepherd's Bush studios and Gaumont-British Distributors were shut down, but a deal with C.M. Woolf and J. Arthur Rank's General Film Distributors led to production continuing at Pinewood and Islington under Black, and one of the directors of the corporation, Maurice Ostrer. At the Gainsborough Annual General meeting the following month, a loss of £97,930 was announced. Chairman Mark Ostrer blamed the Americans for their unwillingness to open their home market to British films: 'This is not due to any lack of merit, but to the fact that they are not accorded playing time in the most important situations, these being almost wholly controlled by American producing interests.'[3] Gainsborough's 1936 productions – three Will Hay films, two films from the Aldwych farce team, a vehicle for Cicely Courtneidge, a modest horror film starring Boris Karloff and the Crazy Gang's *Okay for Sound*, seem unlikely fare for the international market, and one suspects that both Ostrer's remarks and Gainsborough's losses had more to do with general policy decisions at Gaumont-British than with any extravagance at Islington. Certainly Black was untainted by Gainsborough's disappointing financial performance, and he took charge of Gaumont productions such as Hitchcock's *Young and Innocent* (1937) at Pinewood, as well as continuing the series of Will Hay comedies begun a year earlier at Islington with *Boys Will Be Boys* (1935).

Balcon had adopted a cosmopolitan approach to production – making co-productions with Germany until the Nazis made that impossible, and importing American stars and directors to give his films an international appeal. Black concentrated on making films for British audiences. Like his brother George at the London Palladium, Ted had an almost superstitious faith in his ability to divine popular taste and was wary of involving himself with anything that might dilute it. Alfred Roome, Gainsborough's top editor, recalled:

> We often wondered why Ted Black didn't mix with the élite of his profession. I don't think he ever went to a première, star parties and the like. One day he explained his apparent aloofness. He said he didn't want to get contaminated by people outside his band of entertainment. 'If I mix with the intellectual lot, it'll impair my judgement,' he said.[4]

He brought in music hall performers Will Hay, Will Fyffe and the Crazy Gang and the radio comedian Arthur Askey, but he also signed up unknown actors such as Margaret Lockwood, Michael Redgrave and Phyllis Calvert and gave them the opportunity to develop into stars. Above all, he recognized the importance of good scripts. According to Frank Launder:

> Ted believed in writers. To him the screenplay was the be-all and end-all. He enjoyed script conferences and went in for them wholesale, which made it pretty arduous going for the script editor

as well as the writers and directors. ... The small Islington studio soon became a hive of activity. We engaged a number of writers – J.B. Williams, Michael Pertwee and Jack Davies, Val Guest, Marriott Edgar, J.O.C. Orton, Michael Hogan, Gordon Wellesley, Audrey Erskine Lindop, John Cousins and Stephen Clarkson, whilst Sidney [Gilliat] and A.R. Rawlinson, Pat Kirwan, Rodney Ackland, Hans and Wolfgang Wilhelm came in on freelance assignments.[5]

At the end of 1938, Rank took over Denham studios from Alexander Korda and Pinewood was shut down. However, a deal between MGM British and Gainsborough ensured continuing financial support and the MGM distribution of Carol Reed's Jessie Matthews musical, *Climbing High*, and Hitchcock's first Islington film since the 1920s, *The Lady Vanishes*. Both MGM and 20th Century Fox had a substantial stake in Gaumont-British, though relations had hitherto been far from smooth. The success of Gainsborough films such as *Oh Mr Porter!* (1937) and *The Lady Vanishes*, and the looming threat of war, encouraged Fox to close down their small studio at Wembley and enter into a million-pound production agreement with Gainsborough. *Kinematograph Weekly* reported that:

> The deal arranges for the Islington studios to turn out a series of high-class pictures under the control of Twentieth Century Productions. Complete control is to be retained by Maurice Ostrer and Edward Black, who will work in close liaison with Robert T. Kane [hitherto in charge of Fox production]. The staff, which has faithfully served Gainsborough, will be kept in consistent employment for at least twelve months in order to carry out the large-scale production schedule which lies ahead of the producers.[6]

When war broke out in September 1939, Gainsborough, sustained by the Fox contract, continued production. But the Islington studio – with its huge power station chimney and its proximity to the Kings Cross/St Pancras railway junction – was considered too vulnerable to German bombs, and Black moved the Gainsborough team to Shepherd's Bush.

The Shepherd's Bush studio was much bigger than Islington, but the Gainsborough team retained their sense of camaraderie. Phyllis Calvert recalled that:

> The studio was made into a sort of hotel during the war. When the Blitz started people couldn't get there because of the traffic in the mornings and the bombs and the rubble. So they suggested that anyone who wanted to stay in the studio overnight could do. So we

all turned our dressing rooms into bedrooms and whenever we wanted to stay there we did. ... I don't remember any sort of discord at all. The make-up room was an absolute hive of fun and gaiety and laughter. It was like a little club.[7]

The films made by Gainsborough for Fox were not very different from their own programme: Will Hay's *Where's That Fire?* (1939) was followed by two comedy thrillers starring Alastair Sim and Gordon Harker – *Inspector Hornleigh on Holiday* (1939) and *Inspector Hornleigh Goes to It* (1941). But Fox made good use of Carol Reed, whom Black had lured away from Ealing with a £100 a week contract. Reed directed five of the ten Fox films, including the relatively big-budget *Kipps* (1941) and *The Young Mr Pitt* (1942). In its non-Fox films Gainsborough concentrated on comedies, mostly built around the radio star Arthur Askey (see Harper in this volume); thrillers such as *They Came by Night* (1940) with Will Fyffe and Phyllis Calvert; and occasional war films such as *For Freedom* (1940) and *Uncensored* (1942). When the Fox contract ran out in mid-1942, Gainsborough increased production of its own films to take up the slack.

The year 1943 was highly successful for Gainsborough, illustrating Black's policy of developing stars and producing a mixed programme of films. The studio released two serious war films: Anthony Asquith's *We Dive at Dawn*, with John Mills (who had played his first major role in *Tudor Rose*, 1936) as a submarine commander, and *Millions Like Us*, the directorial début of Gainsborough scriptwriters Frank Launder and Sidney Gilliat; two comedies: Arthur Askey in *Miss London Ltd* and Tommy Handley in *It's That Man Again*; an adaptation of Dodie Smith's bitter-sweet stage comedy, *Dear Octopus* with Margaret Lockwood in the major role; and a costume picture based on a novel by Lady Eleanor Smith, *The Man in Grey*, starring Margaret Lockwood, Phyllis Calvert, James Mason and Stewart Granger.

It was the two riskiest ventures, *Millions Like Us* and *The Man in Grey*, which proved the most successful. The inspiration for *Millions Like Us* came from the Ministry of Information, which wanted Gainsborough to produce a documentary about the war effort on the home front. Launder and Gilliat responded with a fictional story about 'mobile women', the young women who were being conscripted into factory work.

The MoI said that they greatly liked the script, but it wasn't the extensive documentary they'd been expecting. However, they strongly recommended Gainsborough to make it with their blessing and co-operation. Ted Black (unlike Maurice Ostrer) was happy to take it on. Kept us reasonably on the straight and narrow, too, and suggested no corn – anything obvious, vulgar or overdone was to be laid at our door.[8]

It was Gainsborough's policy to encourage its writers to turn their hands to directing. Val Guest had made his début with *Miss London Ltd*, and Leslie Arliss, who had made a couple of 'B' films for other studios, was given responsibility for *The Man in Grey*. Despite Maurice Ostrer's hostility and the unease of the some of the actors at having two directors to work with, *Millions Like Us* became a classic of Second World War realism. *The Man in Grey* represented something very different. Black had produced *Tudor Rose*, *Kipps* (1941) and *The Young Mr Pitt* (1942), but these costume films were refined and respectful in their treatment of the past. *The Man in Grey* came from a school of historical fiction which used the past as a setting for romantic fantasy. Amid the danger and discomfort of the war, such fiction found an avid readership. According to the studio correspondent of *Kinematograph Weekly*:

> It is quite plain that civilian and uniformed folk alike are turning more and more to 'period' reading – the classics and near classics, old and new. This trend of public preference cannot be ignored, and who shall say it is not reflected in film audiences? It must continue to be catered for; and let us beware of the derogatory use of the word 'escapist'.[9]

Despite having his finger on the pulse of public taste, it is unlikely that Black was responsible for introducing *The Man in Grey*. Sheridan Morley, in his biography of James Mason, reports that the novel 'had lain gathering dust on library shelves until the writer and producer R.J. Minney brought it to the attention of James's in-laws the Ostrers' (Morley, 1989, p. 55). In fact, Lady Smith's novel had been a bestseller, and Minney had yet to become a producer, but he was enthusiastic about melodrama and close to the Ostrers. It was a subject that fitted easily into Gainsborough's schedule: the story offered good parts for Gainsborough's two female leads, Margaret Lockwood and Phyllis Calvert, and good enough male parts to tempt Mason into a five-film contract and to launch Stewart Granger as a star.

Black responded to the success of *Millions Like Us* and *The Man in Grey* by giving Launder and Gilliat the opportunity to direct, separately, two wartime stories – *2000 Women* (1944), about British women caught in France at the outbreak of war and interned in a camp at Vittel, and

Waterloo Road (1945), with John Mills going AWOL to stop his wife being seduced by a spiv played by Stewart Granger. Anthony Asquith was switched from realist war film to escapist fantasy with *Fanny by Gaslight* (1944), and Askey and Handley were given comedy vehicles which steered them well away from the war, Askey's *Bees in Paradise* and Handley's *Time Flies*, both 1944.

However, the phenomenal success of *The Man in Grey* destroyed the power balance at the studio. In May 1943, Black was made a director of Gainsborough, but all was not well. At the beginning of 1943, Maurice Ostrer had told *Kinematograph Weekly* that Gainsborough was 'refusing to bow to the prevailing tendency to concentrate on war subjects'.[10] With his ideas vindicated by the success of *The Man in Grey*, he grew increasingly impatient of Black's desire for a wide range of subjects, particularly when there were men like Minney eager to produce flamboyant melodramas such as *Madonna of the Seven Moons*.[11] Sidney Gilliat's *Waterloo Road*, the last film produced by Black, seemed to Ostrer to be taking the studio in a realist direction to which he was entirely opposed. According to Gilliat:

> Ostrer thought it an absurd venture and I suspect had no wish to see me or Frank [Launder] established as directors after *Millions Like Us*. The rift between Ostrer and Black grew into a chasm – the tension between the two men had been growing for a long time. Black was not backed by Rank, who had just taken over the group, and he resigned towards the end of the production. But he never let me know during the filming that the picture and myself were a direct cause. He was a man to go tiger-shooting with. Ostrer obstructed the completion of the film after Black's departure, and when I finally managed, through the editor's help, to get the last shots – six or seven months after production was suspended – Ostrer put the film bottom of the dubbing list.[12]

By the end of the year, the trade papers were reporting that Black had been recruited by Alexander Korda for MGM, who were planning an ambitious production programme in Britain.[13] He was to produce a film which would be directed by Carol Reed, but Reed's army duties kept him away from feature production, and Leslie Arliss was eventually brought in to direct *A Man About the House*, which finally emerged in 1947. It is a competent and interesting film, but one that cries out for the subtlety and ambiguity Reed was to employ so successfully in *Odd Man Out* (1947), *The Fallen Idol* (1948) and *The Third Man* (1949). Black's post-Gainsborough career ended sadly. Korda's highbrow extravagance was the antithesis of Black's carefully budgeted populism, and the strain of producing *Bonnie Prince Charlie* (1948), a sprawling, poorly scripted epic, took its toll. In November 1948, shortly after the film had been released to a lukewarm response from critics and audiences, Ted Black died of cancer of the lungs and throat. Alan Wood believed he had worked, and smoked, himself to death (Wood, 1952, p. 146).

Maurice Ostrer

The period when Maurice Ostrer indisputably controlled production policy at Gainsborough lasted only from the end of 1943 to the middle of 1946, but during that time the studio produced most of the popular melodramas it is now remembered for. He was born in 1896 in the East End of London, the youngest of the five sons of Nathan Ostrer, a jeweller's salesman who had left the Ukraine to escape anti-Semitic persecution in the 1870s. One of his brothers, Isidore, described by his son-in-law James Mason as a 'dexterous and imaginative tycoon' and the brain of the family, rose from stockbroker's clerk to banker and set up the Ostrer Brothers Merchant Bank with Maurice and another of the brothers, Mark, in 1921. In the 1920s, the Ostrers were responsible for a number of company flotations, the most important of which was the Gaumont-British Picture Corporation in 1927. The prospects opened up by the 1927 Cinematograph Films Act and the coming of the talkies encouraged Isidore to assume direct control of Gaumont-British. In August 1929 he became chairman, with Mark vice-chairman and Maurice joint managing director.

Having created a circuit of over 350 cinemas, the Ostrers turned their hand to film production. The old Gaumont studio at Lime Grove, Shepherd's Bush, was rebuilt and Michael Balcon was appointed to carry out an ambitious production programme. Isidore had encouraged American investment in Gaumont-British as early as 1929 when William Fox bought a substantial (though not, as he had thought, a controlling) interest in the company. In 1936 another deal was planned with the brothers Joseph and Nicholas Schenck – the heads, respectively, of 20th Century Fox and MGM – but it was disrupted by a hostile counterbid by John Maxwell of the rival Associated-British cinema circuit. In October 1941 the Ostrers sold their shares to J. Arthur Rank, though it was not until 1944 that the conflicting interests in the corporation were sufficiently reconciled for Rank to assume complete control of the Gaumont-British empire.

Maurice's role in the corporation was nebulous, but by the mid-1930s he appears to have been active on the production side at Shepherd's Bush. In his autobiography, Balcon reveals his chagrin at Maurice moving into an office next door to him: 'I obviously had certain responsibilities to Maurice Ostrer as a director of the company and indeed as the Board's representative at the studio, but the arrangement had its complications and it certainly had some influence on my decision to leave' (Balcon, 1969, p. 97). A tetchy quality in the cables Balcon sent Maurice about casting decisions during his trip to Hollywood in 1935 reinforces the impression that he did not welcome having to defer to someone much less experienced than himself in film production.[14]

Balcon left for MGM in December 1936, but it was not until 1939 that Maurice assumed the credit 'In Charge of Production' (on Will Hay's *Ask a Policeman*). It certainly seems to have been Black rather than Ostrer who kept Gainsborough going during the late '30s slump, and until the transfer of Gainsborough's operations to Shepherd's Bush Ostrer appears to have taken his duties lightly.[15] But the deals with MGM and Fox which ensured a steady demand for Gainsborough's films must have been negotiated by the Ostrers.

After Black's departure, Ostrer brought in two producers to help him run the studio: Harold Huth and R.J. Minney. Huth had made his début as an actor in one of Gainsborough's last silent films, *Balaclava* (1928), worked as casting director for MGM British, and directed a low-budget thriller, *Hell's Cargo* (1939), for ABPC. Minney had been editor of *Everybody's Weekly* and of the *Sunday Referee* until Lord Kemsley bought it from Isidore Ostrer in 1939. He had also written a biography of Clive of India which had been turned into a play and then into a Hollywood film, for which Minney wrote the script. He was a staunch advocate of melodrama, telling the British Film Institute Summer School in 1947: 'Melodrama is essential in a film if it is to hit the box office since the film is more akin to the music hall and the circus than to a theatre.'[16]

Most of Gainsborough's 1944 releases were produced by Black, including Launder's *2000 Women* and Asquith's *Fanny by Gaslight*. Black's influence was even apparent in 1945, when *Waterloo Road* finally emerged to a very favourable critical and commercial reception. But Huth's first film as producer, *Love Story*, a contemporary wartime melodrama, was released in time to be one of the most popular films of 1944. Minney got off to a false start with *A Place of One's Own* (1945), allowing James Mason and Barbara Mullen to pretend to be an elderly couple as if they were in a stage play. But he redeemed himself at the box office, if not with the critics, with *Madonna of the Seven Moons* (1944) and *The Wicked Lady* (1945).

At the end of 1944, the process of consolidation within the Rank Organization continued, with an attempt to bring together Rank's disparate interests in film production. For a time it looked as if Filippo del Giudice of Two Cities, which handled Rank's more prestigious films, would assume a controlling position over all Rank productions. This was successfully resisted, but in March 1945 Production Facilities (Films) Ltd (soon disparagingly labelled 'Piffle') was established at Denham with the task of pooling the resources of the Rank studios. This included stars as well as props, and those actors who had signed contracts with Gainsborough were asked to re-sign with the Rank Organization. As Ostrer had narrowed down his production programme to exclude anything but a handful of melodramas, the arrangement had few advantages for Gainsborough. The other Rank companies did not have stars with as much glamour and popular appeal as Mason, Granger, Calvert and Lockwood, while the Gainsborough stars had little regard for the films that had brought them fame and were happy to work on non-Gainsborough subjects.

After directing *The Wicked Lady*, Leslie Arliss was lured away by Korda to continue his collaboration with Ted Black. Val Guest, Launder and Gilliat had already gone, and Ostrer was now dangerously dependent on two men who were outstanding cameramen but less competent as directors: Arthur Crabtree and Bernard Knowles. Phyllis Calvert's low opinion of most of the Gainsborough films she worked on stemmed from her lack of confidence in their directors:

> People thought that if you knew anything about a camera and a bit of light you could be a director. I loved working for Asquith, Reed, Launder and Gilliat. The others were technicians, who were made to look into life deeply, and had never done it before.[17]

And an exclusive diet of fantasy proved to be indigestible. Gainsborough's stars grew restless at being restricted to what they regarded as unchallenging, formulaic roles, and Rank was uncomfortable with the responsibility for a series of salacious films which sat ill with his Methodist principles and his reputation for moral responsibility. A successor to *The Wicked Lady* was vetoed, and little was done to promote the international distribution of *Madonna of the Seven Moons*.[18]

Rumours of Ostrer's increasing discontent with the bureaucracy of the Rank Organization and Rank's dissatisfaction at Gainsborough's low level of production were followed, in May 1946, by an announcement that Ostrer was to resign when his contract ran out in September and that Sydney Box was to take control of the studio.[19] Of the seven films scheduled for release in 1946, only three – *Caravan* (1946), *The Magic Bow* (1946) and *The Root of All Evil* (1947) – appeared, and Sydney Box boasted that he would be able to produce twelve films to Ostrer's three.[20] But this was not entirely fair. Ostrer could hardly be expected to begin production on films he would be unable to see through to completion, and Gainsborough had released six films in 1945, just as it had the two previous years. This compared unfavourably with the number of films Balcon had churned out in the 1930s, but production costs had risen sharply during the war and a fairer comparison is with Balcon's production rate at Ealing, where five films were released in 1943, four in 1944, four in 1945 and only two in 1946. Despite their exoticism, the Gainsborough melodramas were made on tight budgets and Ostrer was a stern enemy of extravagance. In April 1945 he had urged producers to 'settle down and study the subtle relationship of the two factors which govern their balance sheets – the cost of their films and the size of the market for which they are designed'.[21] And Minney, who left Gainsborough with his mentor, claimed it was not the Ostrer regime, but the Rank Organization that was at fault:

> The organisation is too top heavy, and being over centralised all the films cost more to make because they have to carry the very large overheads. For example, a film which I would produce for £100,000 costs £40–50,000 more when made under the Rank Organisation.[22]

Minney and the Ostrers set out to prove their point, floating an independent production company, Premier Productions, and recruiting Leslie Arliss to make *Idol of Paris* (1948) to the Gainsborough formula of bodice-ripping flamboyance. It was produced for less than £100,000 and featured a whip fight between its two female leads. But Christine Norden and Beryl Baxter had none of the talent and charisma of Lockwood and Calvert, and the film failed to make enough to keep the company afloat.[23]

James Mason, who had married Isidore Ostrer's daughter, Pamela Kellino, disparagingly dismissed Maurice as 'Isidore's shadow', and allowed him only limited credit for the successful melodrama formula:

> I believe now that the success of Gainsborough's 'escape' movies represented a victory for the Ostrers. They were fortunate in the fact that Ted Black ran an extremely efficient operation and that their own taste was well suited to the requirements of the time, and

thus they have been unable to repeat the success in different circumstances, but at least we must concede them this one personal victory in the production field (Mason, 1981, pp. 111, 185).

Maurice's subsequent disappearance from the film industry (he joined Isidore in taking control of the textiles conglomerate Illingworth Morris) makes it easy to dismiss him as a dilettante whose success owed more to luck than judgement. The break-up of the partnership with Black was unfortunate, and Gainsborough became severely debilitated in terms of acting, writing and directing talent. But of the ten films for which Maurice Ostrer was directly responsible, seven were big box-office successes, and his vision of an efficiently run studio dedicated to medium-budget entertainment films, with the emphasis on a particular genre, was unique, and was to provide a model for Hammer a decade later.[24]

The Boxes

Sydney Box was born in Beckenham in 1907. He worked as a journalist, at one point becoming editor of the *Christian Herald*, despite his agnostic sensibilities. But his ambitions to write plays and scripts only came to fruition when he teamed up with Muriel Baker, a continuity girl who herself had ambitions to write. Knowing from her own experience that women made up the bulk of the members of amateur dramatics societies, but that most plays had more roles for men than for women, Muriel collaborated with Sydney on a series of one-act plays with female casts. By 1939 they had written over 50 plays, but the outbreak of war disrupted the amateur dramatics scene and left the Boxes without work. They responded with *The Black-Out Book*, a miscellany of jokes, games, puzzles, quizzes and literary snippets, and with the profits they made set up a documentary film company, Verity Films. By the end of 1942 it was the largest organization producing information and propaganda films in the country. With a reputation as an efficient producer, Box grasped the opportunity to break into feature films, co-producing and co-directing *On Approval* (1944) with Clive Brook, and producing three films for Two Cities, *English Without Tears* (1944), *The Flemish Farm* (1943) and *Don't Take it to Heart* (1944). In 1943 he leased Riverside Studios at Hammersmith and ventured into independent production with *29 Acacia Avenue* (1945), a mildly risqué comedy about goings-on in suburbia. It was turned down by Rank for setting young people a bad example, but was successfully distributed by Columbia. Box's next project, *The Seventh Veil*, did win Rank's approval, however, and with dedicated performances from Ann Todd and James Mason it proved to be the top box-office picture of 1945 and won the Boxes a Hollywood Oscar for their screenplay.

Sydney Box, described by one journalist as looking like an 'obese cherub', and by James Mason as having 'the air of a baby rogue elephant', was seen in several quarters as a fresh new voice, a genial, intelligent man, untainted by the extravagance and egocentricity of some of his forbears.[25] However, the problems he faced were formidable. Early in 1947 he submitted a report to Rank, 'Production and Future Planning', in which he pointed out the difficulties of producing a heavy schedule of films using equipment that was 'obsolete or obsolescent'.[26] He put forward suggestions for various stop-gap measures but argued that, as far as sound equipment was concerned, the only long-term solution was:

> That Gainsboro' studios should be equipped with Western Electric sound channels. There is no doubt that the British Acoustic sound is inferior to Western and that some artists are loath to appear in pictures using British Acoustic. A more important point is that the use of Western would create reasonable interchangeability of sound facilities between Denham and Pinewood and Shepherd's Bush and Islington.[27]

Box knew that his proposal was unlikely to be accepted, and suggested as an alternative that he be allowed to produce fewer films, pointing out that this would relieve pressure not only on antiquated studio equipment, but also on the shallow pool of talent, pointing particularly to:

> the difficulty of obtaining twelve first-class scripts each year (we have now used some twenty-four different writers, with mixed results), but we have been forced to work on the majority of the scripts ourselves in order to obtain the standard we require. A reduction of four pictures in the year would enable us to give fifty per cent more time to each script.[28]

Unfortunately for Box, external affairs dictated that he be held to his promise of twelve films a year. The levying of an import duty on films in September 1947 led to a Hollywood boycott and Rank, controlling the Odeon and Gaumont cinema chains, was tempted into expanding production so that his own films would fill the gap left by the dwindling supplies of American films. Abandoning hopes of breaking into the American market – now virtually closed to British films – Rank concentrated on stepping up the production of modest films for the domestic market. Those producers who had been encouraged to make big-budget prestige films were told to be more economical, and many of them turned instead to Korda's revived London Films. Filippo del Giudice left Two Cities, bitterly complaining that 'the sales people' were destroying creative freedom (Wood, 1952, p. 44). But Box rose to the challenge, releasing nine films in 1947 (including Ostrer's *The Root of All Evil*), eleven in 1948 and twelve in 1949.

Predictably, quality was sacrificed to the pressures of time and money. Anthony Asquith, who had made such a good job of the straggling narrative of *Fanny by Gaslight*, was passed over as the director of *The Man Within* (1947) because he demanded a £10,000 fee, and the Boxes fell back on Gainsborough's uninspiring stalwart Bernard Knowles. Ann Todd and Michael Redgrave were allowed to slip away from *The Brothers* (1947) and were replaced by the much weaker Patricia Roc and Maxwell Reed. Corporate politics frustrated James Mason's plan to return from Hollywood to make a film a year with Box, and Dennis Price was cast in the role of Byron which Mason would have filled so well.[29] After the dubbing session for *Miranda* and *Broken Journey* in April 1948, Muriel wrote in her diary: 'However, we've done our best with both pictures but it's depressing when you know they fall short and one hasn't the time to put them right.'[30] And her career as a director stemmed from her experience shooting additional scenes for Gainsborough films which needed to be patched up to make them showable.[31]

Thus a sort of drabness shrouds the Box films, from the gone-wrong-noir of *Daybreak* (1946) to the routine plot mechanics of *Dear Murderer* (1947) and *Broken Journey* (1948) to the bittiness of the Somerset Maugham short story compendium films, *Quartet* (1948) and *Trio* (1950). And though they acted with the best of intentions, the Boxes wrecked Gainsborough's lucrative tradition of costume melodrama. Their first film at Shepherd's Bush, *The Man Within* (1947), based on a Graham Greene homoerotic tale of cowardice and betrayal among a band of smugglers, seemed a very appropriate subject for Gainsborough. Greene's story may have had metaphysical overtones not usually found in costume melodrama but, as the Boultings were to show with *Brighton Rock* (1947), this was not necessarily a bar to popular acceptance. Unfortunately, there was a lack of consonance between Muriel Box's script and Bernard Knowles's direction, and the film is shapeless and unsatisfactory. Despite an excellent cast – Joan Greenwood and Jean Kent, Richard Attenborough and Michael Redgrave – it had little of the popular appeal of *The Man in Grey*. *Jassy* (1947), which followed shortly afterwards, was the one Box film which did conform to the Ostrer formula. But the film's success brought them little joy. Muriel wrote exasperatedly in her diary: 'Bad notices, bad film – huge commercial success.'[32] And Sydney, who had unsuccessfully urged that the film should have a tragic ending if it were to retain any integrity, was accused by the critics of being obsessed with torture, flogging and bloodshed.[33]

The Boxes learned the wrong lessons from the reception of *Jassy*, following the critics in their desire for realism rather than the public in its desire for colourful melodrama, and the next two Gainsborough costume films, *The Bad Lord Byron* and *Christopher Columbus*, both 1949, pleased neither the critics nor the public. Muriel Box testified that:

> When we attempted a costume picture we tried to make it authentically correct in every detail. ... The amount of research that went into *Christopher Columbus* was exceptional, yet it was criticised (unfairly I thought) on account of inaccuracy. *Byron* was also historical in a literary way and was extremely well documented. ... It was most beautifully photographed and everything was totally authentic. Nothing was artificially concocted, everything that was in the film was exactly as Byron described it.[34]

But as Sue Harper points out, the Boxes' yearning for realism 'was fatal to the tone of Gainsborough's enterprises' (Harper, 1994, p. 121). Rejecting Raphael Sabbatini's swashbuckling, and no doubt highly inaccurate, script for *Christopher Columbus*, the Boxes imposed their own authentic but very ponderous script which combined with casting problems, production disasters and poor special effects to sink the film.[35] *Byron* was a much smoother production, but its flashback structure (unlike that of *The Seventh Veil*) robs it of excitement and Dennis Price's Byron, though witty and sophisticated, has little 'Byronic' glamour.

Sydney Box was appointed on the strength of his efficiency as a producer (which proved to be well founded) and the huge success of *The Seventh Veil* (which proved to be an aberration). Much more typical of his – and Muriel's – interests was *29 Acacia Avenue*, the film which Rank had tried to bury.[36] If a Box identity is to be discerned at Gainsborough, it would form around *When the Bough Breaks* (1947), a film about an unmarried mother's attempt to regain the son she allowed to be adopted; *Good Time Girl* (1948) and *Boys in Brown* (1949), about young people in trouble; and, in a more light-hearted vein, *Holiday Camp* (1947) and the Huggett films which grew out of it; *Easy Money* (1948), a compendium of stories about football pools winners; and *A Boy, a Girl and a Bike* (1949). These were films set in the contemporary world and dealt with ordinary people. As Betty Box, producer of *When the Bough Breaks* and the Huggett cycle, put it: 'I suppose they were the equivalent of *Coronation Street*.'[37] The best of these films struck a chord with popular taste that Ted Black would have been proud of, but they were less easy to reproduce than genre films.

Betty Box, who at 26 took over the running of Islington and brought it back to life for the last time, and her husband Peter Rogers, who helped Muriel to re-establish a scenario department for the studio, went on to develop the hit comedy *Doctor in the House* (1954) and its successors, and the *Carry On* films. Muriel Box pioneered a successful career as a director; but her and Sydney's penchant for offbeat subjects gradually shifted them from the centre to the periphery of the film industry.

Betty Box felt no regret at leaving the smelly environs of Islington for the leafy splendour of Pinewood, and considered that 'Gainsborough was not closed down so much as incorporated within the Rank Organization.'[38] Gainsborough had been a pawn in corporate politics since 1928 and – in a time when trade marks and product identities were seen as less important than they are now – it is not surprising that it was merged into the amorphous Rank empire. But for nearly 30 years interesting films were produced at Islington and Shepherd's Bush, and Gainsborough, at least as much as Ealing, contributed significantly to the history of the British film industry.

Notes

1. Phyllis Calvert, interview with Sue Aspinall and Robert Murphy, in Aspinall and Murphy (1983), p. 60.
2. Gaumont-British took over the other major variety circuit, Moss Empires, in 1932, and this too came under George Black's control.
3. Quoted by Wood (1986), p. 50.
4. Quoted in Seaton and Martin (1982), p. 11. Roome co-directed two films for the Boxes, *My Brother's Keeper* (1948) and *It's Not Cricket* (1949), and then returned to editing – most famously of the *Carry On* films.
5. Quoted in Brown (1977a), pp. 75–6.
6. *Kinematograph Weekly*, 2 February 1939, p. 5.
7. Phyllis Calvert, unpublished interview with Sue Aspinall and Robert Murphy, 1983.
8. Sidney Gilliat in Brown (1977a), p. 108.
9. P. L. Mannock, *Kinematograph Weekly*, 22 April 1943, p. 34.
10. *Kinematograph Weekly*, 14 January 1943, p. 121.
11. See Harper (1994), p. 120, for Minney and *Madonna of the Seven Moons*.
12. Quoted in Brown (1977a), p.111.
13. *Kinematograph Weekly*, 18 November 1943, p. 43
14. Ivor Montagu Special Collection, Item 61, lodged in the British Film Institute Library, for the Balcon–Ostrer cables. Balcon seems to have found Maurice's capacity for interference considerably less irksome than that of his next boss, Louis B. Mayer of MGM. See Balcon (1969),

pp. 104–13 for Balcon's view of Mayer.

15. Alan Wood says that Black 'would remark cheerfully, whenever Maurice was missing from the office, "You'll probably find him on the flat at Newmarket"' (Wood, 1952, p. 145).

16. *Today's Cinema*, 27 August 1947, p. 13. Huth's most significant subsequent achievement was as producer of *The Trials of Oscar Wilde* in 1960; Minney wrote a biography of Violette Szabo and turned it into a successful film, *Carve Her Name With Pride* (1958). He stood as Labour candidate for Southend East in 1949 and again at Bexley in 1955, failing to defeat Edward Heath by only a few hundred votes.

17. Phyllis Calvert, interview with Sue Aspinall and Robert Murphy, in Aspinall and Murphy (1983), p. 61.

18. Wood (1952), p. 150, for *The Wicked Lady's Daughter*; Macnab (1993), pp. 117–18, for Ostrer's discontent with the Rank Organization.

19. *Kinematograph Weekly*, 2 May 1946. According to the 'Diary of Muriel and Sydney Box', Sydney took control of the studio on 1 June 1946 'after a blitz-krieg meeting on the previous day by Rank at the studio'. Muriel and Sydney Box Collection, Items 15 and 16, British Film Institute Special Collections.

20. See *Kinematograph Weekly*, 8 August 1946, p. 36.

21. Maurice Ostrer, 'How and Where the Money Should be Spent on British Films', *Kinematograph Weekly*, 19 April 1945, p. 5.

22. *Kinematograph Weekly*, 6 February 1947, p. 20. See also Harold Huth in *Kinematograph Weekly*, 21 March 1946, p. 25.

23. See Leslie Arliss, 'The Only Real Way to Cut Costs Is to Cut Time', *Kinematograph Weekly*, 30 October 1947, p. 33, for the production of *Idol of Paris*.

24. The ten Ostrer films are: *The Man in Grey, Fanny by Gaslight, Love Story, They Were Sisters, Madonna of the Seven Moons, A Place of One's Own, Caravan, The Magic Bow, The Root of All Evil* and *Idol of Paris*.

25. See *Evening Standard*, 7 August 1959 (BFI microfiche) for cherub description; Mason (1981), p. 149, for baby elephant; 'Sydney Box: How he got to the Top', *Leader Magazine*, 1 May 1948 (BFI microfiche) for Box as a new type of producer.

26. Muriel and Sydney Box Collection, Item 12/1.

27. Ibid.

28. Ibid. Muriel Box, who was in charge of the scenario department, makes the same point in her autobiography about the difficulty of getting hold of good scripts (Box, 1974, pp. 185–6).

29. See the letters from Mason to Box in the Sydney and Muriel Box Collection, Item 12/3, in the BFI Library. Mason excludes Box from his general criticism of producers and expresses his desire to return to England on an occasional basis to make films with him.

30. 'The Diary of Muriel and Sydney Box', 4 April 1948.

31. Having re-shot most of *Lost People* (1949) – which had been considered unshowable – Muriel Box received co-director's credit with Bernard Knowles.

32. 'The Diary of Muriel and Sydney Box', 1 February 1947.

33. Paul Dehn, *Sunday Chronicle*, 17 August 1947 (BFI microfiche). Box asserted his innocence of the charge in 'Sadism – It Will Only Bring Us Disrepute', *Kinematograph Weekly*, 27 May 1948, p. 18.

34. Muriel Box, interview with Sue Aspinall and Robert Murphy, in Aspinall and Murphy (1983), p. 64.

35. Muriel asserts that: 'After a good deal of research I found this script both inaccurate and inferior in quality. I passed on my opinion to Sydney and we asked to be excused from producing it but to no avail', Box (1974), p. 197. See 'The Diary of Muriel and Sydney Box' throughout most of 1948, for the Boxes' troubles over *Christopher Columbus* and its American stars Fredric March and his wife Florence Eldridge.

36. See Box (1974), pp. 176–7, for Rank's offer to buy *29 Acacia Avenue* and not show it.

37. Betty Box, interview with Robert Murphy, in Aspinall and Murphy (1983), p. 63.

38. Ibid., p. 62.

10

Wicked Sounds and Magic Melodies: Music in 1940s Gainsborough Melodrama

K. J. Donnelly

Music is one of British cinema history's best-kept secrets. Such attention as has been paid has focused on the prestigious art music composers who dipped their toes into film music in the 1940s. In the case of the Gainsborough melodramas of this period (despite their reliance on lush and powerful scores to achieve dramatic and emotional effects), this aspect of the films has been utterly neglected. What is more, there is virtually nothing in the way of contemporaneous writing about music (apart from John Huntley's informative 1947 book) and almost no surviving recordings of Gainsborough soundtracks (although many were available at the time of release[1]), which leaves the films themselves as the primary resource. But this situation only partly accounts for the critical neglect. Film music historians generally prefer to weave a narrative around an individual musician, an approach that is invalid in Gainsborough's case, because there were no 'great composers' about which to wax lyrical. There was something else: a communal production of music, a production line of sorts, under the aegis of Gainsborough and Gaumont-British musical director Louis Levy.

The music in 1940s Gainsborough melodramas is distinct from the dominant styles and discourses that constituted British film music in the 1930s and '40s. In contrast to those quality productions that used prestige film scores, Gainsborough offered cheap and cheerful music that, in the melodramas in particular, is startling in its brashness and singular in its lack of British restraint. I shall focus on the '40s melodrama cycle; although they cannot be seen as typical of the studio's diverse output, these films feature some extraordinary music that deserves reassessment.

During the 1940s, British film music was put into the service of quality British cinema (Manvell, 1947, p. 91) and was conceived in opposition to Hollywood's industrial modes. A number of concert hall composers wrote music for British films during the 1930s and '40s. Before the Second World War, Arthur Bliss, Benjamin Britten, William Walton and Arthur Benjamin contributed regularly to screen music, while during the war, many more British art music composers were inspired to write film scores as their contribution to the war effort. The most famous of these was Ralph Vaughan Williams, who made his film début at the tender age of 69. Others who tried the water at this time included Sir Arnold Bax, Lord Berners, Lennox Berkeley, Constant Lambert and William Alwyn.

In the mid-1930s Muir Mathieson became the musical director for Korda's London Films. He was in charge of music for all their productions, and he immediately invited respected concert hall composers to supply music for the company's films. Famous composers were a cinematic attraction (Mathieson, 1947, p. 184), and Vaughan Williams's name, for example, appearing boldly on the credits added prestige to the production. By contrast, Gainsborough used musicians of little eminence and employed a musical production line closer to the Hollywood system. During the 1930s Gainsborough's music was masterminded by the music department of Gaumont-British, based at the Lime Grove studios in Shepherd's Bush, and headed by Louis Levy from its inception in the late 1920s.[2] Levy's department employed a number of staff musicians and contracted composers. Among the contributors to Gainsborough music were silent film pioneers such as Hans May, Hubert Bath and Levy himself, along with stalwarts such as Bretton Byrd, the senior music editor. According to John Huntley, Louis Levy ran 'a kind of music casting bureau whereby composers are brought in to score the type of pictures that suit their particular style' (Huntley, 1947, p. 212). Levy's department included arrangers and orchestrators (Levy, 1948, p. 95), a situation reminiscent of Hollywood, where it was common practice for composers to have their music radically rearranged by orchestrators, while other composers provided music for films without receiving credit.

Louis Levy used a wide variety of composers: Bob Busby, who wrote the music for *Waterloo Road*, 1945, had worked for Ufa in Germany and joined the staff in 1942; Henry Geehl (*The Magic Bow*, 1946; *Jassy*, 1947); Cedric Mallabey (*The Man in Grey*, 1943; *Fanny by Gaslight*, 1944); and Jack Beaver, who provided most of the music for the Tom Walls films as well as scoring *Dr Syn* (1937). Levy also collaborated with several European émigrés, including Paul Abraham from Hungary, and Mischa Spoliansky, one-time composer for German theatre director Max Reinhardt on *The Lucky Number* (1933), while German Jewish émigré conductor Walter Goehr provided some music for *The Ghost Train*

(1941). John Greenwood, one of the earliest composers in Britain to become a film specialist, provided scores for Robert Flaherty's celebrated *Man of Aran* (1934) and Gainsborough's Somerset Maugham port-manteau films *Quartet* (1948) and *Trio* (1950). Bretton Byrd was musically self-taught and joined the Gaumont-British music department in 1930 after playing piano in cinemas from the age of fourteen (Huntley, 1947). He was chief music editor for Levy, and his modest background was characteristic of Gainsborough's approach to film scoring.

As head of a music department servicing both Gaumont-British and Gainsborough films, Louis Levy was one of the most influential figures in British film music in the 1930s and '40s. He has, however, received little critical respect. By the time of Manvell and Huntley's book (1957), Gainsborough and Gaumont-British film music had been practically written out of British film music history.[3] This may partly be explained by the fact that Levy did not conform to the dominant paradigm of the artist-composer – there were, for example, widespread (although unsubstantiated) rumours about his lack of musical ability. As musical director for all Gainsborough's output until the late 1940s, his creative position was and has remained unclear to people both inside and outside music.

The production of British film music was dominated by musical directors during the 1930s and '40s. Mathieson was the most famous, while Levy at Gaumont-British was more prolific; Ernest Irving moved from conducting in London's West End theatres to Ealing Studios in 1937.[4] Each of these had a high degree of influence over film music in Britain, choosing composers for films, overseeing the arrangement of their music and often conducting the orchestras, as well as writing and adapting music, and directing the final form in which all the film's music would appear. Levy states:

> The musical director ... is one of the first to start on a picture – and one of the last to finish. I come to things at the very first conferences on the new film. Sometimes a story is altered to suit my needs. Occasionally, even the title is changed.[5]

He cites the example of Gaumont-British's Jessie Matthews film *It's Love Again* (1936), which was renamed from *Say When* to match the title of a prominent song in the film.[6]

Levy's significance cannot be overestimated. Born in 1893, he attained an important position during the years of silent films, becoming the musical director for the Shepherd's Bush Pavilion cinema by 1921. This led directly to his securing a role as head of the Gaumont-British music department with the coming of sound. During silent days he apparently pioneered the use of the theme song before this became habitual in the USA (Huntley, 1947, p. 212), and by 1924 Levy was also a regular on the radio, leading his own orchestra in light music for the BBC. He wrote the 'Music from the Movies March', which not only appeared at the start of his radio show of the same name which began in 1936, but also opened all the Gaumont newsreels of the time. Levy was also responsible for narrative music such as the 'coded' folk music central to the story of Hitchcock's 1938 *The Lady Vanishes* (Chion, 1984, pp. 32–4).

Levy's musical training, like that of many of his staff, had not been via the respectable and expensive London music colleges, but had come through earning a crust accompanying films in cinemas. Levy was from a humble background, and it is tempting to see his class and Jewish background as having militated against him. In addition, he had a pragmatic rather than romanticized vision of composition – that of perspiration outweighing inspiration (Levy, 1948, p. 109). His use of composers without art music reputations, as well as foreign musicians and Hollywood musical styles, was unlikely to win critical admiration in Britain during this period.

While Muir Mathieson, Levy's principal rival and musical Svengali at London Films, seemingly set the standard for British cinema (Manvell, 1947, p. 91), the idea of prestige film music by art music composers was not universally popular. Film producer John Croydon complained about British art music composers, declaring that: 'When they are able to spare the time to score a good British picture, they write their music with one eye on concert hall receipts which may later accrue from the score, and as a result, the unity of the film suffers' (Huntley, 1947, p. 161).[7] Even Mathieson acknowledged that British composers cared less for the drama and tended to lack the technical dexterity of the Americans. He wrote:

> It would, I think, be fair to say that the standard of music in British films is at the present time as high, if not higher than any other country. This applies more especially to the serious type of film. ... I would say that the technique of the Americans is more advanced, or at least infinitely 'slicker' than ours ... [and] their composers seem to have trained themselves to write with precise care and appreciation of the dramatic significance of each turn of the story (Mathieson, 1947, p. 186).

This is stated in more direct terms by Gainsborough producer R.J. Minney:

I do not say that psychology and the work of the great artists and composers should have no place at all in a film. They should. But they should supplement and emphasize the dramatic and the other qualities essential to a story's development and not eclipse or extinguish the story (Minney, 1947, p. 35).

Levy was interested in music as a craft, enhancing the film through blending with it rather than being an attraction in its own right. The 1930s Gainsborough comedies featuring Tom Walls, Jack Hulbert and Will Hay have unassuming music of the quickly produced and functional variety. *Windbag the Sailor* (1936), for example, has a score assembled by Levy. It consists almost entirely of instrumental arrangements of hornpipes and sea shanties that appear at regular intervals to connect scenes or accompany action. A rather utilitarian arrangement is adopted throughout, relying on low volume, similar orchestral textures and with the music taking no unexpected turns. Generally speaking, the music for such relatively cheaply and quickly produced comedies might be expected to have such a mundane character, and Gainsborough is no different in this respect. It is in the 1940s melodramas that the music is most noticeable, often dominating the film.

Levy's proclaimed desire to have well-crafted, functional music in films deserves to be discussed in more detail. Claudia Gorbman has set out the pattern followed by classical Hollywood film music, which involved 'inaudibility' and narrative cueing (Gorbman, 1983, p. 73). She notes that classical Hollywood music effaced itself while emphasizing events taking place on screen, using repeated themes as a structuring device. Gainsborough's employment of integrated music corresponds more closely with Gorbman's schema than do the 'prestige' British scores of the same period. Ralph Vaughan Williams's *Scott of the Antarctic* (1948) score for Ealing, in which the music was quite roughly cut to fit the film, or William Walton's for Two Cities' *Henry V* (1944), where only the music for the battle directly corresponds to screen action, tend to consist of autonomous pieces that could easily be made into suites for the concert hall. According to producer Harold Huth, Gainsborough composer Hubert Bath was 'a master in the art of writing "unobtrusive film music". Instead of hoping the music in *They Were Sisters* [1945] would add to his fame, Bath hoped that it would not be noticed. That, he considered, was the criterion of good background music.'[8] Levy backs up this comment: 'Musical accompaniment should never be consciously heard. ... The music should play subtly on the emotions, and never intrude on the story.'[9]

An example of Gainsborough's use of relatively unassuming music is *Dr Syn*, which was in some ways a precursor of the successful costume drama cycle. The score was largely written by Jack Beaver and Hubert Bath (Huntley, 1947, p. 194), although the sole screen credit is given to Louis Levy as musical director. The music certainly aims to be inconspicuous, with the volume electronically lowered so far that it virtually disappears at times. It tends to match action and, in the manner of Hollywood, there is a large amount of it. Virtually every scene in *Dr Syn* is laden with music, although it remains in the background, and one short theme comprises its repeated material. *Fanny by Gaslight* also has wall-to-wall music – in fact, there is hardly a moment's silence in the film. The score by Cedric Mallabey is functional, with one repeated theme associated with Fanny (Phyllis Calvert), while the rest of the underscore has no structural connection or associations. When Mallabey's underscore is silent, the film bursts with pub songs, stage songs, one bawdy song plus waltzes, can-cans and ballet. Despite its unobtrusive score, this melodrama certainly foregrounds music.

The 1940s cycle of melodramas were among Gainsborough's most notable successes (Aspinall and Murphy, 1983, p. 2). As Thomas Elsaesser points out, melodramas tend to foreground dynamic music that punctuates the emotional turns of the films. They share a 'particular form of dramatic *mise en scène* characterized by a dynamic use of spatial and musical categories' (Elsaesser, 1987, pp. 50–1). Levy seems to have had a melodramatic conception of film music: 'Generally speaking, music is heard to the greatest advantage when the film is trying to create an atmosphere of (a) romance and (b) tension.'[10] In the 1940s melodramas, music is precisely geared towards such ends. Sometimes the demands of the melodramatic material lead to a musical overload that breaks the rule of narrative integration. Indeed, the music in these films is extremely obtrusive, regularly encroaching on the action and fracturing the diegesis, as well as often appearing as diegetic songs that translate into non-diegetic character themes.

I shall now look at four films in some detail: *Caravan* (1946) and *Madonna of the Seven Moons* (1944), which have highly melodramatic musical scores to match their exotic and hyperbolic screen action; and *Love Story* (1944) and *The Magic Bow* (1946), the first of which seems to contain more 'respectable' music in a melodramatic context, and the second of which is an energetic and decidedly populist biopic of an art music hero, Italian violinist and composer Niccolò Paganini.

Caravan concerns Richard (Stewart Granger), who is sent on a mission to Spain, where he is attacked and left for dead by cohorts of Sir Francis

(Dennis Price), who wants Richard's fiancée Oriana for himself. Oriana believes that Richard is dead and marries Sir Francis. Meanwhile, Richard, who is suffering from amnesia, has been saved by gypsy flamenco dancer Rosal (Jean Kent), with whom he lives happily in a cave. Discovering that Richard is alive, Oriana comes to Spain looking for him, and the film climaxes with the deaths of Rosal and Sir Francis, allowing Richard and Oriana to reunite.

The film's exuberance and overstatement allows for music of a similar character, while the Spanish setting motivates the appearance of flamenco songs and dances. These are given a substantial amount of screen time, reflecting composer Walford Hyden's reputation as 'a specialist in Spanish music' (Huntley, 1947, p. 209), although Levy also knew something about flamenco music (Levy, 1948, pp. 64–5). Levy called in Hyden precisely for this specialism; he was not a film music composer and had done more for radio.[11] His work for *Caravan* was bolstered by music written by Bretton Byrd that remains uncredited (Huntley, 1947, p. 200). The flamenco sequences comprise both dances and instrumental performances. Jean Kent's dance numbers are striking (she had started out as a dancer in the 1930s), and there are two flamenco guitar solos as well as the songs sung by the flamenco guitar player. The narrative virtually stops for these interludes, which represent a relatively autonomous succession of musical performances. Sue Harper (Harper, 1987, p. 182) has castigated the dance sequences as pastiche; however, the music sounds quite authentic (to my ears, at least), and Walford Hyden's reputation as an expert in Spanish music, together with Levy's familiarity with flamenco, suggest that the flamenco music has a degree of accuracy.

Caravan's title sequence consists of a Spanish song, which then dominates Hyden's underscore as a melodic theme associated with Rosal. Its manifestation as the title song is within a tight twelve-bar structure and regular song form that plays upon a chord built on the flattened second of the scale, a defining characteristic of flamenco music. It is sung as a serenade, denoted by the image beneath the titles, that of a singing guitar player and a woman on a balcony. It recurs later to underline Rosal's screen presence, occurring first within the diegesis performed as a flamenco song, and appearing finally when she dies. The domination of Rosal's theme supports Harper's suggestion that symbolic elements in these films work to undermine the narrative. The narrative is ultimately concerned with the reunion of Richard and Oriana, but the music privileges Rosal as the key figure in the action. Moreover, the extended screen time of her spectacular dance performances also asserts her power and importance.

At times, *Caravan* comes close to being a musical, as the narrative virtually stalls to foreground musical peformance in its own right. These sequences are, however, motivated by the nominally Spanish setting; Richard goes native when he lives with Rosal, reverting to his mother's Spanish origins and precipitating an extravaganza of non-British emotionality, triggered largely by the rumbustious music. One of *Caravan*'s most striking moments involves Richard having to negotiate a potentially lethal quicksand; he survives by following Rosal's orders and immediately realizes his love for her. The underscore matches the action in the most crass terms, using cymbal crashes to mark each step that Richard takes across the quicksand, replaced by muted violins when he reaches his saviour Rosal. The music in this sequence is distinctly lacking in finesse, but direct in its energetic engagement with the on-screen action. Perhaps reflecting his inexperience as a film composer, Hyden's score is generally unsubtle. Yet his music, from the high-spirited and boisterous flamenco to the brash and stormy underscore, remains distinctive.

Madonna of the Seven Moons also has a striking underscore, provided by Austrian émigré Hans May who, like Levy, was a silent-film pioneer. He worked on Giuseppe Becce's Kinothek of 1919, a groundbreaking library of printed music for silent films. May was a film composer in Germany until the Nazi accession to power in 1933. He arrived in Britain the following year and was involved in the music for films such as *Give Her a Ring* (1934) and *Radio Parade of 1935* (1934) for British International Pictures. After scoring Carol Reed's *The Stars Look Down* (1939), May went on to provide the music for Gainsborough's costume drama *The Wicked Lady* (1945) and the Boulting brothers' *Brighton Rock* (1947). *Madonna of the Seven Moons* centres on Maddalena (Phyllis Calvert), a respectable middle-class housewife living in Rome. The reappearance of her maturing daughter (Patricia Roc), back from school in England, precipitates one of Maddalena's recurring psycho-logical crises, during which she becomes 'Rosanna', a swaggering gypsy-type who lives at the Inn of the Seven Moons in Florence with her cutpurse lover Nino (Stewart Granger). Her 'schizophrenia' is cured only by her death.

The musical underscore for *Madonna of the Seven Moons* is arresting in its dynamism. It mixes autonomous music with Hollywood-style direct matching of the action's nuances. For example, at the film's climax, as Rosanna climbs the stairs to find that Nino's brother (whom she believes to be Nino himself) is attacking her (Maddalena's) daughter, a dissonant but regular tension ostinato (a looped motif) is heard, interrupted only by brutal staccato stabs from the brass. The aggression of the musical stabbing effect (anticipating the imminent mutual death by knives) is decidedly intrusive, but also effective as a signal of the fever pitch of emotion to which the film builds. Immediately after Rosanna is stabbed, the film cuts to a deathbed scene and the music changes character and mode, manifesting a regular structure and relying on musical logic, thus enhancing mood rather than matching action.

Madonna is dominated by Rosanna's theme. This appears in full as the song 'Rosanna' with which Nino serenades her in the garden. The song follows the dominant formal schemes for popular songs, and is accompanied by guitar music; Granger was unhappy that his voice was removed from the soundtrack, to be replaced by one higher in pitch, and perhaps less masculine than his own (Granger, 1981, p. 92). The thematic power of the 'Rosanna' melody underlines the film's concentration upon her character, as well as cueing her escape from middle-class respectability. It appears regularly in the non-diegetic score as an arrangement reliant on lush strings, a common coding for emotion and love in both film music and light music. Although it tends to retain the same arrangement, there is a marked slowing of the melody at certain points, almost like an improvisational rubato, that hangs on to the high notes, both coding and emphasizing desire.

The repeated 'Rosanna' theme overwhelms the film – but there is an organ on the soundtrack that is loosely associated with the Maddalena character, established at the convent near the opening and reappearing at the conclusion when she is given the last rites. Thus the underscore in *Madonna of the Seven Moons* is less systematically thematic than many contemporaneous Hollywood scores, such as those written by Max Steiner or Erich Wolfgang Korngold. The 'Rosanna' melody appears regularly, both as diegetic song, a musical box and whistling, and in the non-diegetic underscore. It not only serves to trigger Maddalena's transformation, but, in signalling the sensual and aggressive half of her character, underlines Rosanna's power in contrast to the weaker melody assigned to the demure Maddalena. In addition, the male lead (Stewart Granger as Nino) is assigned no special music, but becomes a vessel for Rosanna's song, thus further centring her character. Overall, May's underscore is string-heavy and incorporates several 'effects', where the music crudely emphasizes action (a process known in Hollywood as 'mickeymousing') or heightens emotion and suspense. But May's music always sounds purposeful and he varies the orchestral textures admirably throughout, creating one of the most impressive Gainsborough scores.

Love Story, released in the same year, was something of a musical event. The 'Cornish Rhapsody', written by Hubert Bath for the film, was a huge popular success. It became one of the most famous light orchestral pieces of the time, and remains the only piece of Gainsborough film music (underscore) still available as a recording. Many films in the 1940s, inspired by the phenomenal success of the 'Warsaw Concerto', written by Richard Addinsell, that appeared in the RKO film *Dangerous Moonlight* (1941),[12] featured the performance of concert pieces, including what were sometimes termed 'tabloid concertos'. The majority focused on a central character who was a musician, providing the motivation for foregrounded music performance.

Although the format had emerged earlier in British Lion's *The Case of the Frightened Lady* (1940), scored by sometime Gainsborough composer Jack Beaver, the success of *Dangerous Moonlight* can be seen to have had a direct influence on films such as *While I Live* (1947), which featured Charles Williams's 'The Dream of Olwen', Ealing's portmanteau film *Train of Events* (1949), which used Leslie Bridgewater's 'Legend of Lancelot', and *The Woman's Angle* (1952), which included Kenneth Leslie-Smith's 'The Mansell Concerto'. Levy maintained that with the 'Warsaw Concerto' and the 'Cornish Rhapsody', 'We had created an entirely new standard of screen music' (Levy, 1948, p. 90). It was one that drew on radio's popular light orchestral music rather than the highbrow concert hall. While both pieces bore some resemblance to Rachmaninov's orchestral style, neither was the product of Britain's art music intelligentsia – both Addinsell and Bath were primarily film specialists. In the aftermath of the success of 'Cornish Rhapsody', Hubert Bath died in 1945 while sketching music for *The Wicked Lady*.

Originally from Devon, Bath studied at the Royal Academy of Music – in fact, he was one of the few Gainsborough composers who had received such a privileged musical education. He had written some music for the concert hall, but joined the Lime Grove music department full time in 1934 as an arranger and composer. Bath was a pioneer, providing music for the part-sound film *Kitty* (Victor Saville, 1929), and Hitchcock's *Blackmail* (1929), the first all-sound film produced in Britain. In both cases, the score was pared down from the intended music for the silent version. He went on to provide most of the music for Hitchcock's Gaumont-British productions of the 1930s. Today he is remembered solely for the 'Cornish Rhapsody'.

Love Story is about a concert pianist, Lissa (Margaret Lockwood), who, with only a year to live, goes to Cornwall. To her surprise, she falls in love with a man who seems to be dodging the war effort (Stewart

Granger). He becomes the inspiration for her composition of the 'Cornish Rhapsody' and finally redeems himself by saving a group of people trapped in a tin mine. Lockwood leaves him for his own sake, however, and performs the 'Cornish Rhapsody' at the Albert Hall, where Granger turns up to cement their love. The 'Cornish Rhapsody' appears initially over the opening titles, and in its full form. Our next encounter with it is in fragments when Lissa is beginning to compose it in a summerhouse overlooking the cliffs of Cornwall. Finally, we have the full version in the spectacular, climactic Albert Hall concert with Margaret Lockwood at the piano performing in front of a large orchestra. *Love Story* not only contains highly evocative and emotive music; this is matched by a suitably emotional performance from Lockwood as the doomed musician. The 'Cornish Rhapsody' itself is based on two themes and includes 'sea'-coded music and mimicking of seagull cries. While it is arguably clichéd, it is also effective in its primal connotations. The music appears to represent the association of female desire with elemental natural forces.

Gainsborough's historical biopic of violinist Paganini, *The Magic Bow*, was one of the studio's last films before Sydney Box took over the reins of production (Cook, 1996b, p. 63; Harper, 1987, p. 168). Stewart Granger portrays the Italian violinist and composer who, according to popular belief, had sold his soul to the devil. Although the film's subject-matter may smack of the high art that Gainsborough eschewed, their approach to the material conforms to house style. Granger plays Paganini with vigour as an abrasive and unrefined character lacking in middle-class decorum. While there is some historical veracity in this, Granger's performance also fits closely with his persona in other Gainsborough melodramas such as *Caravan*, and particularly, *Madonna of the Seven Moons*.

The hypermasculine Paganini and his musical virtuosity are a sexual magnet. His performances are peppered with reverse shots of adoring women, especially Phyllis Calvert as Jeanne and, to a lesser degree, Jean Kent as his faithful 'companion' Bianchi. Granger emphasizes the spectacular nature of the performer, investing the character with a histrionic dimension that anticipates the behaviour of pop stars of recent times.[13] Also like a pop star, he acquires a large following of female fans. During his European tour, for example, the women in the audience are mesmerized, in thrall to this pied piper and his musical sorcery. The spectacularization of Granger's performance is matched by the superlative violin playing by Yehudi Menuhin, to which the actor mimes convincingly. The publicity material held by the British Film Institute highlights the authenticity of the acting and the music (the virtuosity of both Menuhin and Granger) more than the historical veracity of the film. Indeed, considerable attention was paid to musical accuracy (Levy, 1948, pp. 88–9). Levy attests to the authenticity of the music, seeing it as guaranteed by the 'painstaking research' that went into its production (Levy, 1948, p. 98). For example, Yehudi Menuhin used not only a Stradivarius violin, but also a Guarnieri, Paganini's favourite instrument. This concentration on the music was exploited in the film's promotion. The press book states: 'Selling this film to the public is a pushover if you concentrate on the stars and the music', and also suggests linking up with local musical societies, collaborating with music stores for window and counter displays, and competitions featuring violinists 'who can render pieces from the film' for prizes of tickets.

Gainsborough's perennial concern with class is central to this film. At a soirée at Jeanne's family mansion, Paganini finds out the hard way that music is not appreciated by the idle rich. His performance is initially hampered by broken violin strings, so he performs with the one left on his instrument. The piece he plays is interrupted by the partygoers' conversations and the loud snoring of an elderly man. Disgusted, Paganini serenades his disrespectful audience by creating the noise of a braying ass with his violin, before storming out. The message is populist: sympathy rests with the impoverished musician who has to rely on the patronage of the ignorant ruling class.

The Magic Bow features several sequences of musical performance, including 'Campanella' (Paganini) outside the prison, 'The Devil's Trill' (Tartini), 'La Ronde des lutins' (Brazzini), 'Nel cor pui nom mi senti' (Paganini), Violin Concerto No. 1 (Paganini) at the Parma concert hall,[14] Caprice No. 20 (Paganini) and the final movement of Beethoven's Violin Concerto Op. 61 at the climactic Vatican concert. The repeated main theme, which is associated with the love between Paganini and Jeanne, is based on Paganini's E minor Concerto. It was written by Philip Green, who went on to become one of the most prolific British film composers of the 1950s. Green's love theme ('Romance') is played over the opening titles and finally appears within the diegesis, played by Paganini, triumphantly marking the final union of Granger and Calvert. The piece became highly popular and was performed at the Albert Hall in 1946 (Huntley, 1947, p. 2). This kind of musical tie-in was relatively common during the 1940s, anticipating the pop songs tied-in with films today.

The music in *The Magic Bow* demonstrates the Gainsborough production-line approach: Levy was in overall charge of the film's music, Bretton Byrd was the music editor, David McCallum was the music coach for Granger's miming, Phil Green provided a number of arrangements of the underscore's repeated theme, while Henry Geehl provided the small amount of incidental cues that accompany action.[15] *The Magic Bow* coincided with a cycle of films released in the immediate post-war period that prominently displayed classical music. Shortly before *The Magic Bow*'s release, *The Seventh Veil* (1945), which featured numerous classical piano pieces, and *Brief Encounter* (1945), which popularized Rachmaninov's Piano Concerto No. 2, had both been successful. However, unlike these two films, *The Magic Bow* did not equate classical music with the middle classes; rather, it attempted to win back such music for the masses. *The Magic Bow* demonstrates the interest in class mobility that had been articulated by previous costume dramas,[16] but doubles this by offering art music to everyone.

Gainsborough's mode of production enabled Levy and his crew to produce cheap music quickly, using a number of composers and orchestrators in a production line for some of their scores. That Gainsborough's scores differed radically from the prestige film music of British quality cinema is borne out by the fact that the connections with radio light music (Levy and Hyden) outweighed those with the classical concert hall. The desire for prestigious film music written by established art music composers lost impetus by the early 1950s. Specialist film composers increasingly swamped the small number of art music composers who were still slumming in the film industry. Louis Levy and his cohorts at Gainsborough were the forerunners of these specialists, crafting music for its overall effect within the context of the film rather than for its cultural status.

Once Sydney Box became chief at Gainsborough the films changed character, as did the music department. Levy was no longer used as musical director, and musical production turned to the single-composer system that was and has remained dominant in Britain. In 1947, Levy was replaced as musical director for Gainsborough and Gaumont-British by Felton Rapley.[17] He became musical director to ABPC in 1948 and worked for them at Elstree until his death in 1957.[18] After Levy's exit, some composers with established reputations were imported by Gainsborough, most conspicuously Sir Arthur Bliss, who provided suitably prestigious music for the expensive failure *Christopher Columbus* (1949). Others were Clifton Parker (*When the Bough Breaks*, 1947) and Doreen Carwithen (*Boys in Brown*, 1949), who later married another film composer, William Alwyn; and Benjamin Frankel, once a dance music specialist, who scored *Dear Murderer* (1947) and *So Long at the Fair* (1950) on the way to a mixed career of film and art music.[19] The demise of Levy's music department brought a transformation of Gainsborough's music production, underlined perhaps by the appearance of Muir Mathieson as musical director and conductor on some of the films produced under Box.

In conclusion, it seems extraordinary that the music in Gainsborough melodrama has been so completely neglected. Perhaps, as other writers have suggested, it is that the studio's '40s output went against the grain of the dominant film culture. The music reflects the class address of the Gainsborough films, embodying their populism. Gainsborough's 1940s costume dramas can be seen as contesting the quality consensus films of the time (Cook, 1996b, p. 53). This attitude was also in operation when it came to the film music: Levy led a music department that was unconcerned with concert hall kudos or critical backslapping and focused on the production of effective, integrated and cheap film music. That he managed to oversee the production of a variety of remarkable scores testifies to his position as one of Britain's pioneer film musicians. Levy's humble origins and hustling attitude earned him little in the way of artistic recognition, though they may well have enabled him to understand popular taste. His use of functional music, and his encouragement of suitably unrestrained and expressive music for the exaggerated posturing of Gainsborough's melodramas, may not have helped his case. Such music could not usually be packaged as concert hall suites, though it excelled within the overblown and emotionally charged contexts of the films themselves.

Notes

1. For example, records were issued of music from *Love Story* (1944), *Holiday Camp* (1947), *Miranda* (1948), *Boys in Brown* (1949), *So Long at the Fair* (1950), *Trio* (1950) and *Vote for Huggett* (1949).

2. Gainsborough was absorbed by Gaumont-British in 1928.

3. Manvell and Huntley's pantheon of greats includes only four films from Gainsborough: *Man of Aran, Love Story, The Magic Bow* and *Christopher Columbus*. These appear on an extensive list of ten to twenty of 'the best' from each year (Manvell and Huntley, 1957, pp. 211–24).

4. Although Irving tried to use art music composers, Ealing made some

adventurous commissions: concert pianist Noel Mewton-Wood scored *Tawny Pipit* (1944) and Norman Demuth scored *Pink String and Sealing Wax* (1945).

5. See Levy, L. (1937) 'Music for Every Mood', *Film Weekly*, 7 March, p. 8.

6. Levy was heavily involved in British film musicals of the 1930s, co-ordinating and directing music for Jessie Matthews, and for Gracie Fields's *Shipyard Sally* (1939) and Jack Hulbert's *Sunshine Susie* (1931).

7. Examples include Arthur Bliss's score for *Conquest of the Air*, which appeared as a suite at the Proms in 1938 before the release of that troubled film in 1940. Almost every

composer with a concert hall reputation made their film music into suites – for example, Vaughan Williams's *The Flemish Farm* (1943) and William Alwyn's *Odd Man Out* (1947).

8. See Huth, H. (1945), Hubert Bath's Obituary, *Kinematograph Weekly*, 3 May, p. 21.

9. See Levy, L. (1937), op. cit., p. 9.

10. Ibid., p. 9.

11. Hyden 'contributed music to a number of films, including one based on his famous radio programme, "Café Collette", and a large-scale industrial film on rayon' [!] (Huntley, 1947, p. 209).

12. In many respects, these were the 1940s equivalents of more recent big hit pop song tie-ins, such as Bryan Adams's 'Everything I Do' (from *Robin Hood, Prince of Thieves*, 1991) and Whitney Houston's 'I Will Always Love You' (from *The Bodyguard*, 1992).

13. He even has a hustling manager, Germi, who would not be out of place in a pop musical. *The Magic Bow* anticipates Ken Russell's pop-inspired composer biopics, such as *The Music Lovers* (1970), *Mahler* (1974) and *Lisztomania* (1975),

which attempted to remove the composers from the 'respectable' positions assigned them by the art music establishment.

14. This concert sequence has a bewigged Bretton Byrd conducting the orchestra on stage behind Granger.

15. Henry Geehl also wrote religious music such as 'Crimond', a tune for 'The Lord's My Shepherd'.

16. Paganini's knighthood makes it possible for him to marry Jeanne, reflecting the possibility of social mobility and the malleability of class relations which is apparent in many of the melodramas.

17. See Courtnay, J. (1947) 'Music', *Kinematograph Weekly*, 30 January, p. 47.

18. [Anonymous obituary] 'He Lived to Put Music to Pictures', *Today's Cinema*, 20 August 1957, p. 6.

19. Other, less prominent composers used included Temple Abady (*Easy Money*, 1948, *Miranda*, 1948), Arthur Wilkinson (*The Calendar*, 1948, *Traveller's Joy*, 1949) and Lambert Williamson *(Good Time Girl*, 1948, *Don't Ever Leave Me*, 1949).

11

Filmography: Gainsborough and Related Films, 1924–1950

Denis Gifford

Additional research by Simon Davies

The information in the filmography comes primarily from Gifford (1986), but it includes additional material compiled from a variety of sources.

Details of all Gainsborough films are provided. Because Gainsborough became part of the Gaumont-British Picture Corporation (GBPC) in the late 1920s, Gaumont productions at Shepherd's Bush and elsewhere are listed, along with a number of co-productions and the films made by GBPC for 20th Century Fox at Islington and Shepherd's Bush. Also included is a selection of relevant non-GBPC films, such as some 1930s titles that were distributed by Gaumont, and Sydney Box's Triton and other productions of the 1940s.

The filmography begins in 1924, when the Gainsborough name was first used. (Michael Balcon had made a few earlier films for the production company Balcon, Freedman & Saville, and Gaumont had produced some features at Shepherd's Bush prior to this.) It ends in 1950, when the Gainsborough name ceased to be used; although feature films continued to be made by many ex-Gainsborough people, they were under the Rank name. The date given for individual titles is the initial British Board of Film Classification (BBFC) screening (prior to 1928) or Board of Trade screening. Other sources often use release date or date of production, which may give a different order for the films. In those rare cases where the date is unavailable, an intelligent guess has been made.

In most cases, the film title is that of the British release. French, German and US titles are provided where relevant – for example, in the case of European co-productions and remakes. The production company is usually followed by place of production, where known: either a British studio or the more vague Hollywood, Berlin and so forth. The place of production can be difficult to establish – information given in secondary sources, such as production reports in the trade press or the film credits, is often contradictory. Initially, Gainsborough productions were based at Islington and Gaumont productions at Shepherd's Bush, but for films made in the 1940s it is harder to determine which of the two was used. Beaconsfield and Twickenham were the main other studios used for lower-budget films – for example, British Lion co-productions. With studio rationalization under Rank, the last few Gainsborough films were made at Pinewood after Islington and Shepherd's Bush had closed.

The following credits are generally provided: *pc* is the production company; *p* is the producer; *d* is the director; *sc* is the writer(s), covering any screenwriting credits (screenplay, story, additional dialogue and so forth). If the film is based on a specific work (usually a novel or play, but sometimes a poem, song or opera), the author is given. For some films additional credits are provided: *ad* is the art director; *ap* is the associate producer; *ass d* is the assistant director; *ep* is the executive producer (or in charge of production); *md* is the musical director. The entry usually ends with the generic category as defined by Gifford (1986).

For a small number of titles, further comments have been added – for example, to suggest when sound was added to a film, or to give details of a film that has been remade. The designation 'Foreign' means that the film was registered as foreign rather than British for quota purposes under the Cinematograph Films Act (1927).

Filmography

1924

April: *Claude Duval*. *pc* Gaumont *d* George A. Cooper *sc* Louis Stevens, Mary Bennett. Adventure.

May: *The Prude's Fall* (German title: *Seine zweite Frau*). *pc* Gainsborough (Islington) *p* Michael Balcon *d* Graham Cutts *ad* Alfred Hitchcock *sc* Alfred Hitchcock. Based on a play by Rudolf Besier, May Edginton. Romance.

July: *The Passionate Adventure* (German title: *Ehe in Gefahr*). *pc* Gainsborough (Islington) *p* Michael Balcon *d* Graham Cutts *ass d* Alfred Hitchcock *ad* Alfred Hitchcock *sc* Alfred Hitchcock, Michael Morton. Based on a novel by Frank Stayton. Drama.

July: *The Eleventh Commandment*. *pc* Gaumont (Shepherd's Bush) *d* George A. Cooper *sc* Based on a play by Brandon Fleming. Crime.

1925

January: *The Happy Ending*. *pc* Gaumont *d* George A. Cooper *sc* P.L. Mannock. Based on a play by Ian Hay. Drama.

March: *The Blackguard* (German title: *Die Prinzessin und der Geiger*). *pc* Ufa/Gainsborough (made in Berlin) *p* Michael Balcon, Erich Pommer *d* Graham Cutts *ass d* Alfred Hitchcock *ad* Alfred Hitchcock *sc* Alfred Hitchcock. Based on a novel by Raymond Paton. Drama.

August: *The Rat* (French title: *Le Rat*; German title: *Die Ratte von Paris*). *pc* Gainsborough (Islington) *p* Michael Balcon *d* Graham Cutts *ad* C. W. Arnold *sc* Graham Cutts. Based on a play by Ivor Novello, Constance Collier. Crime.

October: *Settled Out of Court*. *pc* Gaumont (Shepherd's Bush) *d* George A. Cooper *sc* Eliot Stannard. Drama.

November: *Gainsborough Burlesques* (*Battling Bruisers, So This Is Jollygood, Cut It Out, A Typical Budget, The Blunderland of Big Game*). *pc* Gainsborough (Islington) *p* Michael Balcon *d* Adrian Brunel *sc* Adrian Brunel, J.O.C. Orton, Edwin Greenwood. Comedies.

November: *Somebody's Darling*. *pc* Gaumont *d* George A. Cooper *sc* Based on a novel by Sidney Morgan. Comedy.

1926

January: *Steve Donoghue Series* (*Riding for a King, Beating the Book, The Golden Spurs, The Stolen Favourite*). *pc* C&M (Islington) *p* Michael Balcon *d* Walter West. Sport.

January: *The Sea Urchin*. *pc* Gainsborough (Islington) *p* Michael Balcon *d* Graham Cutts *ass d* Leslie Hiscott *ad* C.W. Arnold *sc* Graham Cutts, Charles Lapworth. Based on a play by John Hastings Turner. Romance.

May: *The Pleasure Garden* (German title: *Irrgarten der Leidenschaft*). *pc* Gainsborough/Emelka (made in Munich) *p* Michael Balcon *d* Alfred Hitchcock *ass d* Alma Reville *ad* Ludwig Reiber, C.W. Arnold *sc* Eliot Stannard. Based on a novel by Oliver Sandys. Drama.

July: *London Love. pc* Gaumont (Shepherd's Bush) *d* Manning Haynes
    sc Lydia Hayward. Based on a novel by Arthur Applin. Crime.
September: *The Triumph of the Rat* (German title: *Der Apache, der*
    König der Boulevards). *pc* Gainsborough/Piccadilly (Islington)
    p Michael Balcon, Carlyle Blackwell *d* Graham Cutts *ad* Bertram
    Evans *sc* Graham Cutts, Reginald Fogwell, Roland Pertwee.
    Based on characters created by Ivor Novello, Constance Collier.
    Romance.
September: *The Lodger: A Story of the London Fog* (French title: *Les*
    Cheveux d'or; US title: *The Case of Jonathan Drew*).
    pc Gainsborough (Islington) *p* Michael Balcon *d* Alfred
    Hitchcock *ass d* Alma Reville *ad* C.W. Arnold, Bertram Evans
    sc Eliot Stannard, Alfred Hitchcock. Based on a novel by Mrs
    Belloc Lowndes. Crime.
September: *The Mountain Eagle* (German title: *Der Bergadler*; US title:
    Fear o' God). *pc* Gainsborough/Emelka (made in Munich)
    p Michael Balcon *d* Alfred Hitchcock *ass d* Alma Reville *ad* Willy
    and Ludwig Reiber *sc* Eliot Stannard, Charles Lapworth. Drama.
September: *Mademoiselle from Armentieres. pc* Gaumont (Shepherd's
    Bush) *p* Victor Saville, Maurice Elvey *d* Maurice Elvey
    ad Andrew Mazzei *sc* Victor Saville, V. Gareth Gundrey. War.
December: *Screen Playlets* (*Cash on Delivery, The Escape, Miss*
    Bracegirdle Does Her Duty, The Greater War, Back to the Trees,
    The Woman Juror). *pc* Gaumont (Shepherd's Bush) *d* Milton
    Rosmer, Edwin Greenwood, Jack Raymond *sc* Alfred Barrett,
    Stacy Aumonier, E.F. Parr, W. Townend, H.H. Bashford. Drama.

1927

February: *Hindle Wakes. pc* Gaumont (Shepherd's Bush) *p* Maurice
    Elvey, Victor Saville *d* Maurice Elvey, Victor Saville *ad* Andrew
    Mazzei *sc* V. Gareth Gundrey. Based on a play by Stanley
    Houghton. Romance.
March: *Blighty. pc* Gainsborough/Piccadilly (Islington) *p* Michael
    Balcon, Carlyle Blackwell *d* Adrian Brunel *ass d* Norman Walker
    ad Bertram Evans *sc* Eliot Stannard, Ivor Montagu, Charles
    MacEvoy. War.
April: *The Queen Was in the Parlour* (German title: *Die letzte Nacht*;
    US title: *Forbidden Love*). *pc* Gainsborough/Piccadilly/Ufa (made
    in Berlin) *p* Michael Balcon, Hermann Fellner *d* Graham Cutts

ad Oscar Werndorff *sc* Graham Cutts. Based on a play by Noël Coward. Romance.

April: *Roses of Picardy*. *pc* Gaumont (Cricklewood) *p* Victor Saville, Maurice Elvey. *d* Maurice Elvey *sc* V. Gareth Gundrey, F.V. Merrick, Jack Harris. Based on a novel by R.H. Mottram. War.

May: *Downhill* (US title: *When Boys Leave Home*). *pc* Gainsborough (Islington) *p* Michael Balcon *d* Alfred Hitchcock *ass d* Frank Miles *ad* Bertram Evans *sc* Eliot Stannard. Based on a play by Ivor Novello, Constance Collier. Drama.

May: *The Rolling Road*. *pc* Gainsborough/Piccadilly (Islington) *p* Michael Balcon *ap* Carlyle Blackwell *d* Graham Cutts *ass d* Robert Cullen *ad* Bertram Evans *sc* Violet E. Powell, Boyd Cable. Adventure.

June: *The Glad Eye*. *pc* Gaumont (Twickenham) *p* Victor Saville, Maurice Elvey *d* Maurice Elvey *sc* V. Gareth Gundrey, Maurice Elvey, Victor Saville. Based on a play by Jose Levy, Paul Armont, Nicholas Nancey. Comedy.

July: *Easy Virtue*. *pc* Gainsborough (Islington) *p* Michael Balcon *d* Alfred Hitchcock *ad* Clifford Pember *sc* Eliot Stannard. Based on a play by Noël Coward. Drama.

July: *The Ghost Train* (German title: *Der Geisterzug*). *pc* Gainsborough/Ufa (made in Germany) *p* Michael Balcon, Hermann Fellner *d* Geza von Bolvary *ad* Oscar Werndorff *sc* Benno Vigny, Adolf Lantz. Based on a play by Arnold Ridley. Crime.

September: *The Vortex*. *pc* Gainsborough (Islington) *p* Michael Balcon *ap* S.C. Balcon *d* Adrian Brunel *ass d* S.C. Balcon *ad* Clifford Pember *sc* Eliot Stannard. Based on a play by Noël Coward. Romance.

September: *A Sister to Assist 'Er*. *pc* Gaumont (Shepherd's Bush) *p* Maurice Elvey, Victor Saville, V. Gareth Gundrey *d* George Dewhurst *sc* George Dewhurst. Based on a play by John le Breton. Comedy.

September: *The Flight Commander*. *pc* Gaumont (Shepherd's Bush) *p* Maurice Elvey, Victor Saville, V. Gareth Gundrey *d* Maurice Elvey *ad* Andrew Mazzei *sc* Eugene Clifford, John Travers. Adventure.

October: *A Woman in Pawn*. *pc* Gaumont (Shepherd's Bush) *p* Maurice Elvey, Victor Saville, V. Gareth Gundrey *d* Edwin Greenwood *sc* Based on a play by Frank Stayton. Crime.

October: *The Arcadians*. *pc* Gaumont (Shepherd's Bush) *p* Maurice
Elvey, Victor Saville, V. Gareth Gundrey *d* Victor Saville *sc* Based
on a play by Mark Ambient, Alex Thompson. Fantasy.

November: *One of the Best*. *pc* Gainsborough/Piccadilly (Islington)
p Michael Balcon, Carlyle Blackwell *d* T. Hayes Hunter
ad Clifford Pember *sc* P.L. Mannock. Based on a play by
Seymour Hicks, George Edwards. Crime.

December: *Quinneys*. *pc* Gaumont (Shepherd's Bush) *p* V. Gareth
Gundrey *d* Maurice Elvey *sc* John Longden. Based on a play by
H.A. Vachell. Romance.

1928

January: *Sailors Don't Care*. *pc* Gaumont (Shepherd's Bush) *p* Maurice
Elvey, V. Gareth Gundrey *d* W.P. Kellino *sc* Eliot Stannard. Based
on a novel by Austin Small. Comedy.

February: *The Constant Nymph* (German title: *Die treue Nymphe*).
pc Gainsborough (Islington) *p* Michael Balcon *ap* Basil Dean
d Adrian Brunel *ad* George Harris *sc* Basil Dean, Margaret
Kennedy, Adrian Brunel, Alma Reville. Based on a play by Basil
Dean, Margaret Kennedy. Romance.

May: *The Physician*. *pc* Gaumont (Shepherd's Bush) *p* Maurice Elvey,
V. Gareth Gundrey *d* George Jacoby *sc* Edwin Greenwood. Based
on a play by Henry Arthur Jones. Drama.

June: *Mademoiselle Parley-voo*. *pc* Gaumont (Shepherd's Bush) *p* V.
Gareth Gundrey *d* Maurice Elvey *sc* F.V. Merrick, Jack Harris,
John Longden. Crime.

July: *What Money Can Buy*. *pc* Gaumont (Shepherd's Bush) *p* Maurice
Elvey, V. Gareth Gundrey *d* Edwin Greenwood *sc* Edwin
Greenwood. Based on a play by Arthur Shirley, Ben Landeck.
Drama.

July: *A South Sea Bubble*. *pc* Gainsborough (Islington) *p* Michael
Balcon *d* T. Hayes Hunter *ass d* John Chandos *sc* Angus
MacPhail, Alma Reville. Based on a novel by Roland Pertwee.
Adventure.

July: *Palais de danse*. *pc* Gaumont (Shepherd's Bush) *p* Maurice Elvey,
V. Gareth Gundrey *d* Maurice Elvey *ad* Andrew Mazzei *sc* John
Longden, Jean Jay. Romance.

October: *Smashing Through*. *pc* Gaumont (Shepherd's Bush)
p Maurice Elvey, V. Gareth Gundrey *d* W.P. Kellino *sc* William
Lees, John Hunter, L'Estrange Fawcett. Sport.

The Gallant Hussar (German title: *Der fesche Husar*, also known as *Oberleutnant Noszty*). *pc* Gainsborough/DEFA (made in Berlin) *p* Hermann Fellner, Josef Somlo *d* Geza von Bolvary *ad* Oscar Werndorff, Emil Hasler *sc* Dr A. Bardos, Margarete Maria Langen. Foreign.

October: *The First Born*. *pc* Gainsborough/Mander (BIP, Elstree) *p* Michael Balcon, Miles Mander *d* Miles Mander *ad* C.W. Arnold *sc* Miles Mander, Alma Reville, Ian Dalrymple. Based on a play by Miles Mander. Drama.

November: *You Know What Sailors Are*. *pc* Gaumont (Shepherd's Bush) *p* Maurice Elvey, V. Gareth Gundrey *d* Maurice Elvey *sc* Angus MacPhail, John Longden, L'Estrange Fawcett. Based on a novel by W.E. Townend. Adventure.

December: *The Wrecker* (German title: *Der Würger*). *pc* Gainsborough/FPS Film (Islington) *p* Michael Balcon *ap* S.C. Balcon *d* Geza von Bolvary *ass d* S.C. Balcon *ad* Oscar Werndorff *sc* Angus MacPhail, Benno Vigny. Based on a play by Arnold Ridley, Bernard Merivale. Crime.

December: *A Light Woman*. *pc* Gainsborough (Islington) *p* Michael Balcon *d* Adrian Brunel *sc* Adey Brunel, Adrian Brunel, Angus MacPhail. Adventure.

December: *The Lady of the Lake*. *pc* Gainsborough (Islington) *p* Michael Balcon *d* James A. Fitzpatrick *sc* James A. Fitzpatrick, Angus MacPhail. Based on a poem by Sir Walter Scott. Adventure. Sound added July 1931.

December: *Number Seventeen* (German title: *Haus Nummer 17*). *pc* Felsom (made in Germany) *p* Hermann Fellner, Josef Somlo *d* Geza von Bolvary *ad* Oscar Werndorff *sc* Benno Vigny, Adolf Lantz. Based on a play by J. Jefferson Farjeon. Crime. Sound added August 1929.

December: *Balaclava* (US title: *Jaws of Hell*). *pc* Gainsborough (Shepherd's Bush) *p* Michael Balcon *d* Maurice Elvey, Milton Rosmer *md* Louis Levy *sc* V. Gareth Gundrey, W.P. Lipscomb, Boyd Cable, Angus MacPhail, Milton Rosmer, Robert Stevenson. Based on a poem by Tennyson. War. This silent version was not released. Sound added April 1930.

1929

May: *The Return of the Rat* (German title: *Im Schatten von Paris*). *pc* Gainsborough (Islington) *p* Michael Balcon *d* Graham Cutts *ad* Alan McNab *sc* Angus MacPhail, Edgar C. Middleton, A. Neil Lyons. Based on characters created by Ivor Novello, Constance Collier. Crime. Sound added October 1929.

May: *The Crooked Billet. pc* Gainsborough (Islington) *p* Michael Balcon *d* Adrian Brunel *md* Louis Levy *sc* Angus MacPhail. Based on a play by Dion Titherage. Crime. Sound added March 1930.

In a Monastery Garden. p Michael Balcon *d* Adrian Brunel. Short.

July: *City of Play. pc* Gainsborough (Islington) *p* Michael Balcon *d* Denison Clift *ass d* L.B. Lestocq *sc* Denison Clift, Angus MacPhail. Drama.

July: *Taxi for Two. pc* Gainsborough (Islington) *p* Michael Balcon *d* Alexander Esway, Denison Clift *sc* Alexander Esway, Ian Dalrymple, Angus MacPhail. Comedy.

August: *High Treason. pc* Gaumont (Shepherd's Bush) *p* L'Estrange Fawcett *d* Maurice Elvey *ad* Andrew Mazzei *sc* L'Estrange Fawcett. Based on a play by Noel Pemberton-Billing. Fantasy.

August: *The Devil's Maze. pc* Gaumont (Shepherd's Bush) *p* V. Gareth Gundrey *d* V. Gareth Gundrey *sc* Sewell Collins. Based on a play by G.R. Malloch. Drama.

November: *Woman to Woman. pc* Gainsborough/Burlington/Tiffany-Stahl (made in Hollywood) *p* Michael Balcon, Victor Saville *d* Victor Saville *sc* Victor Saville, Nicholas Fodor. Based on a play by Michael Morton. Romance. Foreign.

November: *Armistice. pc* Gainsborough *p* Michael Balcon *d* Victor Saville *sc* Based on a poem by John McCrae. Musical.

December: *Mickey Mouse. pc* Gainsborough *p* Michael Balcon. Musical.

1930

January: *Gainsborough Gems (Martini and His Band No.1 and 2, Billie Barnes, George Mozart in Domestic Troubles, Hal Swain and His Sax-0-Five, Elsie Percival and Ray Raymond, Pete Mandell and His Rhythm Masters No.1 and 2, Dick Henderson, The Blue Boys No.1 and 2, Lewis Hardcastle's Dusky Syncopaters, The Walsh Brothers, The Volga Singers, Ena Reiss). p* Michael Balcon. Musical. Songs, dances, comedy sketches.

February: *Sugar and Spice (Al Fresco, Toyland, Black and White, Classic v. Jazz, Gypsy Land, Dusky Melodies). p* Michael Balcon *d* Alexander Oumansky. Musical. Made as *The Gainsborough Picture Show* but released as shorts only.

March: *Just for a Song*. *pc* Gainsborough (Islington) *p* Michael Balcon *d* V. Gareth Gundrey *sc* V. Gareth Gundrey, Desmond Carter. Musical.

March: *Alf's Button*. *pc* Gaumont (Shepherd's Bush) *p* L'Estrange Fawcett *d* W.P. Kellino *ad* Andrew Mazzei *sc* L'Estrange Fawcett. Based on a play by W.A. Darlington. Comedy.

March: *The Night Porter*. *pc* Gaumont (Shepherd's Bush) *p* L'Estrange Fawcett *d* Sewell Collins *sc* Sewell Collins, L'Estrange Fawcett. Based on a play by Harry Wall. Comedy.

April: *The Message*. *pc* Gaumont (Shepherd's Bush) *p* L'Estrange Fawcett. *d* Sewell Collins *sc* Brandon Fleming, Sewell Collins, Ralph Gilbert Bettinson. Crime.

April: *Journey's End*. *pc* Gainsborough/Welsh/Pearson/Tiffany-Stahl (made in Hollywood) *p* George Pearson *d* James Whale *ad* Harvey Libbert *sc* Joseph Moncure March, V. Gareth Gundrey. Based on a play by R.C. Sherriff. War. Foreign.

May: *Greek Street* (US title: *Latin Love*). *pc* Gaumont (Shepherd's Bush) *p* L'Estrange Fawcett *d* Sinclair Hill *ad* Andrew Mazzei *sc* Robert Stevenson, Ralph Gilbert Bettinson, Leslie Howard Gordon. Musical.

July: *Symphony in 2 Flats*. *pc* Gainsborough (Islington/ BIP, Elstree) *p* Michael Balcon *d* V. Gareth Gundrey *sc* V. Gareth Gundrey, Angus MacPhail. Based on a play by Ivor Novello. Drama.

August: *Ashes*. *pc* Gainsborough (Islington) *p* Michael Balcon *d* Frank Birch *sc* Angus MacPhail, M.D. Lyon, Claude Soman. Comedy.

September: *The Great Game*. *pc* Gaumont (Shepherd's Bush) *p* L'Estrange Fawcett *d* Jack Raymond *sc* William Hunter, John Lees, W.P. Lipscomb, Ralph Gilbert Bettinson. Sport.

September: *A Warm Corner*. *pc* Gainsborough (B&D, Elstree) *p* Michael Balcon *d* Victor Saville *ad* Walter Murton *sc* Angus MacPhail, Victor Saville. Based on a play by Franz Arnold, Ernst Bach, Arthur Wimperis, Laurie Wylie. Comedy.

November: *Thread o' Scarlet*. *pc* Gaumont *p* L'Estrange Fawcett *d* Peter Godfrey *sc* Ralph Gilbert Bettinson. Based on a play by J.J. Bell. Crime.

December: *Bed and Breakfast*. *pc* Gaumont (Shepherd's Bush) *p* L'Estrange Fawcett *d* Walter Forde *ad* Andrew Mazzei *sc* Sidney Gilliat, H. Fowler Mear. Based on a play by Frederick Witney. Comedy.

1931

January: *PC Josser*. *pc* Gainsborough (Islington) *p* Michael Balcon *d* Milton Rosmer *sc* Con West, Herbert Sargent. Based on a play by Ernest Lotinga. Comedy.

January: *Harry Lauder Songs* (*I Love a Lassie, Somebody's Waiting for Me, I Love to Be a Sailor, Roaming in the Gloaming, Tobermory, Nanny, The Safest of the Family, She Is Ma Daisy, Wee Hoose Amang the Heather*). *pc* Gainsborough/Welsh/Pearson *p* Michael Balcon *d* George Pearson. Musical.

February: *Bracelets*. *pc* Gaumont (Shepherd's Bush) *p* L'Estrange Fawcett *d* Sewell Collins *ad* Andrew Mazzei *sc* Sewell Collins Based on a play by Sewell Collins. Crime.

February: *Hot Heir*. *pc* Gainsborough (Twickenham) *p* Michael Balcon *d* W.P. Kellino *sc* Angus MacPhail, S.C. Balcon. Comedy.

February: *Bull Rushes*. *pc* Gainsborough (Twickenham) *p* Michael Balcon *d* W.P. Kellino *sc* Angus MacPhail, S.C. Balcon. Comedy.

February: *Who Killed Doc Robin?* *pc* Gainsborough (Twickenham) *p* Michael Balcon *d* W.P. Kellino *sc* Angus MacPhail, S.C. Balcon. Comedy.

February: *Third Time Lucky*. *pc* Gainsborough (Islington) *p* Michael Balcon *d* Walter Forde *ad* Walter Murton *sc* Sidney Gilliat, Angus MacPhail. Based on a play by Arnold Ridley. Comedy.

February: *The Stronger Sex*. *pc* Gainsborough (Islington) *p* Michael Balcon *d* V. Gareth Gundrey *sc* V. Gareth Gundrey, Angus MacPhail. Based on a play by John Valentine. Drama.

February: *The Sport of Kings*. *pc* Gainsborough (Twickenham/B&D, Elstree) *p* Michael Balcon *d* Victor Saville *sc* Angus MacPhail. Based on a play by Ian Hay. Comedy.

April: *Aroma of the South Seas*. *pc* Gainsborough *p* Michael Balcon *d* W.P. Kellino *sc* Angus MacPhail. Comedy.

May: *No Lady*. *pc* Gaumont (Shepherd's Bush) *p* L'Estrange Fawcett *d* Lupino Lane *ad* Andrew Mazzei *md* Louis Levy *sc* R.P. Weston, Bert Lee, Lupino Lane, George Dewhurst, L'Estrange Fawcett. Comedy.

May: *Down River*. *pc* Gaumont (Shepherd's Bush) *p* L'Estrange Fawcett *d* Peter Godfrey *ad* Andrew Mazzei *sc* Ralph Gilbert Bettinson. Based on a novel by Austin Small. Crime.

May: *The Ringer*. *pc* Gainsborough/British Lion (Beaconsfield) *p* Michael Balcon *ep* Edgar Wallace *d* Walter Forde *ad* Norman

Arnold *sc* Robert Stevenson, Sidney Gilliat, Angus MacPhail.
Based on a play by Edgar Wallace. Crime.

July: *A Night in Montmartre. pc* Gaumont (Twickenham) *p* Michael
Balcon *d* Leslie Hiscott *sc* Angus MacPhail. Based on a play by
Miles Malleson, Walter Peacock. Crime.

July: *The Hound of the Baskervilles. p* Michael Balcon *pc* Gaumont
(Islington) *d* V. Gareth Gundrey *sc* Angus MacPhail, V. Gareth
Gundrey, Edgar Wallace. Based on a novel by Arthur Conan
Doyle. Crime.

August: *The Man They Could Not Arrest. pc* Gainsborough (Islington)
p Michael Balcon *d* T. Hayes Hunter *sc* T. Hayes Hunter, Arthur
Wimperis, Angus MacPhail. Based on a novel by Austin J. Small
and uncredited material by Edgar Wallace. Crime.

August: *My Old China. pc* Gainsborough *p* Michael Balcon *d* W.P.
Kellino *sc* Angus MacPhail, S.C. Balcon. Comedy.

September: *The Ghost Train. pc* Gainsborough (Islington) *p* Michael
Balcon *ap* Philip Samuel *d* Walter Forde *ad* Walter Murton
sc Angus MacPhail, Lajos Biro, Sidney Gilliat. Based on a play by
Arnold Ridley. Comedy.

October: *The Happy Ending. pc* Gaumont *p* L'Estrange Fawcett
d Millard Webb *ad* Andrew Mazzei *sc* H. Fowler Mear. Based on
a play by Ian Hay. Drama.

October: *Hindle Wakes. pc* Gaumont (Shepherd's Bush) *p* Michael
Balcon *d* Victor Saville *ad* Andrew Mazzei *md* W.L. Trytel
sc Angus MacPhail, Victor Saville. Based on a play by Stanley
Houghton. Romance.

October: *Michael and Mary. pc* Gaumont (Islington) *p* Michael Balcon
d Victor Saville *ad* Alex Vetchinsky *md* Louis Levy *sc* Angus
MacPhail, Robert Stevenson, Lajos Biro. Based on a play by
A.A. Milne. Romance.

October: *The Calendar* (US title: *Bachelor's Folly*).
pc Gainsborough/British Lion (Beaconsfield) *p* Michael Balcon
d T. Hayes Hunter *sc* Angus MacPhail, Bryan Edgar Wallace,
Robert Stevenson. Based on a play by Edgar Wallace. Sport.

December: *Sunshine Susie* (US title: *Office Girl*). *pc* Gainsborough
(Islington) *p* Michael Balcon *d* Victor Saville *ad* Alex Vetchinsky
md Louis Levy *sc* Angus MacPhail, Robert Stevenson, Victor
Saville, Noel Wood-Smith. Based on a screenplay by Franz
Schulz, an operetta by Stefan Bekeffi Jr and a novel by Stefan
Szomahazy. Musical. Remake of the German film *Die*

Privatsekretärin: *pc* Greenbaum *d* Wilhelm Thiele (French and Italian versions of the original were also made).

December: *A Gentleman of Paris*. *pc* Gaumont (Cricklewood/ Shepherd's Bush) *p* Michael Balcon *d* Sinclair Hill *ad* Andrew Mazzei *sc* Sewell Collins, Sidney Gilliat. Based on a novel by Niranjan Pal. Crime.

The Congress Dances (German title: *Der Kongress tanzt*). *pc* Ufa *p* Erich Pommer *d* Erik Charell *sc* Norbert Falk, Robert Liebmann, adapted by Rowland V. Lee *ad* Robert Herlth, Walter Röhrig *md* Werner R. Heymann. Musical. English-language version of German original (a French-language version was also made).

1932

February: *Lord Babs*. *pc* Gainsborough (Islington) *p* Michael Balcon *d* Walter Forde *ad* Alex Vetchinsky *sc* Clifford Grey, Angus MacPhail, Sidney Gilliat. Based on a play by Keble Howard. Musical.

March: *The Frightened Lady* (US title: *Criminal at Large*). *pc* Gainsborough/British Lion (Beaconsfield) *p* Michael Balcon *ap* Herbert Smith *d* T. Hayes Hunter *ad* Norman Arnold *sc* Angus MacPhail, Bryan Edgar Wallace. Based on a play by Edgar Wallace. Crime.

May: *The Faithful Heart* (US title: *Faithful Hearts*). *pc* Gainsborough (Islington) *p* Michael Balcon *d* Victor Saville *ad* Alex Vetchinsky *md* Louis Levy *sc* Robert Stevenson, Victor Saville, Lajos Biro, Angus MacPhail. Based on a play by Monckton Hoffe. Romance.

May: *White Face*. *pc* Gainsborough/British Lion (Beaconsfield) *p* Michael Balcon *d* T. Hayes Hunter *ad* Norman Arnold *sc* Angus MacPhail, Bryan Edgar Wallace. Based on a play by Edgar Wallace. Crime.

June: *Jack's the Boy* (US title: *Night and Day*). *pc* Gainsborough (Islington/Welwyn) *p* Michael Balcon *d* Walter Forde *ad* Alex Vetchinsky *md* Louis Levy *sc* W.P. Lipscomb, Jack Hulbert, Douglas Furber. Comedy.

July: *Love on Wheels*. *pc* Gainsborough (Islington/BIP) *p* Michael Balcon *d* Victor Saville *ad* Alex Vetchinsky *md* Louis Levy *sc* Angus MacPhail, Robert Stevenson, Victor Saville, Douglas Furber. Musical.

October: *Marry Me*. *pc* Gainsborough (Islington) *p* Michael Balcon
d William [Wilhelm] Thiele *sc* Anthony Asquith, Angus
MacPhail, Stephen Zador, Frank Schulz, Ernst Angel. Musical.
Remake of the German film *Mädchen zum Heiraten*: *pc* Fellner
und Somlo *d* Wilhelm Thiele.

October: *Baroud* (US title: *Love in Morocco*). *pc* Rex Ingram (made
in Morocco) *p* Rex Ingram, Mansfield Markham *d* Rex Ingram
sc Rex Ingram, Peter Spencer, Benno Vigny. Adventure. French
and English versions made. Foreign.

October: *Happy Ever After*. *pc* Ufa (made in Berlin) *p* Erich Pommer
d Paul Martin, Robert Stevenson *sc* Jack Hulbert, Douglas
Furber, Walter Reisch, Billy Wilder. Musical. German, French
and English versions made. Foreign.

October: *Tell Me Tonight* (US title: *Be Mine Tonight*). *pc* Cine-Allianz
(made in Germany) *p* Hermann Fellner, Josef Somlo *d* Anatole
Litvak *sc* J.O.C. Orton, Irma von Cube, Albrecht Joseph.
Musical. German, French and English versions made. Foreign.

October: *There Goes the Bride*. *pc* Gainsborough/British Lion
(Beaconsfield) *p* Michael Balcon *d* Albert de Courville
ad Norman Arnold *sc* W.P. Lipscomb, Fred Raymond, Herman
Kosterlitz, Wolfgang Wilhelm. Comedy. Remake of the German
film *Ich bleib' bei dir*, also known as *Marys Start in die Ehe*:
pc Schulz und Wüller *d* Johannes Meyer.

November: *Rome Express* (German title: *Rom-Express*). *pc* Gaumont
(Shepherd's Bush) *p* Michael Balcon *ap* Philip Samuel *d* Walter
Forde *ad* Andrew Mazzei *sc* Sidney Gilliat, Clifford Grey, Frank
Vosper, Ralph Stock. Crime. Not shown in Germany.

December: *After the Ball*. *pc* Gaumont (Shepherd's Bush) *p* Michael
Balcon *d* Milton Rosmer *ad* Alfred Junge *sc* J.O.C. Orton,
H.M. Harwood, Max Neufeldt. Comedy.

December: *The Midshipmaid*. *pc* Gaumont (Shepherd's Bush)
p Michael Balcon *d* Albert de Courville *ad* Alfred Junge
sc Stafford Dickens. Based on a play by Ian Hay, Stephen King-
Hall. Comedy.

1933

January: *The Man from Toronto*. *pc* Gainsborough/British Lion
(Islington) *p* Michael Balcon *d* Sinclair Hill *ad* Alex Vetchinsky
sc W.P. Lipscomb. Based on a play by Douglas Murray. Comedy.

February: *Sign Please*. *pc* Gaumont *p* Clayton Hutton *d* John Rawlins *sc* Sidney Gilliat, John Paddy Carstairs, Louis Dighton. Comedy.

February: *They're Off!* *pc* Gaumont *p* Clayton Hutton *d* John Rawlins *sc* John Paddy Carstairs, Louis Dighton. Comedy.

February: *The Dreamers*. *pc* Gaumont *p* Clayton Hutton *d* Frank Cadman *sc* John Paddy Carstairs, Louis Dighton. Comedy.

February: *Post Haste*. *pc* Gaumont *p* Clayton Hutton *d* Frank Cadman *sc* Sidney Gilliat. Comedy.

February: *Tooth Will Out*. *pc* Gaumont *p* Clayton Hutton *d* Frank Cadman *sc* John Dighton, Hugh Stewart. Comedy.

March: *The Good Companions*. *pc* Gaumont/Welsh/Pearson (Shepherd's Bush) *p* George Pearson, T.A. Welsh *d* Victor Saville *ad* Alfred Junge *sc* W.P. Lipscomb, Angus MacPhail, Ian Dalrymple. Based on a novel by J.B. Priestley and a play by J.B. Priestley, Edward Knoblock. Comedy.

March: *Soldiers of the King* (US title: *The Woman in Command*). *pc* Gainsborough/British Lion (Islington/Beaconsfield/Welwyn) *p* Michael Balcon *d* Maurice Elvey *ad* Alex Vetchinsky *md* Louis Levy *sc* W.P. Lipscomb, Douglas Furber, J.O.C. Orton, Jack Hulbert. Musical.

March: *King of the Ritz*. *pc* Gainsborough/British Lion (Beaconsfield) *p* Michael Balcon *ap* Herbert Smith *d* Carmine Gallone *ad* Norman Arnold *sc* Clifford Grey, Ivor Montagu. Based on a play by Henri Kistemaekers. Musical.

April: *FP1*. *pc* Ufa (made in Berlin) *p* Erich Pommer *d* Karl Hartl *sc* Robert Stevenson, Walter Reisch, Kurt Siodmak, Peter Macfarlane. Based on a novel by Kurt Siodmak. Fantasy. German, French and English versions made. Foreign.

May: *The Only Girl* (US title: *Heart Song*). *pc* Ufa (made in Berlin) *p* Erich Pommer *ap* Robert Stevenson, John Heygate *d* Friedrich Hollaender *sc* Robert Stevenson, John Heygate, Walter Reisch, Robert Liebmann, Felix Salten. Musical. German, French and English versions made. Foreign.

June: *Sleeping Car*. *pc* Gaumont (Shepherd's Bush) *p* Michael Balcon *ap* R.B. Wainwright *d* Anatole Litvak *ad* Alfred Junge *md* Louis Levy *sc* Franz Schulz. Comedy.

June: *Waltz Time*. *pc* Gaumont (Shepherd's Bush) *p* Hermann Fellner *d* William [Wilhelm] Thiele *ad* Alfred Junge *md* Louis Levy *sc* A.P. Herbert. Based on an opera by Johann Strauss. Musical.

June: *The Lucky Number*. *pc* Gainsborough (Islington/Welwyn) *p* Ian Dalrymple, Gilbert Gunn *d* Anthony Asquith *ad* Alex Vetchinsky *sc* Franz Schulz, Angus MacPhail, Anthony Asquith, Douglas Furber. Comedy.

July: *It's a Boy*. *pc* Gainsborough (Islington) *p* Michael Balcon *d* Tim Whelan *ad* Alex Vetchinsky *sc* Austin Melford, Leslie Howard Gordon, John Paddy Carstairs. Based on a play by Austin Melford, Franz Arnold, Ernst Bach. Comedy.

July: *Falling for You*. *pc* Gainsborough (Islington) *p* Michael Balcon *d* Jack Hulbert, Robert Stevenson *ad* Alex Vetchinsky *md* Louis Levy *sc* Jack Hulbert, Robert Stevenson, Douglas Furber, Claude Hulbert, Sidney Gilliat. Comedy.

July: *Britannia of Billingsgate*. *pc* Gaumont (Shepherd's Bush) *p* Michael Balcon *d* Sinclair Hill *ad* Alfred Junge *sc* Ralph Stock. Based on a play by Christine Jope-Slade, Sewell Stokes. Musical.

July: *The Prince of Wales*. *pc* Gaumont.

July: *Orders Is Orders*. *pc* Gaumont (Shepherd's Bush) *p* Michael Balcon *d* Walter Forde *ad* Alfred Junge *sc* Sidney Gilliat, Leslie Arliss, James Gleason. Based on a play by Ian Hay, Anthony Armstrong. Comedy.

July: *Early to Bed*. *pc* Ufa (made in Berlin) *p* Erich Pommer *d* Ludwig Berger *sc* Robert Stevenson, Hans Szekely, Robert Liebmann. Musical. German, French and English versions made. Foreign.

August: *The Ghoul*. *pc* Gaumont (Shepherd's Bush) *p* Michael Balcon *d* T. Hayes Hunter *ad* Alfred Junge *md* Louis Levy *sc* L. DuGarde Peach, Roland Pertwee, John Hastings Turner, Frank King, Leonard Hines. Based on a novel by Frank King. Horror.

August: *I Was a Spy*. *pc* Gaumont (Welwyn/ Shepherd's Bush) *p* Michael Balcon *d* Victor Saville *ad* Alfred Junge *sc* W.P. Lipscomb, Ian Hay. Based on a book by Marthe McKenna. War.

September: *The Fire Raisers*. *pc* Gaumont *p* Michael Balcon *d* Michael Powell *ad* Alfred Junge *sc* Michael Powell, Jerome Jackson. Crime.

September: *Just Smith*. *pc* Gaumont (Shepherd's Bush) *p* Michael Balcon *d* Tom Walls *ad* Alfred Junge *sc* J.O.C. Orton. Based on a play by Frederick Lonsdale. Comedy.

October: *Channel Crossing*. *pc* Gaumont (Shepherd's Bush) *p* Ian Dalrymple, Angus MacPhail *d* Milton Rosmer *ad* Alfred Junge *sc* W.P. Lipscomb, Angus MacPhail, Cyril Campion. Drama.

October: *A Cuckoo in the Nest*. *pc* Gaumont (Shepherd's Bush) *p* Ian Dalrymple, Angus MacPhail *d* Tom Walls *ad* Alfred Junge *sc* A.R. Rawlinson, Ben Travers. Based on a play by Ben Travers. Comedy.

November: *Friday the Thirteenth*. *pc* Gainsborough (Islington) *p* Ian Dalrymple, Angus MacPhail *d* Victor Saville *ad* Alfred Junge, Alex Vetchinsky *md* Louis Levy *sc* G. H. Moresby-White, Emlyn Williams, Sidney Gilliat. Drama.

December: *The Constant Nymph*. *pc* Gaumont (Shepherd's Bush) *p* Michael Balcon *d* Basil Dean *ad* Alfred Junge *sc* Basil Dean, Margaret Kennedy, Dorothy Farnum. Based on a play by Margaret Kennedy, Basil Dean. Romance.

December: *Aunt Sally* (US title: *Along Came Sally*). *pc* Gainsborough (Islington) *p* Michael Balcon *d* Tim Whelan *ad* Alex Vetchinsky *sc* Austin Melford, Guy Bolton, A.R. Rawlinson, Tim Whelan. Musical.

December: *Turkey Time*. *pc* Gaumont (Shepherd's Bush) *p* Michael Balcon *d* Tom Walls *ad* Alfred Junge *sc* Ben Travers. Based on a play by Ben Travers. Comedy.

1934

February: *Jack Ahoy!* *pc* Gaumont (Shepherd's Bush) *p* Michael Balcon *d* Walter Forde *ad* Alfred Junge *sc* Sidney Gilliat, J.O.C. Orton, Jack Hulbert, Leslie Arliss, Gerald Fairlie, Austin Melford. Comedy.

February: *The Night of the Party* (US title: *Murder Party*). *pc* Gaumont (Shepherd's Bush) *p* Jerome Jackson *d* Michael Powell *ad* Alfred Junge *sc* Ralph Smart. Based on a play by Roland Pertwee, John Hastings Turner. Crime.

February: *Red Ensign* (US title: *Strike!*). *pc* Gaumont (Shepherd's Bush) *p* Jerome Jackson *d* Michael Powell *ad* Alfred Junge *sc* Michael Powell, Jerome Jackson, L. DuGarde Peach. Drama.

February: *Waltzes from Vienna* (US title: *Strauss's Great Waltz*). *pc* Tom Arnold (Shepherd's Bush) *p* Tom Arnold *d* Alfred Hitchcock *ad* Oscar Werndorff *md* Louis Levy *sc* Guy Bolton, Alma Reville. Based on a play by Heinz Reichert, Ernst Marischka, A.M. Willner. Musical.

March: *Unfinished Symphony* (US title: *Lover Divine*). *pc* Cine-Allianz (made in Vienna) *p* Arnold Pressburger *d* Willi Forst, Anthony Asquith *sc* Walter Reisch, Willi Forst, Benn W. Levy. Musical. German and English versions made. Foreign.

March: *The Battle* (US title: *Thunder in the East*). *pc* Lianofilm (made in France) *p* Leon Garganoff *d* Nicholas Farkas *sc* Robert Stevenson, Bernard Zimmer, Nicholas Farkas. Based on a novel

by Claude Farrere. War. French and English versions made.
Foreign.

March: *Man of Aran* (French title: *L'Homme d'Aran*; German title:
Die Männer von Aran). *pc* Gainsborough *p* Michael Balcon
d Robert J. Flaherty *sc* Robert J. Flaherty, Frances Flaherty.
Drama.

April: *Princess Charming*. *pc* Gainsborough (Islington) *p* Michael
Balcon *d* Maurice Elvey *ad* Ernö Metzner *md* Louis Levy
sc L. DuGarde Peach, Arthur Wimperis, Laurie Wylie, Robert
Edmunds. Based on a play by F. Martos. Musical.

April: *Evergreen* (German title: *Sensation in London*). *pc* Gaumont
(Shepherd's Bush) *p* Michael Balcon *d* Victor Saville *ad* Alfred
Junge, Peter Proud *md* Louis Levy *sc* Marjorie Gaffney, Emlyn
Williams. Based on a play by Benn W. Levy. Musical.

May: *A Cup of Kindness*. *pc* Gaumont (Shepherd's Bush) *p* Michael
Balcon *d* Tom Walls *ad* Alfred Junge *md* Louis Levy *sc* Ben
Travers. Based on a play by Ben Travers. Comedy.

May: *Wild Boy*. *pc* Gainsborough (Shepherd's Bush) *p* Michael Balcon
d Albert de Courville *sc* Stafford Dickens, Albert de Courville, J.
E. Bradford. Sport.

July: *Chu-Chin-Chow*. *pc* Gainsborough (Islington/Shepherd's Bush)
p Michael Balcon *ap* Philip Samuel *d* Walter Forde *ad* Ernö
Metzner *md* Louis Levy *sc* L. DuGarde Peach, Sidney Gilliat,
Edward Knoblock. Based on a play by Oscar Asche, Frederick
Norton. Musical.

Wings over Everest. *pc* Gaumont (Shepherd's Bush) *p* Michael
Balcon *ap* Ivor Montagu *sc* Geoffrey Barkas, Ivor Montagu.
Featurette.

August: *My Song for You*. *pc* Gaumont (Shepherd's Bush) *p* Jerome
Jackson *d* Maurice Elvey *ad* Alfred Junge *md* Louis Levy
sc Richard Benson, Ernst Marischka, Irma von Cube, Austin
Melford, Robert Edmunds. Drama. Remake of the German film
Ein Lied für dich (1933): *pc* Cine-Allianz *d* Joe May (French and
Italian versions of the original were also made). Foreign.

August: *Little Friend*. *pc* Gaumont (Shepherd's Bush) *ap* Robert
Stevenson *d* Berthold Viertel *ad* Alfred Junge *sc* Margaret
Kennedy, Christopher Isherwood, Berthold Viertel. Based on a
novel by Ernst Lothar. Drama.

October: *Evensong*. *pc* Gaumont (Shepherd's Bush) *p* Michael Balcon
d Victor Saville *ad* Alfred Junge *md* Louis Levy *sc* Edward

Knoblock, Dorothy Farnum. Based on a novel by Beverley
Nichols and a play by Edward Knoblock. Musical.

October: *My Old Dutch*. *pc* Gainsborough (Islington) *p* Michael
Balcon *ap* Ivor Montagu *d* Sinclair Hill *sc* Marjorie Gaffney,
Leslie Arliss, Michael Hogan, Bryan Wallace, Mary Murillo,
Arthur Shirley, Albert Chevalier. Drama.

October: *The Camels Are Coming*. *pc* Gainsborough (Islington)
p Michael Balcon *ap* Robert Stevenson *d* Tim Whelan *ad* Oscar
Werndorff *md* Louis Levy *sc* Guy Bolton, Tim Whelan, Russell
Medcraft, W.P. Lipscomb, Jack Hulbert. Comedy.

October: *Jew Süss* (French title: *Le Juif Suss*). *pc* Gaumont (Shepherd's
Bush/Islington) *p* Michael Balcon *d* Lothar Mendes *ad* Alfred
Junge *md* Louis Levy *sc* A.R. Rawlinson, Dorothy Farnum.
Based on a novel by Leon Feuchtwangler. Drama.

December: *My Heart Is Calling*. *pc* Cine-Allianz (Beaconsfield)
p Arnold Pressburger *ap* Ivor Montagu *d* Carmine Gallone
ad John Harman, Norman Arnold *md* Louis Levy *sc* Richard
Benson, Sidney Gilliat, Robert Edmunds, Ernst Marischka.
Musical. Remake of the German film *Mein Herz ruft nach dir*
(1934): *pc* Cine-Allianz *d* Carmine Gallone (French and Italian
versions of the original were also made). Foreign.

December: *Lady in Danger*. *pc* Gaumont (Shepherd's Bush) *p* Michael
Balcon *d* Tom Walls *ad* Alfred Junge *md* Louis Levy *sc* Ben
Travers. Based on a play by Ben Travers. Comedy.

December: *Road House*. *pc* Gaumont (Shepherd's Bush) *p* Michael Balcon
d Maurice Elvey *ad* Alfred Junge *md* Louis Levy *sc* Leslie Arliss,
Austin Melford. Based on a play by Walter Hackett. Musical.

December: *The Man Who Knew Too Much* (French title: *L'Homme qui
en savait trop*). *pc* Gaumont (Shepherd's Bush) *p* Ivor Montagu
d Alfred Hitchcock *ad* Alfred Junge, Peter Proud *md* Louis Levy
sc Edwin Greenwood, A.R. Rawlinson, Emlyn Williams, Charles
Bennett, D.B. Wyndham-Lewis. Crime.

December: *Dirty Work*. *pc* Gaumont (Shepherd's Bush) *p* Michael
Balcon *d* Tom Walls *ad* Alfred Junge *md* Louis Levy *sc* Ben
Travers. Based on a play by Ben Travers. Comedy.

December: *Temptation*. *pc* Milo (made in France) *d* Max Neufeld. Based
on a play by Melchior Lengyel. Musical. French and English
versions made. Remake of *Antonia, romance Hongroise*. Foreign.

1935

January: *The Iron Duke*. *pc* Gaumont (Shepherd's Bush/Shepperton/Islington) *p* Michael Balcon *d* Victor Saville *ad* Alfred Junge *md* Louis Levy *sc* H.M. Harwood, Bess Meredyth. History.

January: *Things Are Looking Up*. *pc* Gaumont (Shepherd's Bush) *p* Michael Balcon *d* Albert de Courville *sc* Stafford Dickens, Con West, Albert de Courville, Daisy Fisher. Comedy.

January: *The Phantom Light*. *pc* Gainsborough (Islington) *p* Jerome Jackson *d* Michael Powell *ad* Alex Vetchinsky *md* Louis Levy *sc* Austin Melford, Ralph Smart. Based on a play by Evadne Price, Joan Roy Byford. Crime.

February: *Oh Daddy!* *pc* Gainsborough (Islington) *p* Michael Balcon *d* Graham Cutts, Austin Melford *sc* Austin Melford. Based on a play by Austin Melford. Comedy.

March: *Fighting Stock*. *pc* Gainsborough (Islington) *p* Michael Balcon *d* Tom Walls *ad* Oscar Werndorff *md* Louis Levy *sc* Ben Travers. Comedy.

May: *Heat Wave*. *pc* Gainsborough (Islington) *p* Jerome Jackson *d* Maurice Elvey *sc* Austin Melford, Leslie Arliss, Jerome Jackson. Based on a story by Austin Melford. Musical.

May: *Bulldog Jack* (US title: *Alias Bulldog Drummond*). *pc* Gaumont (Shepherd's Bush) *p* Michael Balcon *d* Walter Forde *ad* Alfred Junge *md* Louis Levy *sc* Sidney Gilliat, J.O.C. Orton, Jack Hulbert, Gerard Fairlie, H.C. McNeile. Based on characters created by H.C. McNeile. Comedy.

May: *Forever England* (US title: *Born for Glory*). *pc* Gaumont (Shepherd's Bush) *p* Michael Balcon *d* Walter Forde, Anthony Asquith *ad* Alfred Junge *sc* J.O.C. Orton, Michael Hogan, Gerard Fairlie. Based on a novel by C.S. Forester. War.

June: *The 39 Steps* (German title: *Die 39 Stufen*). *pc* Gaumont (Shepherd's Bush) *ap* Ivor Montagu *d* Alfred Hitchcock *ad* Oscar Werndorff, Albert Jullion *md* Louis Levy *sc* Alma Reville, Charles Bennett, Ian Hay. Based on a novel by John Buchan. Crime.

June: *The Divine Spark* (German title: *Maddalena*). *pc* Alleanza Cinematografica Italiana (made in Rome) *p* Arnold Pressburger *d* Carmine Gallone *sc* Emlyn Williams, Richard Benson, Walter Reisch. Musical. Italian and English versions made. Foreign.

August: *The Clairvoyant* (US title: *The Evil Mind*). *pc* Gainsborough (Islington) *p* Michael Balcon *d* Maurice Elvey *ad* Alfred Junge *md* Louis Levy *sc* Charles Bennett, Robert Edmunds, Bryan Wallace. Based on a novel by Ernst Lothar. Drama.

August: *Me and Marlborough*. *pc* Gaumont (Shepherd's Bush) *p* Michael Balcon *d* Victor Saville *ad* Alfred Junge *md* Louis Levy *sc* Marjorie Gaffney, Ian Hay, W.P. Lipscomb, Reginald Pound. Comedy.

August: *Stormy Weather*. *pc* Gainsborough (Islington) *p* Michael Balcon *d* Tom Walls *ad* Alex Vetchinsky *md* Louis Levy *sc* Ben Travers Based on a play by Ben Travers. Comedy.

August: *Boys Will Be Boys*. *pc* Gainsborough (Islington) *p* Michael Balcon *d* William Beaudine *ad* Alex Vetchinsky *md* Louis Levy *sc* Will Hay, Robert Edmunds. Based on characters created by J.B. Morton. Comedy.

September: *Car of Dreams*. *pc* Gaumont (Shepherd's Bush) *p* Michael Balcon *d* Graham Cutts, Austin Melford *ad* Alfred Junge *md* Louis Levy *sc* Austin Melford, Stafford Dickens, Richard Benson. Musical. Remake of the Hungarian film *Meseauto* (1934): *pc* Reflektor *d* Bela Gaal.

September: *The Passing of the Third Floor Back*. *pc* Gaumont (Shepherd's Bush) *p* Ivor Montagu *d* Berthold Viertel *md* Louis Levy *sc* Alma Reville, Michael Hogan. Based on a play by Jerome K. Jerome. Fantasy.

October: *The Guv'nor* (US title: *Mr Hobo*). *pc* Gaumont (Shepherd's Bush) *p* Michael Balcon *ap* S.C. Balcon *d* Milton Rosmer *ad* Alfred Junge *sc* Guy Bolton, Maude Howell, Paul Lafitte. Comedy. Remake of the French film *Rothschild* (1933): *pc* E.R. Escalmel *d* Marco de Gastyne.

November: *First a Girl*. *pc* Gaumont (Shepherd's Bush) *p* Michael Balcon *ap* S.C. Balcon *d* Victor Saville *ad* Oscar Werndorff *md* Louis Levy *sc* Marjorie Gaffney. Based on a play by Reinhold Schunzel. Musical. Remake of the German film *Viktor und Viktoria* (1933): *pc* Ufa *d* Reinhold Schünzel (a French version of the original, *Georges et Georgette*, was also made).

November: *The Tunnel* (US title: *Transatlantic Tunnel*). *pc* Gaumont (Shepherd's Bush) *p* Michael Balcon *ap* S.C. Balcon *d* Maurice Elvey *ad* Ernö Metzner *md* Louis Levy *sc* L. DuGarde Peach, Clemence Dane, Kurt Siodmak. Based on a novel by Bernhard Kellerman. Fantasy. Remake of the German film *Der Tunnel* (1933): *pc* Vandor *d* Kurt Bernhardt (a French version of the original was also made).

December: *Foreign Affairs*. *pc* Gainsborough (Islington) *p* Michael
Balcon *d* Tom Walls *ad* Alex Vetchinsky *md* Louis Levy *sc* Ben
Travers. Comedy.

1936

January: *King of the Damned*. *pc* Gaumont (Shepherd's Bush)
p Michael Balcon *d* Walter Forde *ad* Oscar Werndorff *md* Louis
Levy *sc* Charles Bennett, Sidney Gilliat, A.R. Rawlinson. Based
on a play by John Chancellor. Crime.
February: *Jack of All Trades* (US title: *The Two of Us*).
pc Gainsborough (Islington) *p* Michael Balcon *d* Jack Hulbert,
Robert Stevenson *ad* Alex Vetchinsky *md* Louis Levy *sc* Jack
Hulbert, Austin Melford, J.O.C. Orton. Based on a play by Paul
Vulpuis. Musical.
March: *First Offence*. *pc* Gainsborough (Islington) *p* Michael Balcon
d Herbert Mason *ad* Walter Murton *md* Louis Levy *sc* Austin
Melford, Stafford Dickens. Crime. Remake of the French film
Mauvaise graine (1934): *pc* CNC *d* Billy Wilder, Alexander
Esway.
March: *Rhodes of Africa* (US title: *Rhodes*). *pc* Gaumont (Shepherd's
Bush) *p* Michael Balcon *d* Berthold Viertel, Geoffrey Barkas
ad Oscar Werndorff *md* Louis Levy *sc* Leslie Arliss, Miles
Malleson, Michael Barringer. Based on a book by Sarah Gertrude
Millin. History.
April: *Pot Luck*. *pc* Gainsborough (Islington) *p* Michael Balcon *d* Tom
Walls *ad* Walter Murton *md* Louis Levy *sc* Ben Travers. Comedy.
May: *Tudor Rose* (US title: *Nine Days a Queen*). *pc* Gainsborough
(Islington) *p* Michael Balcon *ap* Edward Black, Sidney Gilliat
d Robert Stevenson *ad* Alex Vetchinsky *md* Louis Levy *sc* Miles
Malleson, Robert Stevenson. History.
May: *It's Love Again*. *pc* Gaumont (Shepherd's Bush) *p* Michael
Balcon *d* Victor Saville *ad* Alfred Junge *md* Louis Levy *sc* Marian
Dix, Austin Melford, Lesser Samuels. Musical.
May: *The Secret Agent*. *pc* Gaumont (Shepherd's Bush) *p* Ivor
Montagu *d* Alfred Hitchcock *ad* Oscar Werndorff, Albert Jullion
md Louis Levy *sc* Charles Bennett, Ian Hay, Alma Reville, Jesse
Lasky Jr. Based on a play by Campbell Dixon and stories by
W. Somerset Maugham. Crime.
June: *Where There's a Will*. *pc* Gainsborough (Islington) *p* Michael
Balcon *ap* Edward Black, Sidney Gilliat *d* William Beaudine

ad Alex Vetchinsky *md* Louis Levy *sc* Will Hay, William Beaudine, Robert Edmunds, Sidney Gilliat, Leslie Arliss, Ralph Spence. Comedy.

July: *Seven Sinners* (US title: *Doomed Cargo*). *pc* Gaumont (Shepherd's Bush) *p* Michael Balcon *d* Albert de Courville *ad* Ernö Metzner *md* Louis Levy *sc* Sidney Gilliat, Frank Launder, L. DuGarde Peach, Austin Melford. Based on a play by Arnold Ridley, Bernard Merivale. Crime.

August: *Everything Is Thunder*. *pc* Gaumont (Shepherd's Bush) *p* Michael Balcon *ap* S.C. Balcon *d* Milton Rosmer *ad* Alfred Junge *sc* J.O.C. Orton, Marian Dix. Based on a novel by Jocelyn Lee Hardy. War.

September: *East Meets West*. *pc* Gaumont (Shepherd's Bush) *ap* Haworth Bromley *d* Herbert Mason *ad* Oscar Werndorff *md* Louis Levy *sc* Maude Howell. Based on a play by Edwin Greenwood. Drama.

September: *The Man Who Changed His Mind* (French title: *Cerveaux de rechange*; US title: *The Man Who Lived Again*). *pc* Gainsborough (Islington) *p* Michael Balcon *ap* Edward Black, Sidney Gilliat *d* Robert Stevenson *ad* Alex Vetchinsky *md* Louis Levy *sc* John L. Balderston, L. DuGarde Peach, Sidney Gilliat, R.E. Dearing. Horror.

October: *Everybody Dance*. *pc* Gainsborough (Islington) *p* Michael Balcon *ap* Edward Black *d* Charles Reisner *ad* Alex Vetchinsky *md* Louis Levy *sc* Ralph Spence, Stafford Dickens, Leslie Arliss. Musical.

November: *His Lordship* (US title: *Man of Affairs*). *pc* Gaumont (Shepherd's Bush) *ap* S.C. Balcon *d* Herbert Mason *ad* Alfred Junge *sc* L. DuGarde Peach, Edwin Greenwood, Maude Howell. Based on a play by Neil Grant. Drama.

November: *All In*. *pc* Gainsborough (Islington) *p* Michael Balcon *d* Marcel Varnel *sc* Val Guest, Leslie Arliss. Based on a play by Bernard Merivale, Brandon Fleming. Comedy.

November: *Strangers on Honeymoon*. *pc* Gaumont (Shepherd's Bush) *ap* Haworth Bromley *d* Albert de Courville *ad* Ernö Metzner *sc* Ralph Spence, Bryan Edgar Wallace, Sidney Gilliat. Based on a novel by Edgar Wallace. Comedy.

December: *Sabotage* (German title: *Sabotage*; US title: *The Woman Alone*). *pc* Gaumont (Shepherd's Bush) *p* Michael Balcon *ap* Ivor Montagu *d* Alfred Hitchcock *ad* Oscar Werndorff, Albert Jullion *md* Louis Levy *sc* Charles Bennett, Alma Reville, Ian Hay, Helen

Simpson, E.V.H. Emmett. Based on a novel by Joseph Conrad. Crime.

December: *Windbag the Sailor*. *pc* Gainsborough (Islington) *p* Michael Balcon *d* William Beaudine *ad* Alex Vetchinsky, A. Cox *md* Louis Levy *sc* Leslie Arliss, Marriott Edgar, Robert Edmunds, Val Guest. Comedy.

December: *The Flying Doctor*. *pc* Gaumont/National Productions (made in Australia) *d* Miles Mander *ad* Richard Ridgway *sc* Robert Waldron, J.O.C. Orton. Adventure.

1937

January: *OHMS* (US title: *You're in the Army Now*). *pc* Gaumont (Shepherd's Bush) *p* Geoffrey Barkas *d* Raoul Walsh *ad* Edward Carrick *md* Louis Levy *sc* Austin Melford, A.R. Rawlinson, Bryan Wallace, Lesser Samuels, Ralph Gilbert Bettinson. War.

February: *Good Morning, Boys* (US title: *Where There's a Will*). *pc* Gainsborough (Islington) *p* Edward Black *d* Marcel Varnel *ad* Alex Vetchinsky *md* Louis Levy *sc* Leslie Arliss, Anthony Kimmins, Marriott Edgar, Val Guest. Comedy.

February: *Head Over Heels* (US title: *Head Over Heels in Love*). *pc* Gaumont (Shepherd's Bush) *ap* S.C. Balcon *d* Sonnie Hale *ad* Alfred Junge *md* Louis Levy *sc* Marjorie Gaffney, Fred Thompson, Dwight Taylor. Based on a play by François de Croisset. Musical.

February: *The Great Barrier* (US title: *Silent Barriers*). *pc* Gaumont (Shepherd's Bush) *ap* Gunther Stapenhorst *d* Milton Rosmer, Geoffrey Barkas *ad* Walter Murton *md* Louis Levy *sc* Michael Barrington, Milton Rosmer, Ralph Spence. Based on a novel by Alan Sullivan. Adventure.

April: *Okay for Sound*. *pc* Gainsborough (Islington) *p* Edward Black *d* Marcel Varnel *ad* Alex Vetchinsky *md* Louis Levy *sc* Marriott Edgar, Val Guest. Based on a show by R.P. Weston, Bert Lee. Comedy.

May: *Take My Tip*. *pc* Gaumont (Shepherd's Bush) *d* Herbert Mason *ad* Ernö Metzner *md* Louis Levy *sc* Sidney Gilliat, Michael Hogan, Jack Hulbert. Musical.

July: *King Solomon's Mines*. *pc* Gaumont (Shepherd's Bush) *ap* Geoffrey Barkas *d* Robert Stevenson, Geoffrey Barkas *ad* Alfred Junge *sc* A. R. Rawlinson, Charles Bennett, Ralph

Spence, Roland Pertwee, Michael Hogan. Based on a novel by
H. Rider Haggard. Adventure.

July: *Said O'Reilly to McNab* (US title: *Sez O'Reilly to McNab*).
pc Gainsborough (Islington) *p* Edward Black *d* William Beaudine
sc Leslie Arliss, Marriott Edgar, Howard Irving Young. Comedy.

August: *Gangway*. *pc* Gaumont (Pinewood) *d* Sonnie Hale *ad* Alfred
Junge *md* Louis Levy *sc* Dwight Taylor, Lesser Samuels, Sonnie
Hale. Musical.

August: *Dr Syn*. *pc* Gaumont (Islington) *d* Roy William Neill *ad* Alex
Vetchinsky *md* Louis Levy *sc* Michael Hogan, Roger Burford.
Based on a novel by Russell Thorndike. Adventure.

September: *Non-Stop New York*. *pc* Gaumont (Shepherd's Bush)
d Robert Stevenson *ad* Walter Murton *sc* Kurt Siodmak, Roland
Pertwee, E.V.H. Emmett, J.O.C. Orton, Derek Twist. Based on a
novel by Ken Attiwill. Crime.

October: *Oh Mr Porter!* *pc* Gainsborough (Islington) *p* Edward Black
ep Maurice Ostrer *d* Marcel Varnel *ad* Alex Vetchinsky *md* Louis
Levy *sc* Marriott Edgar, Val Guest, Frank Launder, J.O.C. Orton.
Comedy.

November: *Young and Innocent* (US title: *A Girl Was Young*).
pc Gaumont (Shepherd's Bush/Pinewood) *p* Edward Black
d Alfred Hitchcock *ad* Alfred Junge *md* Louis Levy *sc* Charles
Bennett, Edwin Greenwood, Anthony Armstrong, Alma Reville,
Gerald Savory. Based on a novel by Josephine Tey. Crime.

1938

January: *Owd Bob* (US title: *To the Victor*). *pc* Gainsborough
(Islington) *p* Edward Black *d* Robert Stevenson *ad* Alex
Vetchinsky *md* Louis Levy *sc* J.B. Williams, Michael Hogan.
Based on a novel by Alfred Olivant. Drama.

January: *Bank Holiday* (US title: *Three on a Weekend*).
pc Gainsborough (Islington) *p* Edward Black *d* Carol Reed
ad Alex Vetchinsky *md* Louis Levy *sc* Rodney Ackland, Roger
Burford, Hans Wilhelm. Drama.

February: *Sailing Along*. *pc* Gaumont (Pinewood) *d* Sonnie Hale
ad Alfred Junge *md* Louis Levy *sc* Selwyn Jepson, Lesser
Samuels, Sonnie Hale. Musical.

June: *Strange Boarders*. *pc* Gainsborough (Pinewood) *p* Edward Black
d Herbert Mason *ad* Walter Murton *sc* A.R. Rawlinson, Sidney
Gilliat. Based on a novel by E. Phillips Oppenheim. Crime.

June: *Convict 99.* *pc* Gainsborough (Islington) *p* Edward Black *ep* Maurice Ostrer *d* Marcel Varnel *ad* Alex Vetchinsky *md* Louis Levy *sc* Marriott Edgar, Val Guest, Jack Davies, Ralph Smart. Comedy.

July: *Alf's Button Afloat.* *pc* Gainsborough (Islington) *p* Edward Black *d* Marcel Varnel *ad* Alex Vetchinsky *md* Louis Levy *sc* Marriott Edgar, Val Guest, Ralph Smart. Based on a play by W.A. Darlington. Comedy.

September: *The Lady Vanishes* (French title: *Une Femme disparait*). *pc* Gainsborough (Islington) *p* Edward Black *d* Alfred Hitchcock *ad* Alex Vetchinsky, Maurice Carter *md* Louis Levy *sc* Alma Reville, Frank Launder, Sidney Gilliat. Based on a novel by Ethel Lina White. Crime.

October: *Hey! Hey! USA.* *pc* Gainsborough (Islington) *p* Edward Black *d* Marcel Varnel *ad* Alex Vetchinsky, Albert Jullion *md* Louis Levy *sc* Marriott Edgar, Val Guest, J.O.C. Orton, Howard Irving Young, Ralph Spence, Jack Swain. Comedy.

October: *Crackerjack* (US title: *The Man with a Hundred Faces*). *pc* Gainsborough (Pinewood) *p* Edward Black *d* Albert de Courville *sc* A.R. Rawlinson, Michael Pertwee, Basil Mason. Based on a novel by W.B. Ferguson. Comedy.

December: *Climbing High.* *pc* Gaumont (Pinewood) *d* Carol Reed *ad* Alfred Junge *md* Louis Levy *sc* Lesser Samuels, Marian Dix, Stephen Clarkson. Comedy.

December: *Old Bones of the River.* *pc* Gainsborough (Islington/Shepherd's Bush) *p* Edward Black *d* Marcel Varnel *ad* Alex Vetchinsky *md* Louis Levy *sc* Marriott Edgar, Val Guest, J.O.C. Orton. Based on novels by Edgar Wallace. Comedy.

1939

May: *Ask a Policeman.* *pc* Gainsborough (Islington/Shepperton) *p* Edward Black *ep* Maurice Ostrer *d* Marcel Varnel *sc* Val Guest, Marriott Edgar, Sidney Gilliat, J.O.C. Orton. Comedy.

May: *A Girl Must Live.* *pc* Gainsborough/Twentieth Century (Islington) *p* Edward Black *d* Carol Reed *ad* Alex Vetchinsky *md* Louis Levy *sc* Frank Launder, Austin Melford, Michael Pertwee. Based on a novel by Emery Bonnett. Comedy.

August: *Where's That Fire?* *pc* Twentieth Century (Islington) *p* Edward Black *d* Marcel Varnel *sc* Maurice Braddell, Marriott Edgar, Val Guest, J.O.C. Orton. Comedy.

November: *The Frozen Limits. pc* Gainsborough (Islington) *p* Edward
Black *ep* Maurice Ostrer *d* Marcel Varnel *ad* Alex Vetchinsky *md*
Louis Levy *sc* Val Guest, Marriott Edgar, J.O.C. Orton. Comedy.

November: *Inspector Hornleigh on Holiday. pc* Twentieth Century
(Islington) *p* Edward Black *ep* Maurice Ostrer *d* Walter Forde
ad Alex Vetchinsky *md* Louis Levy *sc* Hans W. Priwin, Frank
Launder, Sidney Gilliat, J.O.C. Orton. Based on a novel by Leo
Grex. Crime.

1940

January: *Band Waggon. pc* Gainsborough (Islington/Shepherd's Bush)
p Edward Black *d* Marcel Varnel *sc* Val Guest, Marriott Edgar,
Robert Edmunds, J.O.C. Orton. Musical.

February: *They Came by Night. pc* Twentieth Century (Islington)
p Edward Black *d* Harry Lachman *sc* Michael Hogan, Roland
Pertwee, Frank Launder, Sidney Gilliat. Based on a play by Barre
Lyndon. Crime.

April: *For Freedom. pc* Gainsborough (Shepherd's Bush) *p* Edward
Black, Castleton Knight *d* Maurice Elvey *sc* Miles Malleson,
Leslie Arliss, Castleton Knight. War.

April: *Charley's (Big-Hearted) Aunt. pc* Gainsborough (Shepherd's
Bush) *p* Edward Black *d* Walter Forde *ad* Alex Vetchinsky
md Louis Levy *sc* Val Guest, Ralph Smart, J.O.C. Orton. Based
on a play by Brandon Thomas. Comedy.

May: *Night Train to Munich. pc* Twentieth Century (Shepherd's Bush)
p Edward Black *ep* Maurice Ostrer *d* Carol Reed *ad* Alex
Vetchinsky *md* Louis Levy *sc* Frank Launder, Sidney Gilliat.
Based on a novel by Gordon Wellesley. War.

August: *The Girl in the News. pc* Twentieth Century (Shepherd's Bush)
p Edward Black *ep* Maurice Ostrer *d* Carol Reed *ad* Alex
Vetchinsky *md* Louis Levy *sc* Frank Launder, Sidney Gilliat.
Based on a novel by Roy Vickers. Crime.

November: *Gasbags. pc* Gainsborough (Shepherd's Bush) *p* Edward
Black *d* Marcel Varnel *sc* Val Guest, Marriott Edgar, Val
Valentine, Ralph Spence. Comedy.

November: *Neutral Port. pc* Gainsborough (Shepherd's Bush)
p Edward Black *d* Marcel Varnel *sc* J.B. Williams, T.J. Morrison.
War.

1941

March: *The Ghost Train. pc* Gainsborough (Shepherd's Bush) *p* Edward Black *ep* Maurice Ostrer *d* Walter Forde *ad* Alex Vetchinsky *md* Louis Levy *sc* Val Guest, Marriott Edgar, J.O.C. Orton, Sidney Gilliat. Based on a play by Arnold Ridley. Comedy.

March: *Mr Proudfoot Shows a Light. pc* Twentieth Century *p* Edward Black *d* Herbert Mason *sc* Sidney Gilliat. Comedy.

March: *Inspector Hornleigh Goes to It* (US title: *Mail Train*). *pc* Twentieth Century (Shepherd's Bush) *p* Edward Black *ep* Maurice Ostrer *d* Walter Forde *ad* Alex Vetchinsky *md* Louis Levy *sc* Hans W. Priwin, Val Guest, Frank Launder, Sidney Gilliat, J.O.C. Orton. Crime.

March: *Kipps* (US title: *The Remarkable Mr Kipps*). *pc* Twentieth Century (Shepherd's Bush) *p* Edward Black *ep* Maurice Ostrer *d* Carol Reed *ad* Alex Vetchinsky *md* Louis Levy *sc* Frank Launder, Sidney Gilliat. Based on a novel by H.G. Wells. Comedy.

June: *Once a Crook. pc* Twentieth Century (Shepherd's Bush) *p* Edward Black *d* Herbert Mason *sc* Roger Burford. Based on a play by Evadne Price, Ken Attiwill. Crime.

August: *Cottage to Let* (US title: *Bombsight Stolen*). *pc* Gainsborough (Shepherd's Bush) *p* Edward Black *d* Anthony Asquith *ad* Alex Vetchinsky *md* Louis Levy *sc* Anatole de Grunwald, J.O.C. Orton. Based on a play by Geoffrey Kerr. Crime.

September: *I Thank You. pc* Gainsborough (Shepherd's Bush) *p* Edward Black *d* Marcel Varnel *sc* Howard Irving Young, Val Guest, Marriott Edgar. Comedy.

December: *Hi, Gang! pc* Gainsborough (Shepherd's Bush) *p* Edward Black *d* Marcel Varnel *sc* Howard Irving Young, Val Guest, Marriott Edgar, J.O.C. Orton. Musical.

December: *Rush Hour. pc* Twentieth Century (Shepherd's Bush) *p* Edward Black *d* Anthony Asquith *sc* Arthur Boys, Rodney Ackland. Comedy.

1942

April: *Back Room Boy. pc* Gainsborough (Shepherd's Bush) *p* Edward Black *d* Herbert Mason *sc* Val Guest, Marriott Edgar, J.O.C. Orton. Comedy.

June: *The Young Mr Pitt* (French title: *Le jeune M. Pitt*). *pc* Twentieth Century (Shepherd's Bush) *p* Edward Black *ep* Maurice Ostrer *d* Carol Reed *ad* Alex Vetchinsky *md* Louis Levy *sc* Frank Launder, Sidney Gilliat, Rt Hon Viscount Castleross. History.

June: *Partners in Crime*. *pc* Gainsborough (Shepherd's Bush) *p* Edward Black *d* Frank Launder, Sidney Gilliat *sc* Frank Launder, Sidney Gilliat. Comedy.

July: *Uncensored*. *pc* Gainsborough (Shepherd's Bush) *p* Edward Black *d* Anthony Asquith *ad* Alex Vetchinsky *md* Louis Levy *sc* Wolfgang Wilhelm, Terence Rattigan, Rodney Ackland. Based on a novel by Oscar Millard. War.

August: *The Nose Has It*. *pc* Gainsborough *p* Edward Black *d* Val Guest *sc* Val Guest. Comedy.

December: *King Arthur Was a Gentleman*. *pc* Gainsborough (Shepherd's Bush) *p* Edward Black *d* Marcel Varnel *sc* Val Guest, Marriott Edgar. Comedy.

A Letter from Home. *pc* Twentieth Century *p* Edward Black *d* Carol Reed. Short.

1943

February: *It's That Man Again*. *pc* Gainsborough (Shepherd's Bush) *p* Edward Black *ep* Maurice Ostrer *d* Walter Forde *ad* Walter Murton, John Bryan *md* Louis Levy *sc* Howard Irving Young, Ted Kavanagh. Based on the Tommy Handley radio series. Comedy.

April: *We Dive at Dawn*. *pc* Gainsborough (Shepherd's Bush) *p* Edward Black *d* Anthony Asquith *ad* Walter Murton *sc* J.B. Williams, Val Valentine, Frank Launder. War.

May: *Miss London Ltd*. *pc* Gainsborough *p* Edward Black *d* Val Guest *ad* Maurice Carter *sc* Val Guest, Marriott Edgar. Musical.

July: *The Man in Grey* (French title: *L'Homme en gris*). *pc* Gainsborough (Shepherd's Bush) *p* Edward Black *ep* Maurice Ostrer *d* Leslie Arliss *ad* Walter Murton *md* Louis Levy *sc* Margaret Kennedy, Leslie Arliss, Doreen Montgomery. Based on a novel by Lady Eleanor Smith. Romance.

August: *Dear Octopus* (US title: *The Randolph Family*). *pc* Gainsborough (Shepherd's Bush) *p* Edward Black *d* Harold French *ad* Maurice Carter *sc* R. J. Minney, Patrick Kirwan. Based on a play by Dodie Smith. Romance.

September: *Millions Like Us* (French title: *Ceux de chez nous*). *pc* Gainsborough (Shepherd's Bush) *p* Edward Black *ep* Maurice Ostrer *d* Frank Launder, Sidney Gilliat *ad* John Bryan *md* Louis Levy *sc* Frank Launder, Sidney Gilliat. War.

1944

February: *Time Flies*. *pc* Gainsborough (Shepherd's Bush) *p* Edward Black *ep* Maurice Ostrer *d* Walter Forde *ad* John Bryan *md* Louis Levy *sc* Howard Irving Young, J.O.C. Orton, Ted Kavanagh. Comedy.

March: *Bees in Paradise*. *pc* Gainsborough (Shepherd's Bush) *p* Edward Black *d* Val Guest *ad* Maurice Carter *sc* Val Guest, Marriott Edgar. Musical.

May: *Fanny by Gaslight* (US title: *Man of Evil*). *pc* Gainsborough (Shepherd's Bush) *p* Edward Black *ep* Maurice Ostrer *d* Anthony Asquith *ad* John Bryan *md* Louis Levy *sc* Doreen Montgomery, Aimee Stuart. Based on a novel by Michael Sadleir. Romance.

May: *Victory Wedding*. *pc* Gainsborough (Shepherd's Bush) *p* Maurice Ostrer *d* Jessie Matthews *sc* Doreen Montgomery. Romance.

July: *Give Us the Moon*. *pc* Gainsborough (Shepherd's Bush) *p* Edward Black *d* Val Guest *sc* Val Guest. Based on a novel by Caryl Brahms, S.J. Simon. Comedy.

August: *2000 Women* (French title: *Deux milles femmes*). *pc* Gainsborough (Shepherd's Bush/Islington) *p* Edward Black *ep* Maurice Ostrer *d* Frank Launder *ad* John Bryan *md* Louis Levy *sc* Frank Launder, Sidney Gilliat. War.

October: *Love Story* (US title: *A Lady Surrenders*). *pc* Gainsborough (Shepherd's Bush) *p* Harold Huth *ep* Maurice Ostrer *d* Leslie Arliss *ad* John Bryan *md* Louis Levy *sc* Doreen Montgomery, Leslie Arliss, Rodney Ackland. Based on a novel by J.W. Drawbell. Romance.

December: *Madonna of the Seven Moons*. *pc* Gainsborough (Shepherd's Bush) *p* R.J. Minney *ep* Maurice Ostrer *d* Arthur Crabtree *ad* Andrew Mazzei *md* Louis Levy *sc* Roland Pertwee, Brock Williams. Based on a novel by Margery Lawrence. Romance.

1945

January: *Waterloo Road*. *pc* Gainsborough (Shepherd's Bush)
   p Edward Black *ep* Maurice Ostrer *d* Sidney Gilliat *ad* Alex
   Vetchinsky *md* Louis Levy *sc* Sidney Gilliat, Val Valentine.
   Drama.

March: *A Place of One's Own* (French title: *Le Medaillon fatal*).
   pc Gainsborough (Shepherd's Bush) *p* R. J. Minney *ep* Maurice
   Ostrer *d* Bernard Knowles *ad* John Elphick *md* Louis Levy
   sc Brock Williams, Osbert Sitwell. Based on a novel by Osbert
   Sitwell. Fantasy.

April: *They Were Sisters*. *pc* Gainsborough (Shepherd's Bush) *p* Harold
   Huth *ep* Maurice Ostrer *d* Arthur Crabtree *ad* David Rawnsley
   md Louis Levy *sc* Roland Pertwee, Katherine Strueby. Based on a
   novel by Dorothy Whipple. Romance.

June: *I'll Be Your Sweetheart*. *pc* Gainsborough (Shepherd's Bush)
   p Louis Levy *d* Val Guest *sc* Val Valentine, Val Guest. Musical.

October: *The Seventh Veil*. *pc* Theatrecraft/Ortus (Riverside) *p* John
   Sutro, Sydney Box *d* Compton Bennett *ad* James Carter *md* Muir
   Mathieson *sc* Muriel Box, Sydney Box. Romance.

December: *The Wicked Lady* (French title: *La Masque aux yeux verts*).
   pc Gainsborough (Shepherd's Bush) *p* R. J. Minney *d* Leslie
   Arliss *ad* John Bryan *md* Louis Levy *sc* Leslie Arliss, Gordon
   Glennon, Aimee Stuart. Based on a novel by Magdalen King-
   Hall. Crime.

1946

April: *Caravan*. *pc* Gainsborough (Shepherd's Bush) *p* Harold Huth *ep*
   Maurice Ostrer *d* Arthur Crabtree *ad* John Bryan *md* Louis Levy
   sc Roland Pertwee. Based on a novel by Lady Eleanor Smith.
   Romance.

June: *Bedelia*. *pc* John Corfield (Ealing) *p* Isadore Goldsmith *d* Lance
   Comfort *ad* Duncan Sutherland *md* Ernest Irving *sc* Vera
   Caspary, Moie Charles, Isadore Goldsmith, Herbert Victor, Roy
   Ridley. Based on a novel by Vera Caspary. Crime.

June: *The Years Between*. *pc* Sydney Box (Riverside) *d* Compton
   Bennett *sc* Muriel Box, Sydney Box. Based on a play by Daphne
   du Maurier. Drama.

October: *The Magic Bow*. *pc* Gainsborough (Shepherd's Bush)
   p R.J. Minney *ep* Maurice Ostrer *d* Bernard Knowles *ad* Andrew

Mazzei *md* Louis Levy *sc* Roland Pertwee, Norman Ginsbury. Based on a novel by Manuel Komroff. Musical.

December: *Daybreak*. *pc* Triton (Riverside) *p* Sydney Box *d* Compton Bennett *ad* James Carter *md* Muir Mathieson *sc* Muriel Box, Sydney Box. Based on a play by Monckton Hoffe. Crime.

1947

February: *The Root of All Evil*. *pc* Gainsborough (Shepherd's Bush) *p* Harold Huth *ep* Maurice Ostrer *d* Brock Williams *ad* Maurice Carter *md* Louis Levy *sc* Brock Williams. Based on a novel by J.S. Fletcher. Drama.

April: *The Man Within* (US title: *The Smugglers*). *pc* Production Film Services (Shepherd's Bush) *p* Muriel Box, Sydney Box *d* Bernard Knowles *ad* Andrew Mazzei *sc* Muriel Box, Sydney Box. Based on a novel by Graham Greene. Adventure.

May: *The Brothers*. *pc* Triton (Shepherd's Bush) *p* Sydney Box *d* David MacDonald *ad* George Provis *md* Muir Mathieson *sc* Muriel Box, Sydney Box, Paul Vincent Carroll, David MacDonald. Based on a novel by L.A.G. Strong. Drama.

June: *Dear Murderer*. *pc* Gainsborough (Shepherd's Bush) *p* Betty Box *d* Arthur Crabtree *ad* George Provis, John Elphick *sc* Muriel Box, Sydney Box, Peter Rogers. Based on a play by St John Legh Clowes. Crime.

June: *The Upturned Glass*. *pc* Triton (Riverside) *p* Sydney Box, James Mason *d* Lawrence Huntington *ad* Andrew Mazzei *md* Muir Mathieson *sc* Jon P. Monaghan, Pamela Kellino. Crime.

August: *Holiday Camp*. *pc* Gainsborough (Shepherd's Bush) *p* Sydney Box *d* Ken Annakin *ad* George Provis, A.R. Yarrow *sc* Muriel Box, Sydney Box, Peter Rogers, Godfrey Winn, Ted Willis, Mabel and Denis Constanduros. Comedy.

August: *Jassy*. *pc* Gainsborough (Shepherd's Bush) *p* Sydney Box *d* Bernard Knowles *ad* George Provis, Maurice Carter *md* Louis Levy *sc* Dorothy and Campbell Christie, Geoffrey Kerr. Based on a novel by Norah Lofts. Romance.

November: *When the Bough Breaks*. *pc* Gainsborough (Shepherd's Bush) *p* Betty Box *d* Lawrence Huntington *ad* George Provis, John Elphick *sc* Muriel Box, Sydney Box, Peter Rogers, Moie Charles, Herbert Victor. Drama.

1948

January: *Easy Money*. *pc* Gainsborough (Shepherd's Bush) *p* A. Frank Bundy *d* Bernard Knowles *ad* George Provis, Cedric Dawe *sc* Muriel Box, Sydney Box . Based on a play by Arnold Ridley. Drama.

February: *Idol of Paris*. *pc* Premier *p* R.J. Minney *d* Leslie Arliss *ad* Albert Jullion *sc* Norman Lee, Stafford Dickens, Harry Ostrer. Based on a novel by Alfred Schirokauer. Drama.

March: *Snowbound*. *pc* Gainsborough (Shepherd's Bush) *p* Aubrey Baring *d* David MacDonald *ad* George Provis, Maurice Carter *sc* David Evans, Keith Campbell. Based on a novel by Hammond Innes. Adventure.

April: *Miranda*. *pc* Gainsborough (Islington) *p* Betty Box *d* Ken Annakin *sc* Peter Blackmore, Denis Waldock. Based on a play by Peter Blackmore. Fantasy.

April: *Broken Journey*. *pc* Gainsborough (Shepherd's Bush) *p* Sydney Box *d* Ken Annakin *ad* George Provis, A.R. Yarrow *sc* Robert Westerby. Adventure.

May: *Good Time Girl* (French title: *Les Ailes brulées*). *pc* Triton (Riverside) *p* Sydney Box, Samuel Goldwyn Jr *d* David MacDonald *ad* George Provis, Maurice Carter *sc* Muriel Box, Sydney Box, Ted Willis. Based on a novel by Arthur La Bern. Crime.

June: *The Calendar*. *pc* Gainsborough (Shepherd's Bush) *p* Anthony Darnborough *d* Arthur Crabtree *sc* Geoffrey Kerr. Based on a play by Edgar Wallace. Sport.

July: *My Brother's Keeper*. *pc* Gainsborough *p* Anthony Darnborough *d* Alfred Roome, Roy Rich *sc* Frank Harvey. Crime.

September: *The Blind Goddess*. *pc* Gainsborough (Shepherd's Bush) *p* Betty Box *d* Harold French *ad* Norman Arnold *sc* Muriel Box, Sydney Box. Based on a play by Patrick Hastings. Crime.

October: *Quartet*. *pc* Gainsborough (Shepherd's Bush) *p* Anthony Darnborough, Sydney Box *d* Ken Annakin, Arthur Crabtree, Harold French, Ralph Smart *sc* R.C. Sherriff. Based on stories by W. Somerset Maugham. Drama.

November: *Here Come the Huggetts*. *pc* Gainsborough *p* Betty Box *d* Ken Annakin *sc* Muriel Box, Sydney Box, Peter Rogers, Mabel and Denis Constanduros. Based on characters created by Godfrey Winn. Comedy.

December: *Portrait from Life* (US title: *The Girl in the Painting*).
pc Gainsborough (Shepherd's Bush) *p* Anthony Darnborough
d Terence Fisher *sc* Muriel Box, Sydney Box, Frank Harvey,
David Evans. Drama.

1949

February: *Vote for Huggett*. *pc* Gainsborough *p* Betty Box *d* Ken
Annakin *sc* Allan MacKinnon, Mabel and Denis Constanduros.
Comedy.

March: *The Bad Lord Byron*. *pc* Triton (Shepherd's Bush) *p* Aubrey
Baring, Sydney Box *d* David MacDonald *ad* George Provis,
Maurice Carter *md* Muir Mathieson *sc* Terence Young, Anthony
Thorne, Peter Quennell, Lawrence Kitchin, Paul Holt. History.

April: *It's Not Cricket*. *pc* Gainsborough (Shepherd's Bush) *p* Betty Box
d Alfred Roome, Roy Rich *sc* Bernard McNab, Gerard Bryant,
Lyn Lockwood. Comedy.

April: *A Boy, a Girl and a Bike*. *pc* Gainsborough (Shepherd's Bush)
p Ralph Keene *d* Ralph Smart *ad* George Provis, A.R. Yarrow
md John Hollingsworth *sc* Ted Willis. Drama.

May: *The Huggetts Abroad*. *pc* Gainsborough *p* Betty Box *d* Ken
Annakin *sc* Mabel and Denis Constanduros, Ted Willis, Gerard
Bryant. Comedy.

June: *Marry Me*. *pc* Gainsborough *p* Betty Box *d* Terence Fisher
sc Lewis Gilbert, Denis Waldock. Romance.

June: *Christopher Columbus*. *pc* Gainsborough (Shepherd's Bush)
p A. Frank Bundy, Sydney Box *d* David MacDonald *ad* George
Provis *md* Muir Mathieson *sc* Muriel Box, Sydney Box, Cyril
Roberts. History.

July: *Helter Skelter*. *pc* Gainsborough (Shepherd's Bush) *p* Anthony
Darnborough *d* Ralph Thomas *sc* Patrick Campbell, Jan Read,
Gerard Bryant. Comedy.

July: *Don't Ever Leave Me*. *pc* Triton (Shepherd's Bush) *p* Sydney Box
d Arthur Crabtree *sc* Robert Westerby. Based on a novel by
Anthony Armstrong. Comedy.

July: *Lost People*. *pc* Gainsborough *p* Gordon Wellesley *d* Bernard
Knowles, Muriel Box *sc* Bridget Boland, Muriel Box. Based on a
play by Bridget Boland. War.

October: *Diamond City*. *pc* Gainsborough *p* A. Frank Bundy *d* David
MacDonald *sc* Roger Bray, Roland Pertwee. Adventure.

December: *Boys in Brown*. *pc* Gainsborough (Pinewood) *p* Anthony
Darnborough *d* Montgomery Tully *ad* Douglas Daniels, Gilbert
Chapman *sc* Montgomery Tully. Based on a play by Reginald
Beckwith. Crime.

December: *Traveller's Joy*. *pc* Gainsborough (Shepherd's Bush)
p Anthony Darnborough *d* Ralph Thomas *sc* Bernard Quayle,
Allan MacKinnon. Based on a play by Arthur Macrae. Comedy.

1950

March: *The Astonished Heart*. *pc* Gainsborough (Pinewood)
p Anthony Darnborough *d* Terence Fisher, Anthony
Darnborough *sc* Noël Coward. Based on a play by Noël Coward.
Romance.

May: *So Long at the Fair*. *pc* Gainsborough (Pinewood) *p* Betty Box
d Terence Fisher, Anthony Darnborough *ad* Cedric Dawe
sc Hugh Mills, Anthony Thorne. Based on a novel by Anthony
Thorne. Drama.

July: *Trio*. *pc* Gainsborough (Pinewood) *p* Anthony Darnborough
d Ken Annakin, Harold French *sc* R.C. Sherriff, Noel Langley.
Based on stories by W. Somerset Maugham. Drama.

Bibliography

compiled by Justine King

The bibliography lists books, articles in books and journals, and unpublished material cited in the text. References to newspapers, periodicals, yearbooks and trade journals are dealt with in endnotes to individual contributions.

Adburgham, A. (1983) *The Silver Fork Society: Fashionable Life and Literature from 1814 to 1840.* London: Constable.

Aldgate, A. and Richards, J. (1986) *Britain Can Take It: The British Cinema in the Second World War.* Oxford: Blackwell.

Allen, R.C. and Gomery, D. (1985) *Film History: Theory and Practice.* New York: McGraw-Hill.

Altman, R. (ed.) (1981) *Genre: The Musical.* New York and London: Routledge.

Altman, R. (ed.) (1992) *Sound Theory, Sound Practise.* New York and London: Routledge.

Anger, K. (1975) *Hollywood Babylon.* London: Arrow Books.

Anger, K. (1986) *Hollywood Babylon II.* London: Arrow Books.

Armes, R. (1978) *A Critical History of British Cinema.* London: Secker & Warburg.

Askey, A. (1975) *Before Your Very Eyes.* London: Woburn.

Aspinall, S. and Murphy, R. (eds) (1983) *BFI Dossier 18: Gainsborough Melodrama.* London: BFI Publishing.

Aspinall, S. and Murphy, R. (1983) Unpublished interview with Phyllis Calvert.

Balcon, M. (1969) *Michael Balcon Presents ... A Lifetime of Films.* London: Hutchinson.

Balcon, M., Lindgren, E., Hardy, F. and Manvell, R. (1947) *Twenty Years of British Films 1925–1945.* London: Falcon Press.

Balio, T. (1976) *United Artists: The Company Built by the Stars.* Madison: University of Wisconsin Press.

Balshofer, F.J. and Miller, A. (1967) *One Reel a Week.* Berkeley and Los Angeles: University of California Press.

Barr, C. (1983) '*Blackmail*, silent and sound', in *Sight and Sound* (Autumn).

Barr, C. (ed.) (1986) *All Our Yesterdays: 90 Years of British Cinema.* London: BFI Publishing.

Barr, C. (1989) 'War record', *Sight and Sound* (Autumn).

Barr, C. (1993) *Ealing Studios.* London: Studio Vista. Revised edition.

BECTU. *BECTU Oral History Project.* Held by Broadcasting Entertainment Cinematograph and Theatre Union, London.

Benjamin, W. (1992) *Illuminations.* London: Fontana.

Bennett, C. (1921) 'Technical survey of 1920', in *Kinematograph Year Book 1921*.

Bergfelder, T. (1996) 'The production designer and the *Gesamtkunstwerk*', in Higson (ed.) *Dissolving Views*. London: Cassell.

Bock, H.M. and Töteberg, M. (eds) (1992) *Das Ufa Buch*. Frankfurt: Zweitausendeins.

Bordwell, D., Staiger, J. and Thompson, K. (1985) *The Classical Hollywood Cinema: Film Style and Mode of Production to 1960*. New York and London: Routledge.

Bouchier, C. (1995) *Shooting Star: The Last of the Silent Film Stars*. London: Atlantis.

Box, M. (1974) *Odd Woman Out*. London: Frewin.

Brandlmeier, T. (1993) 'Deutsche Kameraschule im britischen Film', in Schöning (ed.) *London Calling*. Munich: Edition Text und Kritik.

Bretschneider, J. (ed.) (1992) *Ewald André Dupont: Autor und Regisseur*. Munich: Edition Text und Kritik.

Brook, C. (n.d.) *The Eighty Four Ages*. Unpublished autobiography held by the British Film Institute, London.

Brown, G. (1977a) *Launder and Gilliat*. London: BFI Publishing.

Brown, G. (ed.) (1977b) *Walter Forde*. London: BFI Publishing.

Brown, G. (ed.) (1981) *Der Produzent: Michael Balcon und der englische Film*. Berlin: Volker Spiess.

Brown, G. and Low, R. (1984) 'Filmography', in Fluegel (ed.) *Michael Balcon: The Pursuit of British Cinema*. New York: Museum of Modern Art.

Brunel, A. (1949) *Nice Work*. London: Forbes Robertson.

Burnett, R.J. (1932) *The Devil's Camera: Menace of a Film-ridden World*. London: Epworth Press.

Buscombe, E. (1974) 'Walsh and Warner Bros', in Hardy (ed.) *Raoul Walsh*. Edinburgh: Edinburgh Film Festival.

Carrick, E. (1948) *Art and Design in the British Film*. London: Dobson.

Chion, M. (1984) 'Chiffre de destinée: Une Femme disparait d'Alfred Hitchcock', *Cahiers du Cinéma*, No. 358 (April).

Claus, H. (1996) *Der Kongress tanzt: The Ufa Sound Film Operetta and Its Language Versions*. Unpublished paper delivered at the musicals conference at Southampton University.

Cook, P. (1996a) *Fashioning the Nation: Costume and Identity in British Cinema*. London: BFI Publishing.

Cook, P. (1996b) 'Neither here nor there: national identity in Gainsborough costume drama', in Higson (ed.) *Dissolving Views*. London: Cassell.

Courtneidge, C. (1953) *Cicely*. London: Hutchinson.

Davies, S. (1993) *A Gainsborough/Gaumont Chronology*. Unpublished database.

Davy, C. (ed.) (1937) *Footnotes to the Film*. London: Lovat Dickson & Thompson.

Dibbets, K. (1988) 'L'Europe, le son, la tobis', in *Le Passage du muet au parlant panorama mondial de la production cinématographique (1925–1935)*. Toulouse: Cinémathèque de Toulouse/Editions Milan.

Dixon, W.W. (1994) 'The doubled image: Montgomery Tully's *Boys in Brown* and the independent frame process', in Dixon (ed.) *Re-Viewing British Cinema 1900–1992*. Albany, NY: State University of New York Press.

Dixon, W.W. (ed.) (1994) *Re-Viewing British Cinema 1900–1992*. Albany, NY: State University of New York Press.

Doyle, G.R. (1936) *25 Years of Films*. London: Mitre Press.

Ďurovičová, N. (1992) 'Translating America: The Hollywood Multilinguals 1929-1933', in Altman (ed.) *Sound Theory, Sound Practise*. New York and London: Routledge.

Dyer, R. (1981) 'Entertainment and Utopia', in Altman (ed.) *Genre: The Musical*. New York and London: Routledge.

Edgar, M. (1937) *Jill Darling*. London: French's Acting Edition.

Edgar, M. (1938) *Albert and Balbus and Samuel Small*. London: Francis, Day & Hunter.

Ellis, J. (1978) 'Art, culture and quality: terms for a cinema in the forties and seventies', *Screen*, vol. 19, no. 3 (Autumn).

Ellis, J. (1996) 'The quality film adventure: British critics and the cinema 1942–1948', in Higson (ed.) *Dissolving Views*. London: Cassell.

Elsaesser, T. (1987) 'Tales of sound and fury: observations on the family melodrama', in Gledhill (ed.) *Home Is Where the Heart Is*. New York and London: Routledge.

Elsaesser, T. (1993) 'Heavy traffic: Perspektive Hollywood: Emigranten oder Vagabunden', in Schöning (ed.) *London Calling*. Munich: Edition Text und Kritik.

Fisher, J. (1973) *A Funny Way to Be a Hero*. London: Muller.

Flanagan, B. (1961) *My Crazy Life*. London: Fred Miller.

Fluegel, J. (ed.) (1984) *Michael Balcon: The Pursuit of British Cinema*. New York: Museum of Modern Art.

Gifford, D. (1986) *The British Film Catalogue 1895–1931*. London: David and Charles.

Gledhill, C. (ed.) (1987) *Home Is Where the Heart Is: Studies in Melodrama and the Woman's Film*. London: BFI Publishing.

Gledhill, C. (ed.) (1991) *Stardom: Industry of Desire*. New York and London: Routledge.

Gledhill, C. and Swanson, G. (eds.) (1996) *Nationalising Femininity: Culture, Sexuality and British Cinema in the Second World War*. Manchester: Manchester University Press.

Gomery, D. (1976) 'Tri-Ergon, Tobis-Klangfilm, the coming of sound', *Cinema Journal*, vol. 16, no. 1.

Gomery, D. (1980) 'Economic struggles and Hollywood imperialism: Europe converts to sound', *Yale French Studies*, no. 60.

Gorbman, C. (1983) *Unheard Melodies: Narrative Film Music*. London: BFI Publishing.

Granger, S. (1981) *Sparks Will Fly*. London: Granada.

Hake, S. (1993) *The Cinema's Third Machine: Writing on Film in Germany 1907–1933*. Lincoln: University of Nebraska Press.

Handley, T. (1938) *Handley's Pages*. London: Stanley Paul.

Hardy, F. (ed.) (1981) *Grierson on the Movies*. London: Faber.

Hardy, P. (ed.) (1974) *Raoul Walsh*. Edinburgh: Edinburgh Film Festival.

Hare, R. (1956) *Yours Indubitably*. London: Robert Hale.

Harper, S. (1987) 'Historical pleasures: Gainsborough costume melodrama', in Gledhill (ed.) *Home Is Where the Heart Is*. London: BFI Publishing.

Harper, S. (1994) *Picturing the Past: The Rise and Fall of the British Costume Film*. London: BFI Publishing.

Higson, A. (1986) '"Britain's outstanding contribution to the film": the documentary–realist tradition', in Barr (ed.) *All Our Yesterdays*. London: BFI Publishing.

Higson, A. (1992) 'Film-Europa: Dupont und die britische Filmindustrie', in Bretschneider (ed.) *Ewald André Dupont: Autor und Regisseur*. Munich: Edition Text und Kritik.

Higson, A. (1993) '[The] Way West: Deutsche Emigranten und die britische Filmindustrie', in Schöning (ed.) *London Calling*. Munich: Edition Text und Kritik.

Higson, A. (1995) *Waving the Flag: Constructing a National Cinema in Britain*. Oxford: Clarendon Press.

Higson, A. (1996a) 'Film Europa: Kulturpolitik und industrielle Praxis', in Sturm and Wohlgemuth (eds) *Allo? Berlin? Ici Paris!*. Munich: Edition Text und Kritik.

Higson, A. (ed.) (1996b) *Dissolving Views: Key Writings on British Cinema*. London: Cassell.

Higson, A. and Maltby, R. (eds) (1998) *'Film Europe' and 'Film America': Cinema, Commerce and Cultural Exchange, 1920–1939*. Exeter: University of Exeter Press.

Hitchcock, A. (1937) 'Direction', in Davy (ed.) *Footnotes to the Film*. London: Lovat Dickson & Thompson.

Hulbert, J. (1975) *The Little Woman's Always Right*. London: W.H. Allen.

Huntley, J. (1947) *British Film Music*. London: Skelton Robinson.

Jackson, A. (1929) *Writing for the Screen*. London: A. & C. Black.

Jacobsen, W. (1989) *Erich Pommer: Ein Produzent macht Filmgeschichte*. Berlin: Argon.

Kardish, L. (1984) 'Michael Balcon and the idea of a national cinema', in Fluegel (ed.) *Michael Balcon: The Pursuit of British Cinema*. New York: Museum of Modern Art.

Kavanagh, T. (1949) *Tommy Handley*. London: Hodder and Stoughton.

Kavanagh, T. (1974) *The ITMA Years*. London: Woburn Press.

Kieswetter, B. (1930) 'The European sound-picture industry', *Electronics*, vol. 1, no. 9.

Krazsna Kransz, A. (1928) 'The European Kino-Congress', *Close Up*, vol. 3, no. 4.

Kuhn, A. (1996) 'Cinema, culture and femininity in the 1930s', in Gledhill and Swanson (eds) *Nationalising Femininity*. Manchester: Manchester University Press.

Landy, M. (1991) *British Genres: Cinema and Society 1930–1960*. Princeton: Princeton University Press.

Lasky, J.L. (1957) *Blow My Own Horn*. New York: Doubleday.

Lee, N. (1937) *Money for Film Stories*. London: Isaac Pitman.

Levy, L. (1948) *Music for the Movies*. London: Sampson Low.

Lovell, A. (1969) *British Cinema: The Unknown Cinema*. London: BFI Education.

Low, R. (1950) *The History of the British Film 1914–1918*. London: Allen & Unwin.

Low, R. (1971) *The History of the British Film 1918–1929*. London: Allen and Unwin.

Low, R. (1981) 'Die Anfänge: Gainsborough und Gaumont-British', in Brown (ed.) *Der Produzent: Michael Balcon und der englische Film*. Berlin: Volker Spiess.

Low, R. (1985) *Film-making in 1930s Britain: The History of the British Film 1929–1939*. London: Allen and Unwin.

Macnab, G. (1993) *J. Arthur Rank and the British Film Industry*. London: Routledge.

MacQueen-Pope, W. (1952) *Ivor*. London: W.H. Allen.

Manvell, R. (1947) 'British feature films from 1925 to 1945', in Balcon *et al. Twenty Years of British Films 1925–1945*. London: Falcon Press.

Manvell, R. and Huntley, J. (1957) *The Technique of Film Music*. London: Focal Press.

Marshall, M. (ed.) (1979) *The Stanley Holloway Monologues*. London: Elm Tree.

Mason, J. (1981) *Before I Forget*. London: Hamish Hamilton.

Mathieson, M. (1947) 'Aspects of film music', in Huntley *British Film Music*. London: Skelton Robinson.

Medhurst, A. (1986) 'Dirk Bogarde', in Barr (ed.) *All Our Yesterdays*. London: BFI Publishing.

Midwinter, E. (1979) *Make 'Em Laugh: Famous Comedians and Their Words*. London: Allen and Unwin.

Minney, R. J. (1947) *Talking of Films*. London: Home and Van Thal.

Morley, S. (1989) *James Mason: Odd Man Out*. London: Weidenfeld and Nicolson.

Murphy, R. (1983) 'A brief studio history', in Aspinall and Murphy (eds) *BFI Dossier 18: Gainsborough Melodrama*. London: BFI Publishing.

Murphy, R. (1984) 'The coming of sound to Britain', *Historical Journal of Film, Radio and Television* vol. 4, no. 2.

Murphy, R. (1989) *Realism and Tinsel: Cinema and Society in Britain 1939–1949*. London: Routledge.

Noble, P. (1951) *Ivor Novello*. London: Falcon Press.

Oakley, C. (1964) *Where We Came In*. London: Allen & Unwin.

O'Regan, T. and Shoesmith, B. (eds) (1987) *History on/and/in Film*. Perth: History and Film Association of Australia (WA).

Pearson, G. (1957) *Flashback*. London: Allen & Unwin.

Petrie, D. (1996) *The British Cinematographer*. London: BFI Publishing.

Poole, J. (1980) 'Independent frame', *Sight and Sound* (Spring).

Powell, M. (1986) *A Life in Movies: An Autobiography*. London: Heinemann.

Pudovkin, V.I. (1958) *Film Technique and Film Acting*. London: Vision.

Quirk, L.J. (1971) *The Films of Fredric March*. New York: Citadel.

Reynolds, F. (1937) *Off to the Pictures*. London: Collins.

Richards, J. (1984) *The Age of the Dream Palace: Cinema and Society in Britain 1930–1939*. London: Routledge.

Richards, J. and Sheridan, D. (eds) (1987) *Mass Observation at the Movies*. London: Routledge.

Rother, R. (1992) 'Zwischen Parodie und poetischem Wachtraum: *Die Drei von der Tankstelle*', in Bock and Töteberg (eds) *Das Ufa Buch*. Frankfurt: Zweitausendeins.

Ryall, T. (1986) *Alfred Hitchcock and the British Cinema*. Beckenham, Kent: Croom Helm. Revised edition 1996, London and Atlantic Highlands: Athlone Press.

Sainsbury, F. (1941–2) 'Close-ups: No. 14 – Arthur Crabtree', *Cine-Technician* (November–January).

Salmi, M. (ed.) (1982) *National Film Archive Catalogue of Stills, Posters and Designs*. London: BFI Publishing.

Salt, B. (1992) *Film Style and Technology: History and Analysis* (second edition). London: Starword.

Saville, V. (n.d.) *Shadows on the Screen*. Unpublished memoirs of Victor Saville. Typescript held at the British Film Institute, London.

Schatz, T. (1989) *The Genius of the System*. New York: Pantheon.

Schöning, J. (ed.) (1993) *London Calling: Deutsche im britischen Film der dreissiger Jahre*. Munich: Edition Text und Kritik.

Seabury, W. (1929) *Motion Picture Problems: The Cinema and the League of Nations*. New York: Avondale.

Seaton, R. and Martin, R. (1978) *Good Morning, Boys: Will Hay, Master of Comedy*. London: Barrie and Jenkins.

Seaton, R. and Martin, R. (1982) 'Gainsborough: the story of the celebrated film studio', *Films and Filming* (May) and 'Gainsborough in the 40s', *Films and Filming* (June).

Spoto, D. (1983) *The Dark Side of Genius: The Life of Alfred Hitchcock*. London: Collins.

Staiger, J. and Gomery, D. (1979) 'The history of world cinema: models for economic analysis', *Film Reader* no. 4.

Sturm, S.M. and Wohlgemuth, A. (eds) (1996) *Allo? Berlin? Ici Paris!: Deutsch-französische Filmbeziehungen 1918–1939*. Munich: Edition Text und Kritik.

Taylor, J. R. (1978) *Hitch: The Life and Work of Alfred Hitchcock*. London: Faber & Faber.

Thompson, K. (1985) *Exporting Entertainment: America in the World Film Market 1907–1934*. London: BFI Publishing.

Thompson, K. (1987) 'The end of the "Film Europe" movement', in

O'Regan and Shoesmith (eds) *History on/and/in Film*. Perth: History and Film Association of Australia (WA).

Thompson, K. and Bordwell, D. (1994) *Film History: An Introduction*. New York: McGraw-Hill.

Tims, H. (1989) *Once a Wicked Lady: A Biography of Margaret Lockwood*. London: Virgin Books.

Truffaut, F. (1968) *Hitchcock*. London: Secker and Warburg. Also (1978) London: Granada.

Vincendeau, G. (1988) 'Hollywood Babel', *Screen*, vol. 29, no. 2 (Spring).

Weiss, A. (1991) 'A queer feeling when I look at you', in Gledhill (ed.) *Stardom: Industry of Desire*. New York and London: Routledge.

Wilcox, H. (1967) *25,000 Sunsets*. London: Bodley Head.

Wilson, S. (1975) *Ivor*. London: Michael Joseph.

Wood, A. (1952) *Mr Rank*. London: Hodder and Stoughton.

Wood, L. (1986) *British Films 1927–1939*. London: BFI Library Services.

Worsley, F. (1949) *ITMA 1939–1948*. London: Vox Mundi.

Index